Practicing Legal Design

MARCO IMPERIALE

Commissioning editor
Alex Davies

Managing director
Sian O'Neill

Practicing Legal Design
is published by

Globe Law and Business Ltd
3 Mylor Close
Horsell
Woking
Surrey GU21 4DD
United Kingdom
Tel: +44 20 3745 4770
www.globelawandbusiness.com

Practicing Legal Design

ISBN 978-1-83723-119-5
EPUB ISBN 978-1-83723-120-1
Adobe PDF ISBN 978-1-83723-121-8

GPSR Compliance: EU Authorised Representative: Easy Access System Europe - Mustamäe tee 50, 10621 Tallinn, Estonia, gpsr.requests@easproject.com

Contents

Acknowledgments

First and foremost, my family. Your unwavering patience and encouragement have been invaluable throughout this journey.

To all our clients. Without your insights, challenges, and trust, this book would not have been possible. Your experiences and feedback have shaped its direction and depth.

To the Better Ipsum team, along with the incredible contractors who have contributed their expertise and dedication. Your commitment has been instrumental in bringing this project to life.

To Sian, Alex, and the entire team at Globe Law and Business. Your insights, collaboration, and encouragement have been both inspiring and essential. Moreover, and most important, thanks for dealing with my natural tendency to procrastinate.

To Michael, Ashleigh, Maclen, Matthew, and Sally. Your interviews are the cherry on top of the book. This work wouldn't have been the same without your help.

To Heidi, thanks for the preface. And for the support. Sometimes you don't need lots of words to express gratefulness.

I also want to acknowledge LCA, Mondora, and Design Rights, with whom I shared the first steps of my journey in this field. Your influence has played a key role in my professional growth, and I am grateful for the foundation you helped build.

Then there's the legal design community. All the teams at the *Legal Design Journal*, the Legal Design Summit, the Legal Design Labs around the world, and everyone pushing the boundaries of innovation in this space. Your work continues to elevate and redefine what legal design can achieve, inspiring practitioners and thinkers worldwide.

Finally, to you, the reader. Whether you are a law firm partner, a corporate counsel, a designer, a student, or simply someone curious about the future of law, I hope this book inspires you to be more user-centric, empathetic, and innovative.

May your work contribute to building a better legal world.

About the author

Marco Imperiale is the founder and managing director of Better Ipsum, a benefit corporation providing innovative services to law firms, institutions, and corporate legal departments.

Before starting Better Ipsum, Marco was a copyright/entertainment lawyer and the head of Innovation at LCA, one of the major Italian law firms.

In his legal design journey, Marco has worked with law firms, institutions, and corporate companies in various industries, such as pharma, automotive, logistics, insurance, fintech, energy, apparel, and telecommunications.

He has lectured on legal design at the Harvard Graduate School of Design (*J-Term 2023 and 2024*), spoken various times at the Legal Design Summit, the most important legal design event globally, and is currently part of the case studies team at the *Legal Design Journal*, the only academic journal dedicated to legal design.

Aside from legal design, Marco teaches AI for Business and Fashion Law at Polimoda, and is a Teaching Fellow for CopyrightX, the copyright course offered by Harvard Law School in conjunction with the Berkman Center for Internet and Society. He is a mindfulness trainer, a long-time advocate of wellbeing in the legal profession, and serves as president of the UIA Committee for Wellbeing and Mental Health.

For more information about his work, visit www.marcoimperiale.net and www.betteripsum.net

fostering accountability while making the process more engaging. It's smart. It's efficient. It works.

Drawing inspiration from outside the legal world, the book highlights successes such as Oral-B's toothbrush redesign, which prioritized user needs by simplifying features. This same principle – clarity over complexity – drives the new design vision for legal tools. The goal extends beyond mere functionality to create usability that truly resonates.

Beyond tools and processes, the book confronts the cultural barriers that often hold legal innovation back. It challenges the "We've always done it this way" mindset and champions inclusivity and equity. Legal design invites a shift in thinking that centers systems around the people they serve.

Technology also plays a pivotal role in this vision. While AI is not a substitute for human expertise, it serves as an enhancer – streamlining collaboration and simplifying complex tasks. By freeing up time and space for creativity, these tools enable lawyers and designers to focus on what truly matters – solving problems and delivering value.

Whether you're a lawyer mired in legalese, a designer eager to make an impact, or a policymaker striving for change, this book offers a roadmap you can follow.

Legal design has evolved from a trend into a movement. It's about creating a legal system that is inclusive, effective, and built for real people. *Practicing Legal Design* provides an inspiring and actionable guide for anyone ready to embrace that vision. If you've ever questioned what's possible in law or sought to make the system work better for everyone, this book is your call to action.

Dr Heidi K. Gardner
Bestselling author of *Smarter Collaboration: A New Approach for Breaking Down Barriers and Transforming Work* (2022) and *Smart Collaboration* (2016), a distinguished fellow at Harvard Law School, and chief executive officer of Gardner & Co.

Introduction:
Why this book?

As the field of legal design continues to evolve, one might wonder, why do we need a book on the subject? The answer lies in the complexity and significance of this emerging discipline, which is still in a state of flux. Legal design is a distinctive and rapidly developing field, yet it remains somewhat nebulous in terms of definitions, frameworks, and objectives. Even the concept of discipline is potentially a matter of discussion. Is it an approach? A methodology? A discipline? All of the above?

Unlike more established matters, legal design has yet to settle into a shared definition. Some see it as a way to simplify and humanize the law, making it clearer and more accessible to those without legal training. Others consider it a subject worthy of academic investigation, one that calls for structured research within universities and legal theory. There are also those who focus on its potential to streamline legal processes more generally, moving beyond policies and contracts to bring about a wider cultural shift in the legal field.

This lack of consensus has both fueled the buzz around legal design and complicated its development. The absence of common definitions or agreed-upon frameworks, together with a (supposed) general lack of use cases, means that practitioners mostly work in silos, developing their own methodologies and approaches without a shared language or set of best practices. On the other hand, something is moving. We have more than a decade of experience, lots of projects involving clients and institutions, and an official academic *Legal Design Journal*. Lancaster University established the first legal design tenure worldwide, and labs, initiatives, and courses on the matter are flourishing around the world.

The goal of this book is not just to provide another addition to the growing body of literature on legal design. It seeks to fill critical gaps, clarify misconceptions, and provide practical guidance that is currently lacking in the field. Many existing texts and articles discuss the concept of legal design in abstract terms, but few provide detailed instructions or case studies on how to apply legal design principles in real-world situations. This lack of practical guidance leaves many practitioners, especially those new to the field, struggling to translate theory into practice. Moreover, some practitioners who have developed successful legal design methodologies are hesitant to share their "secret tricks". This reluctance may stem from a desire to maintain a competitive edge or simply from the fact that their techniques are still evolving. As a result, there is a dearth of concrete, actionable information available to those who want to implement legal design in their work.

In response to these gaps, this book offers a step-by-step guide to legal design projects, drawing on our extensive experience in the field. I will share our unique methodology for contracts, policies, and documents, which has been refined through years of practice, as well as practical tips and examples to help readers apply legal design principles effectively. Is it the only way of doing legal design? Not at all. But it is working for us.

I would also stress another critical aspect that is often overlooked in existing legal design literature – the role of artificial intelligence (AI), especially concerning generative AI. As AI technology continues to advance, it is poised to have a profound impact on the legal profession, potentially rivalling the Industrial Revolution in its scope and significance. Despite this, most legal design articles and texts currently available do not adequately address the intersection of AI and legal design. In this book, we will explore how AI can be integrated into legal design processes, enhancing efficiency, accuracy, and accessibility. I will examine the opportunities and challenges that AI presents, as well as its potential to revolutionize the way legal services are delivered. By incorporating AI into the discussion, I hope to provide a forward-looking perspective that prepares readers for the future of legal design.

Legal design has the potential to bring about a Copernican Revolution in the legal profession, fundamentally changing the way legal services are conceived, delivered, and experienced. This book is an invitation to join that revolution, equipping readers with the knowledge and tools they need to navigate and shape the future of law.

You might wonder why this book refers to a limited amount of legal design works. This is for three reasons. Firstly, I didn't want it to be a collection of legal design work from all over the world, but a practice manual (at the end of the day, the title should speak for itself). Secondly, there was a risk of self-promotion, which I don't like. This is not our brochure, but a book for current and future practitioners. Third, I don't want to refer to the current status of legal design works as the only way to do legal design. This is your manual, and your introduction to the legal design world. I hope that one day you'll fill the world with your examples.

Now, use it as much as you find it useful and enjoy the ride!

Part I:
Ontology

Introduction to Part I:
Opening the door

How can we begin to discuss legal design without first understanding what it entails? This is not a rhetorical exercise. It is the most appropriate starting point. Despite the growing attention paid to legal design in conferences, academic publications, professional events, and online discussions, the concept itself remains either elusive or misunderstood by a considerable portion of the legal community. Many lawyers, whether in private practice or working within corporate legal departments, have come across the term (perhaps during a keynote address, a social media exchange, or an innovation workshop) but have not truly grasped what legal design is, let alone the transformative potential it carries.

This book has a clear ambition – to offer concrete guidance for the application of legal design in real-world contexts. However, to do so without first addressing its theoretical foundations would be methodologically shallow and intellectually careless. Legal design is not a technique to be applied mechanically, nor a collection of templates to be followed. It is a field rooted in a broad and evolving terrain of study, drawing on law, design theory (with particular attention to the evolution of design thinking in legal contexts), behavioral and social sciences, economics, and various other areas of knowledge. Without this foundation, any practical implementation risks becoming a façade – pleasing in form, but lacking substance and coherence.

For this reason, Part I is devoted to the theory of legal design. The intention is neither to produce an abstract philosophical tract nor to prescribe rigid taxonomies. Rather, it is to provide the structure, clarity, and academic grounding required to enable a genuine understanding of what legal design is, how it has developed, and why it matters. Only by acquiring this foundational knowledge can legal professionals move from vague enthusiasm to informed and effective engagement.

The first chapter addresses the ontology of legal design. It retraces the evolution of the concept, its definitional uncertainties, and the current state of scholarly debate. The aim is to move away from generic slogans and instead offer a rigorous and coherent analysis of legal design as both a methodology and a cultural shift within the legal field. The second chapter explores the principles underpinning legal design. These are not mere suggestions or inspirational statements – they serve as the essential pillars for ensuring coherence, reproducibility, and a shared language across projects and practitioners. They allow legal professionals to critically assess whether their work is grounded in the values and methods that define the field. The third chapter addresses the question of why legal design has become necessary. It examines the forces that have placed growing pressure on traditional legal systems and practices. In doing so, it provides the context in which legal design is not only relevant but urgently needed. The fourth chapter turns to one of the most visible and discussed dimensions of legal design – the abandonment of legalese in favor of plain language. Far from being a superficial adjustment, the adoption of clear, inclusive, and human-centered language is a profound transformation in how the law communicates its intentions and obligations. This chapter also addresses concepts such as tone of voice, multilingualism, and the nuances of intercultural contracting.

Chapter 1:
So, this is legal design

Law and the Oral-B toothbrush[1]

For several years, I've started most of my presentations, workshops, and lectures on legal design with an intriguing story about the Oral-B toothbrush.[2] According to the story, when Oral-B was preparing to launch its electric toothbrush on the market, the initial idea was to deliver a revolutionary and cutting-edge product. The first prototype, designed by engineers, was packed with technological features – it provided data regarding the status of your mouth and even played music while you brushed your teeth. It was innovative, but something was missing.

Recognizing the need for a different perspective, Oral-B brought in a renowned design company to reimagine the product and propose new solutions. What emerged from this collaboration was a complete departure from the original concept. The consultancy focused on the actual needs and desires of users, uncovering two simple yet critical features people wanted – a long-lasting battery and interchangeable heads, allowing a family to share one toothbrush instead of buying several.

This was a tough decision for Oral-B. The proposed changes were drastically different from the original concept and involved a significant market risk. Yet, it decided to prioritize user needs over technological showmanship, and the results speak for themselves. The Oral-B electric toothbrush became one of the company's most successful products, setting the standard for electric toothbrushes and solidifying Oral-B's place as a market leader.

I return to this story whenever someone asks what legal design really means. Imagine applying that same approach to a contract, a regulation, or a legal service. Begin with the person on the receiving end. Understand how they read, decide, struggle, or disengage. Let their needs guide the way forward. This is not about simplifying the law for the sake of it, nor about dumbing things down. It is about designing with care, purpose, and attention. The law, like a toothbrush, works best when it is built not just to impress, but to be used.

Legal design is not aesthetics

It is true that legal design often results in visually appealing documents or platforms – beautiful contracts, engaging workflows, or clear policies. However, aesthetics is a byproduct, not the primary focus. Legal design emphasizes functionality, clarity, and usability. It is about creating legal solutions that work effectively for their intended users, with beauty emerging as a natural consequence of good design principles.

Legal design is not legal tech

Legal design is not synonymous with legal technology, although the two often intersect. Legal design focuses on improving the usability and accessibility of legal processes, and its outcome may include a technology-based solution like a platform or app, or not. However, it is not limited to technological outputs – it can involve physical documents, processes, or even workshops aimed at addressing systemic challenges in law.

Legal design is not contract simplification

Contract simplification represents just one expression of legal design, but it does not capture its full breadth. Legal design reaches further, engaging with the redesign of legal processes, the development of digital platforms, and the improvement of entire systems. While simplified contracts often attract the most attention (precisely because they offer a tangible and immediate result) they are only part of a larger movement aimed at rethinking how people interact with law across all stages, from negotiation and drafting to compliance and conflict management.

It is important to stress that the ambition of legal designers is not simplification for its own sake, but clarity. A legal design-informed contract might in fact be longer than its predecessor. It may include more examples, more structure, and more explicit explanations. This is not a failure of conciseness, but a success in communication. A ten-page agreement that is clear, navigable, and readable serves its users far better than a one-pager obscured by jargon and ambiguity. Clarity demands choices about language, tone, hierarchy, visual layout, and user flow. It requires stepping into the shoes of the reader and anticipating their questions, hesitations, and misunderstandings. In that sense, legal design is not about reducing; it is about revealing. It aims to make the law visible and workable, not by stripping it down, but by giving it shape in a way that respects its purpose and the needs of those who depend on it.

Legal design is not visual law

Visual law refers to the use of visual elements like diagrams, charts, and infographics to make legal information more accessible. In terms of scope, visual law focuses narrowly on the visual representation of legal content, while legal design encompasses a broader application, including redesigning legal processes, systems, and documents. Moreover, while visual law is primarily about clarity and communication, legal design also aims to foster engagement, usability, and efficiency in navigating legal frameworks.

A panacea for all evil? Well, no...

Despite the enthusiasm that surrounds legal design and the dedication of its most passionate practitioners, it would be misleading to present it as a universal remedy for all that ails the legal sector. Legal design is not a fix all. It cannot, on its own, resolve the deeply rooted issues of accessibility, procedural inertia, or inefficiency that pervade many legal systems. It is a powerful tool, but one that works best when integrated into a wider effort, one that includes thoughtful policy change, reform in legal education, and the responsible use of technology. Legal design can illuminate and support this transformation, but only if the ground is ready and the conditions are conducive. To succeed, it requires a coalition of professionals, institutions, and organizations willing to reimagine the status quo. Without this collective investment, its reach will remain limited.

In this sense, many legal design projects falter not because the methodology is weak, but because the environment in which they are implemented is resistant or unprepared. Several recurring pitfalls emerge.

First, without genuine commitment, legal design cannot take root. In many initiatives, priorities shift rapidly. What begins as a promising endeavor is quickly sidelined by internal urgencies, political hesitations, or more conventional ways of thinking. When organizations treat legal design as a box ticking exercise, or as a trendy experiment to be showcased rather than absorbed, the results are superficial at best.

Second, a lack of transparency can quietly erode the entire process. Legal design thrives on clarity, and clarity is incompatible with strategic ambiguity. If a contract, for example, contains deliberate vagueness or room for interpretive maneuver, the design effort becomes a mere aesthetic gesture. Real clarity demands honesty, not only in language but also in intent. Without the willingness to be fully open about rights, duties, and consequences, even the most beautifully designed artefact fails to serve its purpose. I talk more about ambiguity and transparency in Chapter 4.

Third, the absence of humility can be fatal. Legal design, like any meaningful process of change, begins with the recognition that we do not have all the answers. No discipline is above learning from others, and no professional should consider themselves immune to critique. Those who approach legal design as a decorative addition to their already "perfect" work misunderstand its nature. It is not a finishing touch, but a fundamental reconsideration of how legal communication operates.

Fourth, if the true motivation behind a project is to impress rather than to improve, failure is almost inevitable. Legal design is not performance. It is not about shiny slides, colorful diagrams, or design trophies. If the primary goal is visibility rather than usability, the result may look good, but it will not function.

Finally, the unwillingness to question oneself remains one of the greatest obstacles. Legal professionals are trained to defend, to argue, to persuade. But legal design requires a different stance – the courage to question, to listen, and to rethink. This means being open to the possibility that one's contracts, policies, or processes may be flawed, not in their legality, but in their legibility, purpose, and fairness.

A global movement

Legal design has rapidly evolved from a niche concept into a global movement, reflecting a widespread recognition of the need to make legal systems more accessible and user-friendly. Today we have multiple labs all over the world,[6] the first tenure in legal design at Lancaster university in the UK,[7] and lots of university courses all around the world.[8]

One of the most meaningful accomplishments of the legal design community has been the creation of the *Legal Design Journal (LDJ)*.[9] More than a publication, it is a collective project – a reflection of the energy, plurality, and shared ambition that define this evolving field. Emerging from conversations, collaborations, and a common urgency to give shape to a new discipline, the LDJ embodies the community's commitment to document, question, and advance legal design in ways that are both rigorous and accessible.

In September 2024, we released the first issue of the journal, available both online and as open access. This launch marked an important milestone – the beginning of a dedicated space for reflection, critique, and experimentation within the legal design ecosystem. The *LDJ* is not the product of a single institution or editorial board. It is, in every sense, a work of community. Its pages reflect the diversity of voices and approaches that make legal design such a vital and dynamic field. It was not created to claim authority, but to invite dialogue – to offer a shared space where lawyers, designers, technologists, and researchers can question assumptions, exchange practices, and contribute to a more open and collaborative legal culture.

The global movement of legal design is evidenced by a growing number of initiatives, conferences, and workshops dedicated to the field, spanning continents from North America to Europe, Asia, and Australia. These events serve as platforms for legal professionals, designers, academics, and technologists to share insights, strategies, and best practices for integrating design thinking into legal practices. For example, the Legal Design Summit, held in Helsinki, Finland,[10] has become a focal point for this burgeoning field, attracting participants worldwide who are eager to explore innovative ways to deliver legal services.

The growing international interest in legal design is not simply a matter of embracing new tools or technological trends. At its core, this shift reflects a broader aspiration towards legal systems that are not only fair and impartial, but also transparent, comprehensible, and genuinely accessible to the people they serve. Legal design, with its emphasis on user-centered thinking, speaks directly to global efforts aimed at improving access to justice and strengthening legal literacy. Across different jurisdictions, from civil law countries to common law systems, there is a mounting recognition that procedural fairness must be matched by clarity in communication. In response, legal design projects have begun to reshape how law is presented and experienced, from simplifying public-facing legal language to redesigning institutional websites for greater navigability or introducing interactive formats that guide users through their rights and responsibilities.

What makes this shift even more compelling is the shared understanding across legal cultures that traditional modes of legal expression often obstruct, rather than facilitate, meaningful engagement. The conventional legal document – dense, abstract, and intimidating – remains a major barrier for most citizens, regardless of education or socioeconomic status. In this context, the principles of legal design offer a valuable toolkit. Not a fixed methodology, but a flexible set of approaches that can be adapted to local contexts while relying on shared foundations of clarity, structure, and usability. Whether applied to court forms, tenancy agreements, or policy disclosures, legal design works to reduce friction between legal content and its users, enabling more active participation in legal processes.

This evolution is not happening in a vacuum. It coincides with the broader digital transformation of public and private services, including the legal sector. As more people interact with the law online – whether through e-government portals, automated legal services, or digital dispute resolution mechanisms – expectations for clear and intuitive experiences are rising. Legal design responds to these expectations by rethinking not only the look and feel of legal information, but also its architecture and delivery.

At the same time, I would like to stress that legal design's flexibility allows it to address highly specific needs in different parts of the world, while staying grounded in universal principles of design and plain language. In the United States, legal design has been applied to the simplification of legal aid documents for non-native speakers or the unhoused. In various European countries, it has been used to enhance transparency in digital consent forms in line with GDPR requirements or to comply with regulatory requirements. In parts of Asia, where institutional formality and deference to authority can discourage legal inquiry, design has been used to create more approachable communication channels that encourage citizen engagement. These examples underscore not only the range of issues legal design can respond to, but also its cultural sensitivity, its capacity to adjust to local norms while still seeking to empower individuals.

Nonetheless, challenges persist. Legal design still meets resistance from more traditional corners of the profession, where it is sometimes dismissed as superficial or secondary to substantive law. There are also practical tensions – how to balance usability with doctrinal exactitude, how to ensure inclusiveness without diluting legal protection, and how to integrate design sensibilities into legal education and policymaking in a sustainable way. These tensions are not flaws, but necessary frictions in a maturing field that is learning how to situate itself among long-established structures.

Prototyping in the legal world

Prototyping, in the legal context, represents a small revolution. Borrowed from other disciplines, it introduces a working method that sharply contrasts with the cautious, definitive mindset most legal professionals have been trained to adopt. The idea of creating a draft version of a legal product – not to polish it endlessly behind closed doors, but to expose it to real-world scrutiny and feedback – may feel not only uncomfortable but fundamentally counterintuitive. And yet, in legal design, it is precisely this step that often brings the most clarity. A prototype, whether it is a simplified contract, a redesigned interface for a compliance process, or a new onboarding flow for clients, becomes a tool for learning, rather than a final deliverable. It invites criticism, highlights misunderstandings, and brings to the surface assumptions we did not know we were making. It allows us to listen before we speak.

Yet for many lawyers, especially those shaped by traditional models of education and practice, prototyping can feel almost impossible. The obstacles are not technical. They are cultural, psychological, and professional. Perfectionism is often the first barrier – lawyers are trained to deliver polished, correct, final outputs. The very concept of a "draft" is usually seen as a step toward perfection, not an instrument of exploration. Pessimism is another – the belief that any deviation from the traditional model may backfire, create risk, or reduce the seriousness of our work. Added to that is a deeply rooted individualism – the idea that the lawyer must solve problems alone, relying on their own knowledge and expertise, rather than through iteration with users and collaboration with others. And then there is backward thinking – a professional culture that often looks to precedent, to what has already been done and accepted, rather than to what might be possible. These attitudes do not come from nowhere. They are the product of decades of professional socialization, of hierarchical structures, and of legal education systems that still reward solitary perfection over shared creativity.

And yet, despite all these barriers, prototyping remains one of the most powerful ways to reconcile the apparent contradiction between compliance with legal standards and meaningful engagement with users. It allows us to test how a clause is read, not just how it is written. It gives us the chance to understand whether a service is understood, not just whether it is delivered. It helps us shape legal products that do not only tick the boxes of legality but also serve the people they are meant to protect.

Prototyping also has ripple effects far beyond the product itself. It encourages a shift in the internal culture of legal organizations. It opens doors to collaboration with professionals who are rarely invited into legal processes – project managers, service designers, developers, but also secretaries and paralegals. It brings together diverse teams and promotes a more inclusive way of working, where legal knowledge is only one part of the equation. This is especially valuable in large firms and in-house legal departments, where new ideas often struggle to surface due to rigid hierarchies or fear of failure. A prototyping approach can gently disrupt that, making room for iteration, shared responsibility, and collective learning.

From a client perspective, prototyping reinforces relationships. When clients are invited into the process – not merely at the end when the final version is presented, but at the beginning when things are still open and malleable – they develop a clearer understanding of the legal reasoning behind choices. They see how and why trade-offs are made. This creates not only more usable outputs but also more trust. Clients who are listened to early are more likely to stay engaged, and more likely to feel that the final product reflects their concerns. In this sense, prototyping becomes not just a design tool but also a conversation tool, one that helps translate legal reasoning into something human, situated, and real.

There is also a pedagogical dimension. Exposing law students and young professionals to prototyping methods expands their mindset and their toolkit. It invites them to think in systems, to question assumptions, to engage in feedback loops, and to learn from disciplines traditionally considered outside the legal domain. They not only become better at solving legal problems, but also more capable of asking the right questions. They are equipped for a professional future where the ability to connect, test, and communicate may matter as much as the ability to draft a flawless memo.

Still, we should not underestimate how hard it is to introduce prototyping into the legal profession. My suggestion is not to give up on prototyping, but to reframe it. It is not a lack of professionalism. It is a different form of professionalism – one based on openness, responsiveness, and the willingness to learn. The more we normalize prototyping, the more we enable lawyers to work with, rather than against, the complexity of their environments. It becomes not a risk, but a safeguard.

Prototyping is not a silver bullet. It requires structure, facilitation, time, and above all a shift in attitude. But its potential is not limited to isolated innovation projects. It represents a way of working that could gradually redefine the legal profession itself – more porous, more relational, and more attuned to the needs of the world it claims to serve.

The legal designer – a new job?

In his book, *Tomorrow's Lawyers*,[11] Richard Susskind identifies the legal designer as one of the emerging roles in the legal world. It is an interesting suggestion, but also a controversial one. The figure of the legal designer is still debated – is it really possible for a single professional to cover such a role, or does legal design, by its very nature, require the contribution of multiple and diverse types of knowledge? My answer comes from direct experience, not from theory. Over the years, I have often been asked, sometimes not under the label of Better Ipsum but simply as Marco, to help companies revise and simplify legal documents. These were not abstract or theoretical questions. They were practical requests: can you make this easier to understand, more human, more accessible? The market, even when it does not call it legal design, is clearly asking for it. But this leads back to the original question: who is a legal designer? Is it someone who knows how to simplify a contract and can use Canva or InDesign fluently? In part, yes. And if that person has a legal background, all the better. Many designers struggle with the language of regulation or the internal logic of compliance. But for me, legal design is not something that can be embodied by a single profile. It requires a mix of skills, methods, and sensitivities. Visual design, information architecture, legal reasoning, behavioral science, plain language writing, service thinking. It is not a solo discipline. A legal designer should not be seen as a lone creative problem solver, but as a connector, a weaver of competences who knows how to listen, translate, mediate, and make things happen. In this sense, the legal designer is not a defined professional identity, but a collaborative role that thrives in the space between departments – legal, communication, product, compliance, tech – and gives shape to something that none of them could fully realize alone.

When law firms offer legal design services

In recent years, a growing number of law firms across the globe have started including legal design in their service offering. Some have built dedicated teams combining lawyers, visual designers, and content strategists. Others integrate legal design into specific practice groups, relying on professionals with a dual background. On paper, this move positions firms as forward-thinking and client-centered, ready to speak the language of innovation. It supports the idea of a more collaborative, feedback-oriented culture and can appeal to clients looking for clear, accessible, and user-friendly legal documents. There is also a clear advantage in terms of expertise – firms often have lawyers who are deeply specialized in sectors such as pharmaceuticals, finance, or technology. This makes it easier to tackle highly regulated areas, where legal design must be rigorous as well as accessible. However, offering legal design within a traditional law firm structure comes with its share of contradictions. The first is credibility. It is difficult to present yourself as a legal design champion if your standard output remains a 70-page, text-heavy contract that only another lawyer can decipher. Clients notice these inconsistencies, and the gap between what is promised and what is delivered can damage trust. The second is operational. Legal design, when done well, is not fast. It takes time, iteration, testing, and often a rethinking of internal processes. This has an impact on costs and resource allocation. If the firm's internal culture and business model are not ready to absorb this shift, legal design risks being treated as a decorative layer rather than a substantial change. It becomes a label rather than a method. Integrating legal design into a law firm can open new opportunities, but only if it is backed by coherence, investment, and a genuine willingness to work differently. Without that, the risk is to promise innovation while continuing to deliver more of the same.

References

1   Although I know this story might feel more at home in a product design context, I believe it captures something essential about the shift we need in the legal field. We often assume we understand our users, but the truth is we probably don't. And the real step forward is learning to create with them, not just for them.

2   https://www.fastcompany.com/3060197/how-two-industrial-design-titans-are-helping-brands-simplify-tech

3   In my first book on Legal Design, co-authored with Barbara de Muro and focused on the Italian context, we described legal design as a discipline, not as an approach aimed at creating legal products that are both understandable for end users and reliable from a legal point of view (*Legal Design, Come il Design può semplificare il Diritto.* Giuffrè Francis Lefebvre, 2021).

4   ISO ISO 24495-2:202 (Draft) on plain language and legal communication defines legal design as the application of design principles and methods to create more human-centric legal products and services.

5   A preliminary note: we will address all the relationship with other designs in chapter two.

6   Among the most important are the Legal Design Lab at Stanford, the NuLawLab at Northeastern University, and the Legal Design Lab at Seton Hall University, NJ.

7   www.lancaster.ac.uk/arts-and-social-sciences/people/michael-doherty

8   Including Queen Mary University, Bond University, University of Kent, Venice International University, and many more.

9   www.legaldesign-journal.com

10   www.legaldesignsummit.com

11   R. Susskind. *Tomorrow's Lawyers. An Introduction to Your Future*, Oxford, 2013.

Chapter 2:
Principles of legal design

Why do we need to speak about principles?

A critical aspect of legal design that warrants attention is the tendency of stakeholders to overemphasize the tangible outcomes of the process – such as documents, policies, or contracts – while underestimating the underlying principles that guide it. However, engaging with these foundational principles is as crucial as exploring the intricate methodologies of legal design, for several reasons.

Firstly, principles serve as the North Star of the discipline, providing practitioners with a guiding structure amidst strategic, methodological, or procedural uncertainties. In moments of ambiguity, referring back to these core principles offers clarity and direction, ensuring alignment with the overarching goals of legal design.

Second, legal design represents a paradigm shift in the legal profession, fundamentally transforming how legal content is conceived, communicated, and experienced. In this transformative process, principles function as the pivotal axis around which change orbits, facilitating the transition from traditional legal frameworks to more user-centered and accessible solutions.

Third, principles possess a universal and adaptable nature, transcending the specificity of individual cases or contexts. Whether applied within public administration, corporate environments, or law firm departments, the foundational principles of legal design remain relevant and applicable, regardless of the diversity and complexity of stakeholders involved. Their adaptability ensures consistency in approach while accommodating the unique needs of different sectors.

Finally, principles act as a litmus test for assessing progress and evolution within the field of legal design. Given the discipline's resistance to conventional metrics and quantifiable evaluations, periodically revisiting these principles provides an invaluable means of measuring the true impact and development of legal design initiatives over time.

It is important to note that the principles I include in this chapter reflect a personal interpretation, albeit one that has been positively received by both practitioners and the audience at the Legal Design Summit in 2023.[1] In keeping with legal design's intrinsic commitment to continuous improvement through feedback, I always welcome comments and suggestions to refine and expand upon these ideas further.

Some preliminary aspects are worth clarifying. In developing this framework of principles, I have chosen to highlight not only the individual principles but also the balance that exists among them. A holistic view is essential – just as a music album gains meaning through the interplay between each track and the sequence in which they are presented, the principles of legal design should be understood both on their own and in relation to one another. I considered whether certain elements from legal design practice – such as active listening, a mindset open to feedback, and a non-judgmental stance – should be included as standalone principles. However, I believe these elements are already embedded within the broader structure. Rather than being explicitly listed, they run through and support several of the existing principles, forming an integral part of the framework even if not always immediately visible.

Principle no. 1: Human-centrism

Despite the different views and priorities in the legal design scenario (both in academy and practice), it seems that human-centrism is a core starting point. Indeed, we notice the necessity of putting the human at the center of legal communication and a detachment – whether at a corporate or institutional level – between the final user and the legal contents. This also considering that the human-centric revolution is touching every aspect of our life. We buy items on Amazon, watch movies on Netflix, rent rooms on Airbnb. All these are human-centered platforms, built with a user perspective and working backwards.

But how can we reach human-centrism in legal documents or contracts? As we will see in the following paragraphs, the tools are many – we can use personas, customer journeys, or surveys to validate our assumptions. We can work on the architecture of information or play with a Canva map. We can (indeed, we should) also involve users directly in the design process, gathering their feedback not as an afterthought but as a fundamental part of the workflow. Even better, we can use all of them.

The core, in any case, is putting the final user of the document at the center of our process. In the design thinking world, there is a tale about Amazon meetings,[2] where an empty chair is always present that represents the final user. How about using the same kind of mentality with our projects?

Principle no. 2: Co-creation

Most legal professionals, particularly those in law firms, genuinely believe they are client-centric. Their brochures and websites frequently emphasize bespoke and tailor-made services, hallmarks of exclusivity that not only serve as a marketing tool but also justify premium fees. However, co-creation is something fundamentally different from merely interviewing a client and delivering a personalized service. It goes beyond customization; it transforms the client from a recipient of legal expertise into an active participant in shaping solutions.

Co-creation requires a shift in power dynamics. Instead of viewing clients as end-users who consume legal services, legal professionals must see them as partners in an evolving process. This approach means fostering dialogue, exploring alternatives together, and designing solutions through shared insights. It is not just about providing a legal product that meets expectations. It is about redefining those expectations through collaboration.

At a practical level, co-creation takes many forms, from co-design workshops to collaborative brainstorming sessions where clients and other stakeholders contribute directly to the development of legal solutions. In the best cases, client and provider may work together for the production of legal contents and services. This participatory approach extends beyond consultation – it actively involves users in testing prototypes, refining workflows, and even shaping success metrics. By embedding user feedback into iterative design cycles, co-creation ensures that the final outcome is not only functional but also meaningful, fostering trust and deeper engagement.

Pro tip:

Too often, when we present our services or products, we do most of the talking. And even when the client speaks, our attention is usually on problem-solving or analyzing a specific situation. But what if we paused that instinct for a moment? A dedicated listening session - with no pitch, no agenda, just space to hear - can shift the dynamics of the relationship. Sometimes, being truly heard is more powerful than being helped.

Yet, co-creation is as much a challenge as it is an opportunity. It forces law firms and legal professionals to rethink their value proposition, moving away from a purely expertise-driven model to one that prioritizes shared problem-solving. This shift demands openness, adaptability, and a willingness to embrace new methods of collaboration. But for those willing to engage, the reward is significant – legal solutions that are not only more effective but also more aligned with the needs and realities of those they serve.

Principle no. 3: Diversity and inclusion

Legal design fosters diversity for its own nature. In each project (and assuming we are not undertaking a solo effort) we have different professionals, different backgrounds, different languages. Legal design is also highly inclusive. Whether in terms of language, icons, or decision-making, we always tend to welcome different points of view and work with the final users in our mind. If we are able to manage properly the process, we will be able to benefit from this treasure.

Diversity and inclusion, in legal design, are two sides of the same coin. If diversity allows us to benefit from different opinions at the table, inclusion is the tool that we need so that everyone not only has a seat at the table, but is listened to as well.

Unfortunately, there are downsides. As we will see in the next few chapters, having different voices at the table could be the best possible scenario, but also the worst possible nightmare, especially if the process is badly managed.[3] We need professionals to promote dialogue, tools to avoid silos and stagnation, and – more generally – the sincere belief from each participant that every voice not only matters, but deserves to sit at the table as well. As a manager who daily works with designers, tech professionals, and engineers, I have witnessed how difficult this balance is to reach.

Principle no. 4: A non-hierarchical approach

This is one of my favorite principles, and one of the most challenging, at least for legal professionals. For some, it could be a corollary of the previous principle, but I decided to treat it as a separate entity for its relevance in the old-school, often elitist, world that is legal.

It is challenging to speak about a non-hierarchical approach, especially with the idea of classic law firms in mind. If most of them are willing (at least on paper) to put people first, listen to the outcomes of the various professionals, and invest in work–life integration, adopting a non-hierarchical approach requires a further leap. Basically, it means assuming that not only every voice matters but that every voice has the same value. How can we welcome opinions if the managing partner is the first to speak in a meeting and sets the tone of a project? How can we be sure that all professionals are able to speak with their own mind and will not be afraid of the reaction? Are we able to consider the agendas of senior partners, designers, and trainees in the same way?

The non-hierarchical approach brings with it a characteristic of our current moment – reverse mentoring. Sometimes we forget that this is the first time in human history that younger generations have been allowed to lecture – at least on specific topics – rather than only to listen. In practical terms, younger professionals – in their area of expertise – could have a stronger added value than more experienced ones.

If we believe that the world of tomorrow will not rely on yesterday's patterns, and that we need a new way to deal with future challenges, then we need to welcome different and innovative points of view, despite the source. As with everything in legal design, this is easier said than done.

Principle no. 5: Process first

The "process first" principle is multi-faceted. Firstly, it means coming to legal design sessions and workshops with a mind that is open, eager to discover, and not prone to judgment. As we will see in part three of this book, not jumping directly to conclusions is very important for a good final outcome.

Second, it means assuming that the outcome is the result of a series of steps and not a goal. Paradoxically, if a process is well managed, the final product is not only a consequence, but a not-so-important element. Many times, we start a session with the intention of redefining a policy or a document, and we finish by analyzing the internal process that led to it.

Third, it means relying on a specific and defined path. This is very important, especially considering the leap of faith that is required from all participants in a legal design project. We need to structure a process, communicate it to the various participants, and stick to it.

In the legal design field there is a general concern regarding the lack of a common framework. To avoid this, we propose a new methodology that takes into account the various applications of this discipline. Yet, the lack of a common framework should not be an excuse to avoid focusing on the process part, especially because there are ways to avoid this pitfall. We can rely on the experience of seasoned professionals in order to be guided and also to create a new methodology. Indeed, one of the appealing factors in legal design is its always evolving dynamic. When doing this, we should be careful to avoid the risk of confusion and disorder that can arise if the basic principles are not followed.

Principle no. 6: Divergence and convergence

A crucial yet often overlooked principle in legal design is the dynamic interplay between convergence and divergence – concepts that originate from design thinking and are essential for fostering innovation. Legal design, by its very nature, is an iterative and exploratory process that requires both expansive thinking to generate possibilities (divergence) and focused thinking to refine and implement the best solutions (convergence).

Divergence refers to the phase in which legal professionals, stakeholders, and users are encouraged to explore a wide range of ideas, solutions, and approaches without constraints. This phase promotes creativity, openness, and inclusivity, allowing diverse perspectives to surface and fostering a deeper understanding of the problem at hand. Divergence is particularly valuable in the early stages of a legal design project when traditional legal mindsets – often constrained by precedent and risk aversion – can hinder innovation. Techniques such as brainstorming, ideation workshops, and scenario mapping play a pivotal role in ensuring that all possible options are considered, including unconventional ones that might challenge the status quo.

Convergence, on the other hand, involves narrowing down ideas, synthesizing insights, and refining potential solutions to align with practical realities, business goals, and legal constraints. In this phase, participants of legal design projects apply critical thinking and structured methodologies to assess feasibility, compliance, and user impact. Convergence requires prioritization and decision-making, focusing on what can realistically be implemented within the given legal and organizational framework. This phase emphasizes the importance of balancing innovation with legal rigor, ensuring that solutions are not only creative but also actionable, effective, and sustainable.

The synergy between divergence and convergence is critical in achieving user-centered legal solutions that are both forward-thinking and pragmatic. However, striking the right balance between these two modes of thinking is often challenging for legal professionals accustomed to linear processes and definitive answers.

Principle no. 7: Fail fast

In the legal world, we are generally behind in terms of quick decision-making.

We tend to analyze scrupulously the alternatives, to think several times before sending an email or providing an opinion. This is absolutely understandable. As a managing partner once told me, if a business man makes the right decisions 60 percent of the time in his career he is a good manager, but if a lawyer makes three bad decisions, he's a bad lawyer.

Unfortunately, this contrasts with the quick, creative approach proposed by legal design.

Firstly, because "fail fast" means working in an MVP way.[4] We start, we test, we redefine, we listen to feedback. Everything is imperfect. Everything can be improved. And, quoting a Maroon 5 song, nothing lasts forever. It is up to us to see it as a positive or negative element.

Second, "fail fast" means working on different skills and, according to neuroscience, different brain areas. Whether we are speaking about proposing solutions or accepting failure, this is something in which lawyers need to be properly trained.

Lastly, "fail fast" means, in its deepest form, "think less/feel more". Most of the intuitions during the legal design process do not come from deep reflections. They come from tiredness, laughs, and surprising eureka moments. Balancing deep work and intuition is by far one of the hardest tasks for session facilitators.

Principle no. 8: How might we?

If there are three magic words in the legal design world, I believe that they are these. "How might we?" represents the forward-thinking approach, the dynamics in a static world, and true "thinking outside of the box".

If most of the lawyers I know define themselves as creative, what I see in practice is quite the opposite. We need templates, we work with the same team, we rely on pre-defined structures. Looking at our behavior with a Langerian[5] perspective, most of our working time in a design project is mindless.

"How might we?" and "fail fast" are a perfect match. Like beer and pretzels, or pasta and ragù. "Fail fast" means pushing lawyers to create, and "How might we?" to think about different ways of doing things. The combo will show that we are not afraid of mistakes. That we are eager to invest in a specific process despite the outcome. That we want to test possible solutions and change our actions. In the world of legal, disinclined to R&D, it is music to clients' ears.

Principle no. 9: Productification

Lawyers tend to identify themselves (and like to be recognized) as service providers. As trusted professionals who provide legal advice to clients who need it. However, the rise in exponential innovation and generative artificial intelligence, the expanding presence of the Big Four, and investments made by key players in legal tech start-ups and scale-ups, forced them to broaden their horizons. Are they providing a service or a product?

Legal design work is something concrete, usable, and improvable – whether it's a better contract, a playbook, or a policy. For this reason, in considering our role as consultants and the process outcome of a legal design project, we have a better perspective of our work if we consider it as a product.

Productification is not only a change of term, but a change of mindset as well, because products are tangible and developed with the final user in mind. When working on a service, we normally are more focused on the work itself, and sometimes on how to present the outcome of the work that we have done to the user.

Instead, when developing a product, the "user in mind" attitude becomes almost obsessive. From the first moment, we try to think what the user is going to think and how it will approach the experience.

Also, this change of mindset puts the legal element at the same level to other services - not above or below. We are just a part of a big puzzle that includes design thinking, visual design, project management and sometimes more fields (including economics, cognitive psychology, and organizational behavior).

Principle no. 10: KISS (Keep It Simple Stupid!)

Leonardo da Vinci (1452-1519) was an Italian Renaissance painter, draughtsman, engineer, scientist, and theorist. Many people know him for his achievements as a painter, but he studied many subjects, including anatomy, astronomy, botany, and cartography. He is considered by designers to be the first modern designer and the greatest. We have given his name to our Framework for Legal Design, to honor him and his heritage. We give more details of the Framework in Chapters 18, 19, 20 and 21 in Part IV of this book. Leonardo used to say that simplicity is the ultimate sophistication. Truth is, reaching simplicity is way harder than it seems. Only when complex concepts are clear in our mind, and shaped by our experience, are we able to explain them in a simple way. Legal design is hard for everyone, but especially for lawyers, because they are the ones taking the highest risks. If in a legal design process we are not precise on personas or the customer journey, the legal design product won't be perfect, but if we cut out the wrong article, or paraphrase a legal term or concept incorrectly, the stakes are way higher. A contract can be void. A court can consider us liable. The audience for which we have done the work could misinterpret our efforts.

The positive element is that – through legal design – we can become better lawyers as well. Because being simple requires us to be clear in our minds as to what to say and how to say it, what is material and what is not, and how it will be received.

One element I would like to stress is that legal design is not a matter of cutting up lines of text. The final focus should be the clarification of the document. Paradoxically, we could create longer content in order to make it clearer.

Principle no. 11: Dignity

I have to thank Robert de Rooy for reminding me of the necessity of this principle. It is great to see great legal designers like Margaret Hagan at the Stanford Lab and Dan Jackson at the Northeastern Lab working on it.

If we want citizens and clients to be involved in the definition of the future world, we need to provide them with the relevant tools. Legal design is not only an instrument to make legal content understandable, it is a way to create a better society and to involve stakeholders in the process of creating it.

Maybe because of bias, we sometimes overestimate the abilities of a common citizen to understand the legal details of a banking statement, an energy bill, or a smart working agreement. Legal design is an element to rebalance this inequality. This principle can be considered in contrast with the idea of the lawyer as the repository of knowledge, but I am convinced that in the future, and maybe already now, knowledge won't be lawyers' main asset. Our added value will be the trust we create with clients.

Principle no. 12: +1

This is my favorite.

Plus 1 is the awareness that the special chemistry (shall we call it alchemy?) among different professionals is more valuable than the sum of their char-acters. If you put the lawyer, the designer, the client, and the client of the client in a room, the alchemy is what really makes the difference. And it is also the hardest element to reach.

I often think of a legal design team as a rock band. Some elements are crucial for the success of a project. Some elements can be substituted, but their role has to be filled. Some professionals are better than others, but only in their specific field. What really matters, however, is that the combination of all the personalities and backgrounds is crucial for the success of the show. Without a good combination, it is possible that the project will be a decent learning experience, but it is not going to be a blast.

Plus 1 means also that every project is different, and this is something worth mentioning. I have worked with dozens of institutions and corporations in many different industries, and I can guarantee that the combination provided by the teams is different every time. Of all the reasons that keep me excited to get out of bed in the morning and willing to push the boundaries, this is one of the strongest.

Insight:

While we tend to focus on the outcome of legal design projects, I believe that principles are equally, if not more, important for the success of legal design as a discipline in the long-term. The positive externalities of legal design are difficult to highlight, because the more we delve into it, the more we can see its potential impact on consumers, citizens, and society in general. Principles, therefore, could represent a serious starting point to foster a discussion on the matter and spread the seeds of a groundbreaking discipline.

Future principles

If principles help us navigate the present, they must also point us toward what lies ahead. Legal design, by its very nature, is a work in progress – not just a method, but a posture. It is a field that resists crystallization, because it grows in direct proportion to the changes around it. What we call future principles, then, are not predictions. They are signs of where legal design might be heading, or better still, what it needs to stay relevant, serious, and human in a world that is rapidly changing.

The first element to consider is resilience. Not in the diluted, managerial sense of the word, but as a capacity to respond (not react) to sudden shifts. The rise of generative artificial intelligence, the increasingly polarized digital public sphere, the growing complexity of global systems – these are not future problems, they are current tensions that will only intensify. A legal design process that pretends they do not exist, or that simply ignores the discomfort they bring, is missing the point. Future principles must allow space for contradiction and friction, rather than rush to simplify them. This calls for a stronger connection between legal design and ethical reflections. We need to be more deliberate in asking ourselves not just what we are designing, but why, and for whom. This requires grounding our work in values that are not decorative or aspirational, but chosen, revisited, and enacted. Every single time.

Second, future principles must include a new relationship with technology. Legal design can no longer afford to treat digital tools as optional extras or external layers. Technology is not just a means of execution – it shapes the very logic of the systems we are working within. The design of prompts, the training of models, the data that is excluded or included – all of this has legal meaning. In this context, legal designers need a seat at the table not only when drafting the interface, but when designing the architecture itself. That also means deeper, more structured collaboration with data scientists, engineers, and policy-makers. Legal design has to become more fluent in the languages of the future, or it risks becoming a translation exercise for products already made by others.

Third, future principles will require stronger ecological awareness. For too long, the legal world has been treated as a closed universe, detached from the environmental and social urgencies of our time. Legal design must break this loop. What if we treated every legal product not only as a tool of communication but also as part of a broader ecosystem? What if we started to ask what resources were used to produce a document, how inclusive it truly is, and how it will live in the hands of those who use it? Thinking ecologically also means thinking about time – not only the deadlines of delivery, but the long-term consequences of the systems we are building. If we are not taking this into account, we are not designing. We are decorating.

Lastly, and perhaps most importantly, future principles will require a renewed humility. The legal world has often been built on the illusion of control – the idea that we can regulate, predict, and systematize every outcome. Legal design, especially in its future expressions, should stand for the opposite. For openness. For listening. For discomfort. For not knowing. It should resist the temptation to become another method to be mastered, and instead remain what it was meant to be from the start – a conversation. One that continues, and changes, and hopefully becomes better – not because we know more, but because we are willing to question what we thought we knew. That, in the end, is the principle that might matter the most.

References

1   In addition to the list presented at the Legal Design Summit in 2023, I have included co-creation. Regarding sustainability (removed from the original list), I dedicate an entire chapter to the topic in part two of this book.

2   www.inc.com/john-koetsier/why-every-amazon-meeting-has-at-least-one-empty-chair.html

3   Regarding benefits of collaborations and its risks, I highly suggest H. Gardner's books: *Smart Collaboration* (Harvard Business Review Press, 2017), *Smarter Collaboration* (Harvard Business Review Press, 2022) and *Smart Collaborations for In-House Legal Teams* (Ark, 2020).

4   A minimum viable product (MVP) is a version of a product with just enough features to be usable by early customers who can then provide feedback for future product development: www.techopedia.com/definition/27809/minimum-viable-product-mvp

5   Ellen Langer is tenured professor at the Harvard psychology department, and is considered the mother of non-meditative mindfulness. For further information, see https://ellenlanger.com

Chapter 3:
Why legal design?

New context, new demand

The emergence of legal design is a structural response to a changing environment in which complexity, velocity, and uncertainty have become dominant traits. Today, legal systems are required to operate in conditions that are more fragmented and fast-moving than ever before. Regulatory frameworks intersect, collide, and mutate at increasing speed, exposing organizations and individuals to a level of legal opacity that traditional models struggle to manage. What once felt predictable is now variable. What once seemed stable is now unsettled. The legal profession is required to speak the language of responsiveness, iteration, and flexibility.

Legal documents themselves bear the signs of this pressure. They are becoming denser, more technical, and less intelligible to the very people they are supposed to serve. Our discipline does not respond by simplifying for the sake of appearance. It proposes a change in orientation – a move from rigidity to clarity, from authority to usability, from abstraction to real-world application. The aim is not to weaken legal rigor, but to make it work in a world that no longer accepts obstacles to comprehension. Instead of reacting to change from the outside, we offer a new way of producing legal meaning within conditions of ambiguity.

At the same time, legal design leverages the fact that expectations of legal users, whether clients, regulators, colleagues, or citizens, have shifted. People no longer accept exclusion from legal processes on the basis of obscurity or inherited convention. They demand legal information that is not only correct but also understandable. They expect legal professionals to act not as custodians of arcane language, but as translators, mediators, and guides. They seek participation, not passive reception. This is a cultural change, shaped by new expectations of access, transparency, and responsiveness across all sectors, from public administration to finance, from healthcare to digital services.

Example:

Think about this for a moment. You use Amazon for your purchases, you use Airbnb for your vacations, you use Netflix for your entertainment, you use Uber to move in a crowded city. Your children use Instagram, Snapchat, and TikTok, and spend hundreds of hours playing with videogames. All these platforms have something in common – they know customers pretty well, they use visuals more than content, and they are created to be engaging and user-friendly. How long before clients and citizens will ask institutions, law firms, and companies to provide the same kind of service?

These pressures do not only come from outside the legal field. They reflect a deeper questioning within it. Many lawyers, especially those working within organizations or multidisciplinary teams, are beginning to acknowledge the limitations of traditional legal thinking. They are witnessing the disconnect between legal advice and operational needs, between compliance schemes and business goals, between documents and how users actually behave. These mismatches produce friction, inefficiency, and risk.

Lastly, there is growing demand for legal work to be not only convincing, but demonstrably effective. Clients, organizations, and institutions want to see how legal frameworks perform, based on evidence – how users navigate documents, how much time is gained or lost, how mistakes are avoided, how trust is created or undermined. What is the added value provided? On that note, I see a half-full glass. Emphasis on data is not going to dilute legal reasoning but reinforce it, providing that added value not in theory, but in visible and traceable ways.

A form of innovation – or innovations
The English word "innovation" comes from the Latin "innovatio". In the verb "innovare" it is possible to see the two roots "In" (to bring inside, to include) and "novare" (give a content of novelty, to apply a change, to have a new approach).[1] Today, very often the use of this concept is limited to "add a technique, a content, a technology that has already been developed, and include it into an existing subject".

While this action can be very useful in spreading the use of new and promising technologies, or an interesting cross-fertilization that adds value to existing things, we should be careful not to lose the meaning of looking at things in a new way. As an example: in the last 50 or 60 years, innovation, to use this word, in the automotive industry has been very wide and diffused. Yet, in many cases this has meant adding technologies (electronics, microelectronics, computing, sensors) to an object that we call a "car", that really has not been changed very much in its way of being used, but that has been improved and refined.

Yet, some of the really "innovative" designs in the history of cars (think about the Volkswagen Beetle, or the original Mini) were not focused on incorporating new technologies, but were about the complete project of the car, and so they were able to change the way of looking at the car and of using it. From this perspective, legal design is a structural way of rethinking legal practice that challenges assumptions, reshapes tools, and reframes culture.

Legal design expresses itself in many forms of innovation. The first is incremental innovation. This discipline brings gradual but concrete improvements to existing legal products and services. Terms and conditions become easier to navigate. Privacy policies become comprehensible. Legal documents shift from internal archives to usable tools. The law remains intact, but its form becomes accessible, iterative, and open to feedback.

The second is radical innovation. In this case, legal design goes beyond improving what already exists and proposes alternative formats. Contracts may become interactive dashboards, service touchpoints, or collaborative frameworks. Legal journeys may be redesigned around experiences rather than procedure. The shift is not in the layout, but in the way that law is delivered and perceived.

The third is disruptive innovation. Here, legal design intervenes when the dominant logic of legal services is no longer suitable. Tools like AI-driven legal interfaces can change the rules of legal access, bringing law closer to those who were previously excluded, not by lowering its quality, but by changing its mode of delivery.

The fourth is architectural innovation. Why architecture? Because legal design maintains the legal substance of documents but most of the time reorganizes their structure. The sequencing, layout, and visual hierarchy of legal documents are redesigned to match the way people actually read and decide. A visual contract may include the same terms as a traditional one, but its interface transforms the reading experience. The user is guided, not overwhelmed. The law becomes navigable, structured, and human-readable.

The fifth is sustainable innovation. Legal design strengthens what is already working, refining existing processes to their clarity, speed, and usability. A redesigned NDA can simplify onboarding. A human-centric policy can enable better communication with non-legal teams. Through new products we remove friction between intention and result.

The sixth is open innovation. Legal design draws from other disciplines to enrich the legal process. It borrows from behavioral science, service design, psychology, visual communication, and more. We are opening the legal field to methods, rules, and sensibilities that law has often ignored. This way, we allow it to evolve with intelligence, awareness, and plurality.

Each of these six expressions – incremental, radical, disruptive, architectural, sustainable, and open – offers a different way for legal design to respond to change. None of them is better than the others. They serve different needs, timelines, and ambitions. What matters is to understand that innovation in law is not a single act, but a range of strategies. An alternative lens through which we understand problems, devise responses, and deliver legal value.

Pro tip:
Curious about legal design and eager to broaden your perspective beyond the pages of this book? Take a look at the legal design podcast repository. It gathers dozens of practitioners who share their experiences, methods, and concrete strategies for bringing human-centered thinking into the legal field.[2]

The legal experience
Legal documents such as contracts, policies, and agreements are often perceived as static artefacts, mere collections of words intended to fulfil formal obligations rather than dynamic instruments of interaction. We tend to treat them as dead letters, textual entities tied to compliance rather than active elements capable of shaping human behavior, guiding decisions, and structuring relationships. This perspective is both widespread and limiting. A contract is not only a written record. It is an experience that unfolds across time, beginning with its presentation and extending through negotiation, execution, and eventual enforcement. It affects how individuals and organizations relate to one another, how expectations are formed and adjusted, and how legal certainty is created or eroded. The meaning of a legal document lies not just in its wording, but in how it is perceived, used, and remembered.

Example:
Have you ever reflected on the role of elements such as signatures, attachments, annexes, or authorization steps? Although they may lie outside the core body of the contract, they shape the way the agreement is understood, accessed, and completed. These elements, often treated as marginal,

frequently create the most friction for users. Unclear instructions on how to sign, disorganized file structures, or missing approvals can cause confusion, frustration, and delay.

A legal experience is shaped by many factors – how a document or system is perceived, how it is structured and negotiated, how it fits within existing workflows, how users engage with it over time. What if we started to view legal documents and systems not as static, text-heavy artefacts, but as interfaces for human collaboration? This shift would allow us to move beyond a narrow, textual conception of legal agreements and towards a more integrated, experiential approach – one that also considers risk management as part of the design process. The real challenge is therefore not only to draft clearer contracts, but to design contractual ecosystems that support understanding, facilitate interaction, and contribute to better legal outcomes.

Insight:

Regarding the concept of contract experience, I have been intrigued by the work of the WCC (World Commerce and Contracting) in terms of relational contracting[3] – a model that does not discard formal agreements, but complements them with frameworks designed to support trust, adaptability, and mutual responsibility. WCC, indeed, stresses that traditional transactional contracts underperform by an average of 27 percent against expectations. This shortfall is due to a fundamental mismatch between the nature of the relationship and the legal tools used to manage it. In order to solve the problem, the WCC proposes a clear path – first, align on values and governance structures; second, formalize these into a relational contract or companion document; and third, ensure that all stakeholders understand and uphold the behavioral expectations that sustain cooperation. This integrated approach allows us to shift the focus from strict enforcement to shared outcomes.

The illusion of reading legal texts

Think about the last time you were asked to accept the terms and conditions of a social media platform. Or the moment you received a new bank policy update. Or the moment you glanced, perhaps briefly, at the fine print tucked into the last page of your electricity bill. Did you read them? Did you even consider doing so? If you're like most people, the answer is no. And not because you're careless, lazy, or disengaged. Rather, the truth is more unsettling – the way these documents are written and presented makes reading them virtually impossible for the vast majority of users.[4]

Multiple studies consistently confirm that people do not read contracts or legal texts in their entirety, and often not at all. These findings are robust and span sectors, regions, and professions. According to the World Commerce and Contracting Purpose of Contracts report, 69 percent of professionals find contracts unclear, citing their excessive length and complexity as key obstacles.[5] Moreover, 90 percent of business professionals report that they find contracts hard or very hard to understand, even though many of them work with such documents regularly.[6]

The numbers are even more revealing when we shift to everyday digital interactions. Consider the Microsoft Service Agreement covering its products.[7] If one were to read it aloud from start to finish, the task would take several hours, without breaks. Worse still, if you were to read every privacy policy you encounter in a year, it would take an estimated 76 full working days.[8] And how about this: 97 percent of users routinely accept terms and conditions without reading them.[9]

Example:
A controlled experiment took place in which participants were asked to sign up for a new service.[10] Hidden in the terms was a clause requiring them to surrender their first-born child. Nearly every participant clicked "accept" without noticing it. The clause was absurd by design. But its invisibility to users was entirely real.

On average, users spend just over one minute reviewing privacy policies that exceed 7,000 words.[11] The UK's Competition and Markets Authority has reached a similar conclusion, warning that complex terms and small print can confuse or mislead consumers, limiting their capacity to make informed decisions.[12] But there are many examples. In October 2016, the CMA published research indicating that 54 percent of UK businesses did not fully understand the rules on unfair contract terms, which could lead to the inclusion of unfair terms in consumer contracts.[13] A parallel study by the European Commission confirmed that overly dense and lengthy contract terms discouraged reading and undermined fairness in contractual relationships.[14] A 2024 MIT study went further, demonstrating that the linguistic complexity of legal documents, commonly referred to as legalese, is not only a barrier for non-lawyers but also for legal professionals themselves.[15] That research showed that legalese acts like a kind of incantation – it signals insti-tutional power and formal authority, but does so at the expense of comprehension.

To put it bluntly: the system is broken.

F-patterns and scanning – how we actually read

Reading is a complex cognitive act, and when it comes to screens, it is rarely linear. Eye-tracking research reveals that people tend to scan rather than read, especially online. In my workshops, I usually mention Jakob Nielsen's landmark study in 2006, which uncovered what became known as the F-shaped reading pattern.[16] By observing 232 users browsing thousands of pages, the study found that readers typically begin with a full horizontal scan at the top (usually reading the headline or first line), followed by a shorter horizontal scan further down, and then a vertical scan along the left margin.[17] This forms the shape of an "F", which Nielsen referred to it as "F for fast" (to say that users are quick and selective. Instead of reading every word, they skim for useful content, and words located towards the right side of a para-graph or lower on the page are far less likely to be noticed). Variants of this behavior include the E-pattern, the inverted L-shape, and other variations depending on layout. The same scanning tendencies appeared on pages as different as Google search results, corporate websites, and product listings. These behaviors, however, are not conscious. We are not drawing an "F" inten-tionally. Rather, we are seeking value and minimizing cognitive effort.[18, 19]

Example:

While the F-pattern remains dominant, other eye-tracking studies have documented alternative scanning strategies. In the layer-cake pattern, eyes jump from heading to heading, ignoring the text beneath. In the spotted pattern, users look for keywords, numerals, or visual anchors such as links. On mobile, the marking pattern is typical, in which the eyes fixate in place while the content scrolls beneath. In the bypassing pattern, repeated phrases at the beginning of lines are skipped entirely. Not surprisingly, the commitment pattern, where readers engage deeply with every line, is highly rare. Take into account that patterns like these[20] are shaped by both layout and intent – the more unstructured and denser the content, the more readers revert to scanning.[21]

Eye-tracking also highlights that people treat web pages not as destinations but as transient points of passage. What may seem careless from the perspective of a single page (skipping half the content) is often a rational strategy in the broader context of navigating the web. Readers optimize the cost–benefit ratio of their attention. If the page does not immediately offer clarity or relevance, they move on. Eye-tracking studies also confirm what most lawyers are already aware of – scanning behavior is related to intent. A user hunting for a price or keyword will therefore behave differently from one seeking to understand an argument or policy.

Example:

A growing body of research has examined how digital reading differs from paper-based reading in terms of speed, comprehension, and cognitive engagement. One study found that students read eight percent slower on an iPad compared to paper, with longer fixation durations and reduced comprehension for longer or complex texts.[22] A 2024 meta-analysis of 17 studies concluded that paper-reading generally leads to better understanding, particularly for academic or informative material.[23] Moreover, eye-tracking studies show that print readers often re-read sections, pause, or jump back; behaviors that are rare in digital reading.[24] Paper also offers spatial cues – readers know where a chart or paragraph appeared physically, which aids memory. Screens, especially with endless scrolling, offer few stable anchors. The result is a sensation of disorientation and lower recall. The digital environment adds distractions, from alerts to hyperlinks, increasing cognitive load and undermining sustained attention.[25]

A neurological case for legal design

One of most persuasive foundation for legal design comes from what neuroscience and cognitive psychology have taught us about how the human brain works. Legal design responds to a biological truth – our cognitive system is not optimized for parsing endless paragraphs of dense, unstructured text. It is, however, remarkably adept at decoding visual patterns. Research has long shown that the brain processes images up to 60,000 times faster than text,[26] and our visual system is constantly active: our eyes register approximately 36,000 images per hour.[27] Visual and spatial processing involves an integrated network across both hemispheres, particularly in the occipital and parietal lobes. While the right hemisphere often plays a stronger role in non-verbal and spatial perception, these processes are distributed, not unilateral. Visual and spatial processing involves an integrated network across both hemispheres, particularly in the occipital and parietal lobes. It is no surprise, then, that visual communication reaches us more quickly, more directly, and more effectively than verbal alternatives.

This neurological bias toward the visual has concrete effects on attention, memory, and comprehension. Content that includes infographics is shared three times more frequently on social platforms than text-only posts.[28] Memory studies confirm that while people typically recall only ten percent of what they hear after three days, that retention rate increases to 65 percent when the message is accompanied by a relevant image.[29] Online, users read at most 28 percent of the content on a page, and often far less.[30] In this context, writing alone cannot carry the communicative burden. Structure, layout, and visual orientation become essential tools to navigate the complexities of current communication.

Legal design acknowledges this shift, rethinking the architecture of communication. Our aim is to present information in a way that the human brain can grasp, retain, and use. Visual cues, such as icons, color schemes, spacing, flowcharts, typography, and timelines serve a functional role, creating rhythm, establishing hierarchy, reducing cognitive strain, and supporting the user's journey through the document. When used in legal documents, these visual strategies can draw attention to obligations, compare options, clarify timelines, and flag exceptions. They support orientation and prevent the kind of confusion that gives rise to disengagement or misunderstanding.

One of my favorite insights on this topic comes from Temple Grandin's *Thinking in Pictures*.[31] Grandin, who processes the world through images rather than words because of her autism, argues that a significant portion of the population, up to two-thirds, relies primarily on visual thinking.[32] Not surprisingly, lawyers (as journalists) are mostly part of the other third – the verbal thinkers. For this reason, the legal profession remains trapped in a textual paradigm, where players assume that traditional linear form is both neutral and sufficient. How about challenging a *de facto* exclusion, acknowledging the diversity of human cognition and crafting content that is not just legally valid but cognitively accessible?

A nudging law

Another reason why legal design has gained traction in recent years is its capacity to integrate behavioral insights. One of the most powerful tools in this respect is nudging – a concept rooted in behavioral economics that refers to subtle interventions in the decision-making environment that guide users toward desired outcomes without restricting their freedom of choice.[33] In legal systems burdened by complexity, procedural opacity, and administrative inefficiency, nudging offers a pragmatic, ethical, and user-centered approach to improving interaction with the law by restructuring choice architecture – setting helpful defaults, reducing friction in beneficial actions, and increasing the salience of critical information. In the legal world, this might mean designing an online form where the most protective options are pre-selected but editable, where progress indicators reduce cognitive overload, or where users receive real-time feedback to correct errors before submission.

At its core, nudging operates on four main principles. The first is choice architecture – the deliberate organization of decision environments to highlight better options without eliminating alternatives. The second is simplification, which reduces procedural clutter and enhances comprehension. The third is feedback, which helps users navigate legal steps with real-time support, increasing confidence and accuracy. The fourth is salience of information, which ensures that key terms, obligations, or deadlines stand out, improving compliance and reducing misunderstandings.

Insight:

These interventions may be especially relevant in domains where the law intersects with everyday users, such as social services, licensing, healthcare, or consumer protection. Poorly designed systems in these areas often deter compliance, increase administrative costs, and ultimately frustrate the objectives they were meant to serve.[34]

Nudging does not replace regulation, but surely complements it, helping reducing administrative burdens such as the cognitive load, time, and compliance costs users face when interacting with public or private legal systems.[35] Think about excessive documentation, convoluted procedures, and vague instructions. By applying nudging strategies such as default options, simplified forms, opt-out decisions, and interactive guidance, legal processes may become more intuitive, resulting in higher compliance, reduced error rates, and lower dropout.[36] Similarly, streamlined application processes for social services, coupled with better interface design, may improve completion rates and reduce processing errors.[37]

Pro tip:

From a legal design perspective, the integration of nudging requires careful implementation. Nudges have to be transparent, respectful of user autonomy, and subject to ethical review. Although they may empower users, uphold fairness, and reduce friction without sacrificing freedom, they may also be manipulative or exclusionary.

In a legal culture historically centered on deterrence, nudging offers an alternative logic – one that invites, supports, and enables. That helps users experience less frustration, and institutions benefit from reduced enforcement costs and improved legitimacy. The transition from command to design, however, is not superficial, because it redefines the very role of law in shaping behavior. As legal designers, we are not only offering a method of improving documents or services, but a strategy where law might meet people where they are – cognitively, emotionally, practically – and help them get where they need to go.

Is legal design just for B2C?

That is, quite literally, a million-dollar question – especially in a world where contracts are evolving from static legal artefacts into dynamic business tools, and where compliance is no longer a back-office function but a strategic asset. Legal design has often been framed as a solution for business-to-consumer (B2C) scenarios, where clarity, trust, and transparency are essential for engaging non-expert users. But is that the full picture? Or are we missing something in the business-to-business (B2B) space?

First, we need to unpack the question. What kind of legal design are we talking about? Are we speaking about full-contract redesigns or targeted interventions, like clause-level rewording or visual enhancements for specific sections? Are we referring to legal design in terms of underlying principles or in terms of visual communication, iconography, and workflows? Are we imagining the legal designer as a lone in-house innovator or as a cross-functional team embedded in product, sales, legal, and compliance functions?

The answer depends – unsurprisingly – on context. In B2C, the use of legal design is increasingly accepted, if not expected. Users demand clarity. Regulatory bodies enforce it. The benefits are visible. But in B2B, the picture is more nuanced. One recurring objection is that lawyers draft contracts for other lawyers, and that legal professionals within companies are trained to read complexity, not fear it. So, the argument goes: if the audience is fluent in legal language, why insisting on clarifying it?

And yet, this objection misses a fundamental point. Contracts, especially in B2B environments, are rarely confined to the legal department. They are negotiated by sales, reviewed by procurement, enforced by operations, and lived by business units. A manufacturing agreement might be implemented by supply chain managers, not attorneys. A SaaS contract might be activated and operationalized by product and engineering teams. In this ecosystem, legal design is about opening up legal work. It's about making sure contracts are not just legally valid, but strategically usable. We've already seen emerging examples – contract playbooks that visually map fallback positions, modular frameworks for cross-jurisdictional clauses, one-page deal summaries for internal alignment, visual timelines embedded into SLAs. These are current strategies in procurement teams, tech companies, fast-growth scale-ups and global enterprises alike. Legal design, in these contexts, is not only possible – it's desirable.

Example:

One example of research into contract environment design that intrigues me particularly is that by the WCC regarding the most negotiated terms.[38] The research reveals many elements we may expect – for example, price and liability are at the front of most negotiations. However, we may not be aware of how much scope and specification or IP assets influence the business scenario. As I often mention in my LinkedIn posts: this is required reading!

References

1   www.etymonline.com/word/innovation
2   The podcast is available at https://open.spotify.com/ show/68AtgS63X8JJFQaNai8QPJ
3   www.worldcc.com/Portals/IACCM/Resources/Relational%20Contracting %20and%20Governance%20Guide%20-%202024.pdf
4   It is worth mentioning that the paper "Poor writing, not specialized concepts, drives processing difficulty in legal language" (https://pubmed.ncbi.nlm.nih.gov/35257980/) won the 2022 IG Nobel Prize on Literature. IG Nobels are a satirical parody of Nobel Prizes, celebrating weird achievements in scientific research. https://improbable.com/ig/about-the-ig-nobel-prizes/
5   Deloitte and World Commerce & Contracting, "The Purpose of Contracts" (WorldCC, September 2024) https://info.worldcc.com/purpose-of-contracts
6   IACCM, "Ten Pitfalls to Avoid in Contracting" (World Commerce & Contracting, 4 February 2015) www.worldcc.com/Resources/Content-Hub/View/ArticleID/3972
7   Microsoft services agreement that covers all Microsoft products: www.microsoft.com/en-in/servicesagreement

8   Aleecia M McDonald and Lorrie Faith Cranor, "The Cost of Reading Privacy Policies" (2008) I/S: A Journal of Law and Policy for the Information Society http://www.is-journal.org/. The number is calculated based on actual reading speeds and the average length of standard policies across services and platforms, and reflects the impossible demand placed on users in the name of informed consent.

9   Deloitte, 2017 Global Mobile Consumer Survey: US Edition – The Dawn of the Next Era in Mobile (Deloitte 2017) www2.deloitte.com/us/en/pages/technology-media-and-telecommunications/articles/global-mobile-consumer-survey-us-edition.html; Jonathan A Obar and Anne Oeldorf-Hirsch, "The Biggest Lie on the Internet: Ignoring the Privacy Policies and Terms of Service Policies of Social Networking Services" (2018) Information, Communication & Society 1, presented at TPRC 44: The 44th Research Conference on Communication, Information and Internet Policy, 2016 https://ssrn.com/abstract=2757465

10   European Commission, Consumers, Health, Agriculture and Food Executive Agency and others, Study on Consumers' Attitudes Towards Terms and Conditions (T&Cs) – Final Report (Publications Office of the European Union 2016) 44 https://data.europa.eu/doi/10.2818/950733

11   European Commission and others (n. 21) 44.

12   Competition and Markets Authority, Unfair Contract Terms Guidance: Guidance on the Unfair Terms Provisions in the Consumer Rights Act 2015 (CMA37, 31 July 2015) www.gov.uk/government/publications/unfair-contract-terms-cma37

13   www.gov.uk/government/news/over-half-of-businesses-dont-know-unfair-contract-rules-well

14   Civic Consulting, Study for the Fitness Check of EU Consumer and Marketing Law – Final Report Part 1 – Main Report (European Commission, Directorate-General for Justice and Consumers 2017) 153-154 https://data.europa.eu/doi/10.2838/016391

15   Anne Trafton, "MIT Study Explains Why Laws Are Written in an Incomprehensible Style" (MIT News, 19 August 2024) https://news.mit.edu/2024/mit-study-explains-laws-incomprehensible-writing-style-0819

16   Jakob Nielsen, "F-Shaped Pattern for Reading Web Content (Original Study)". Nielsen Norman Group, 16 April 2006. www.nngroup.com/articles/f-shaped-pattern-reading-web-content/

17   *Ibid*.

18   *Ibid*.

19   Even in follow-up studies conducted over a decade later, the pattern persists – on desktop and mobile alike -whenever content is text-heavy. Kara Pernice, "F-Shaped Pattern of Reading on the Web: Misunderstood, But Still Relevant (Even on Mobile)". Nielsen Norman Group, 12 November 2017. www.nngroup.com/articles/f-shaped-pattern-reading-web-content/

20   *Ibid*.

21   TY Chiu and D Drieghe, "The Role of Visual Crowding in Eye Movements During Reading: Effects of Text Spacing" (2023) 85 *Attention, Perception, & Psychophysics* 2834 https://doi.org/10.3758/s13414-023-02787-1

22 A Feis and others, "Reading Eye Movements Performance on iPad vs Print Using a Visagraph" (2021) 14(2) *Journal of Eye Movement Research* https://doi.org/10.16910/jemr.14.2.6

23 Yiren Kong, Young Seo and Ling Zhai, "Comparison of Reading Performance on Screen and on Paper: A Meta-Analysis" (2018) 123 *Computers & Education* https://doi.org/10.1016/j.compedu.2018.05.005

24 YC Jian, "Reading in Print versus Digital Media Uses Different Cognitive Strategies: Evidence from Eye Movements during Science-Text Reading" (2022) 35 *Reading and Writing* 1549 https://doi.org/10.1007/s11145-021-10246-2

25 If you want to know more about this topic I suggest the works of Maryanne Wolf. Her concept of the "bi-literate brain" encourages training ourselves to switch between fast browsing and deep reading, depending on context. She also highlights that the medium affects physical comfort. Screens can cause eye fatigue and dryness, due to pixelation and lower blinking rates. Paper, by contrast, reflects light naturally and tends to be less tiring, especially over long periods. Maryanne Wolf, *Reader, Come Home: The Reading Brain in a Digital World* (Harper, 2018).

26 Douglas Rudy Vogel, "Persuasion and the Role of Visual Presentation Support: The UM/3M Study," Working Paper Series 86/11, Management Information Systems Research Center, University of Minnesota, 1986.

27 Eric P. Jensen, *Brain-Based Learning: The New Science of Teaching & Training* (Corwin Press, 2000).

28 Content Whale, "Benefits of Using Infographics in Content Marketing", Content Whale, 2023. https://content-whale.com/us/blog/benefits-of-using-infographics-content-marketing/

29 John Medina, *Brain Rules* (Pear Press, 2009).

30 Jakob Nielsen, "How Little Do Users Read?" Nielsen Norman Group, 1 May 2008. www.nngroup.com/articles/how-little-do-users-read/

31 Temple Grandin, *Thinking in Pictures: My Life with Autism* (Vintage Books, 2006).

32 *Ibid.*

33 Richard Thaler and Cass Sunstein, *Nudge: Improving Decisions About Health, Wealth, and Happiness* (Penguin Books, 2009).

34 Joseph J Cordes, Susan E Dudley and Layvon Q Washington, *Regulatory Compliance Burdens: Literature Review and Synthesis* (George Washington University Regulatory Studies Center, October 2022). https://regulatorystudies.columbian.gwu.edu/regulatory-compliance-burdens-literature-review-and-synthesis

35 Elizabeth Linos, Lisa T Quan and Elspeth Kirkman, *Nudging Early Reduces Administrative Burden: Three Field Experiments to Improve Code Enforcement* (Preprint, University of California, Berkeley, 2019). www.researchgate.net/publication/333663419 accessed 10 April 2025

36 Ministry of Finance, *Economic Survey 2018–19, Volume 1* (Government of India, 2019) ch 2. www.indiabudget.gov.in/economicsurvey

37 Katie Sullivan, Sara Soka, Lena Selzer and Gabriela Dorantes, *Preparing for Human-Centered Redesign: A Readiness Guide for State and Local Public Benefits Agencies Looking to Improve Applications, Renewals, and Correspondence* (Civilla and Beeck Center for Social Impact + Innovation at Georgetown University, Fall 2021). https://beeckcenter.georgetown.edu/project/social-safety-net-benefits-research

38 www.worldcc.com/Portals/IACCM/Reports/Most-Negotiated-Terms-2024.pdf

Chapter 4:
Abandoning the legalese – communicating plainly

A short introduction to plain language

The emergence of the plain language movement can be seen as a timely and necessary response to the growing demand for transparency in legal and administrative texts. Born out of the recognition that legal language had become a barrier rather than a bridge, this movement calls for a style of writing that prioritizes clarity without compromising precision. The reasons are easy to understand – when legal documents are drafted in ways that exclude or confuse, they fail to perform their basic communicative functions and the role of law as a public good is compromised at its core. At the end of the day, the ability to understand the law shapes the relationship between institutions and citizens, reinforcing trust, participation, and the proper exercise of rights and responsibilities.[1,2] A legal text that is readable, respectful of its audience, and mindful of linguistic clarity becomes a vehicle of inclusion, capable of reaching individuals with different educational paths, social conditions, or cognitive styles.

This shift is no longer confined to isolated efforts. Legal systems across the globe are increasingly institutionalizing the use of plain language as a structural element of fairness and public trust. Authorities, courts, legislative bodies, and consumer protection agencies have begun to view clarity not merely as a stylistic preference but as a foundation of ethical legal practice. In the United States, the Plain Writing Act of 2010 obliges all federal agencies to produce public documents that are "clear, concise, well-organized, and appropriate to the intended audience".[3] In the United Kingdom, HM Courts and Tribunals Service follows guidance developed in collaboration with the Plain English Campaign, ensuring that forms and judicial communications are free from jargon and understandable to lay users.[4] At the European level, the Commission has promoted a Joint Practical Guide that explicitly encourages drafters to prioritize clarity in multilingual contexts.[5] Elsewhere, the Canadian province of British Columbia rewrote its Employment Standards Act using plain language in 1997, making it one of the first full legislative texts to undergo such transformation, a case still studied internationally.[6] In South Africa, the very Constitution is praised for its clear and accessible drafting, and institutions such as the Financial Sector Conduct Authority have issued plain language guidelines for insurance and credit industries.[7] Australia's Office of Parliamentary Counsel has published a Plain English Manual, supporting legislative drafters in producing statutes that citizens can actually understand.[8] Finally, New Zealand offers perhaps the most emblematic example with the complete rewrite of its Income Tax Act, a process guided by the principle that the law must be written "so that users can find it, understand it, and apply it".[9] These examples (and there could be many, many more) make it increasingly difficult to dismiss plain language as a peripheral trend. Rather, they show it as an emerging standard, one that signals a broader institutional commitment to accessibility and legal dignity. Moving away from legalese is a sign that legal systems are beginning to reorient themselves not around their own internal codes, but around the people they claim to serve. It's more than just a communication choice.

Insight:

Have you ever considered the possibility of using a comic to draft a contract? While it might seem unconventional at first glance, there are numerous examples of contracts presented entirely in comic form. One of the most cited and influential examples comes from South African lawyer Robert de Rooy,[10] who developed legally binding visual contracts to improve accessibility for people with limited literacy. His work, originally aimed at agricultural workers, replaced dense legal prose with narrative-driven illustrations, allowing parties to fully grasp the content before signing. But this is not an isolated case. Similar approaches have been adopted in various jurisdictions and fields, from employment agreements to informed consent documents in clinical settings.[11] These agreements replace or support text with sequences of drawings that illustrate the key obligations, rights, and expectations. Once both parties sign the comic, it becomes a valid and enforceable agreement, provided the essential elements of a contract are present. In doing so, the comic format transforms what is often perceived as obscure or intimidating into something that can be followed, understood, and genuinely agreed upon.

What does it mean to communicate clearly?

Across a world that speaks over 7,000 languages and uses more than 300 writing systems,[12] there is one ability that surpasses borders, professions, and cultural settings – the capacity to communicate clearly. But what does communicating clearly mean? Well, it means conveying information in a way that can be understood and acted upon, with minimal friction and maximum precision. While this may sound intuitive, the sheer volume of self-help books, online courses, and training programs dedicated to the topic reveals a deeper truth – clarity is hard to achieve. And yet, it remains essential.

Miscommunication, on the other hand, is not merely inconvenient. It is costly. According to the State of Business Communication Report 2024, poor communication habits account for a loss of 7.47 hours per employee per week, across sectors and company sizes.[13] That is nearly a full working day lost – not only in productivity, but in missed conversations, flawed processes, abandoned ideas, and strained collaboration.

Communicating clearly begins with precision in thought. One must know exactly what needs to be said, why it matters, and to whom. From there, the method becomes just as important as the message – choosing words, tone, format, and channels that reflect not only the content, but the audience's expectations, background, and cognitive habits.

Pro tip:

People often say, "Just use plain language – it's simple". But, as the famous proverb goes, "the devil is in the detail" and even a single term can become a minefield. Take "self-represented litigant". Is it clear? Technically, yes. But does it resonate with someone facing a court process alone, overwhelmed and unassisted? Not always.

When we write for clarity, we're not just simplifying. We're balancing nuance, accuracy, tone, and emotion. And every word we choose can include, or exclude, entire groups of people.

If legal language is a map, then plain language forces us to ask, who are we mapping for? And who gets left out?

Think about it:

Court user may sound neutral, but does it include family members, interpreters, or those still outside the system?

Legal consumer sounds inclusive, until it starts to feel like academic jargon to someone reading a form at 2am.

Customer brings in user-centered thinking but can feel out of place in a justice context – too commercial, too transactional.

Litigant is legally precise but may alienate people who don't even identify with the legal system yet.

Unrepresented is clear and widely used but defines someone by what they lack – and can sound clinical or even cold.

Community member or *person* feels human and accessible, but risks being too vague for legal accuracy.

People navigating legal problems is plain and relatable but may fall short in legal analysis or procedural contexts.

Plain language isn't just about simplifying – it's about making deliberate, thoughtful decisions, one word at a time.

The benefits of clarity and comprehension

The roots of legalese can be traced back to medieval legal traditions, where Latin phrases and arcane formulations were markers of exclusivity and gatekeeping. These linguistic habits persisted, not for clarity or necessity, but to signal institutional authority, a tradition that continues today. However, there are several benefits associated with the use of plain language in legal documents and interactions. These benefits extend beyond readability, influencing trust, compliance, dispute prevention, and institutional credibility. Among the most relevant advantages, there are the following.

Less ambiguity

For those without legal training, traditional legal language can be obscure and intimidating. Plain language enhances understanding by reducing ambiguity and enabling individuals to grasp their rights and obligations more easily, lowering the risk of non-compliance or unintentional breaches.

In healthcare, simplifying consent forms may help patients better understand treatment options. In consumer banking, clearer credit agreements could support clients in grasping repayment terms and interest conditions, potentially reducing defaults. Tenancy agreements written in plain language might lead to fewer misunderstandings regarding maintenance duties or termination clauses.

Trust and reputational safeguards

When people understand the documents they are asked to sign, they are more likely to trust the institution or professional behind them. This is particularly relevant in consumer contracts, employment agreements, and public-facing documents.

A clearly written employment contract – detailing working hours, salary, and leave entitlements – could strengthen employee confidence and might reduce the number of routine HR queries. In e-commerce, transparent return policies written in plain language may increase customer satisfaction and could reduce the volume of complaints. Public notices drafted with accessible language, including visually structured explanations of tax or traffic regulations, might contribute to higher compliance rates and may lower the risk of litigation.

Fewer disputes and faster resolution

Complex language increases the likelihood of conflicting interpretations, which can easily lead to disputes. Plain language makes agreements easier to interpret consistently and may expedite the resolution of disagreements.

Think about construction contracts involving multiple subcontractors. Clearly written clauses on timelines and deliverables could reduce operational confusion and may improve coordination. In family law, custody agreements that use accessible language might help parents better understand their responsibilities, possibly reducing the need for judicial intervention. During mediation, plain language can allow parties to focus more directly on substantive issues, rather than diverting attention to the interpretation of ambiguous legal terms.

Regulatory compliance

Clarity is increasingly a legal requirement. The GDPR explicitly requires that information be provided in "a concise, transparent, intelligible and easily accessible form, using clear and plain language".[14] Healthcare regulations stress that informed consent must be based on real understanding. Plain language, in this sense, could serve as both a preventive and enabling tool, while non-compliance may result in sanctions.

Examples, especially in highly regulated scenarios, could fill entire pages of this book. I chose just one. After the 2008 financial crisis, the US Securities and Exchange Commission (SEC) introduced stricter rules[15] for mutual fund prospectuses, requiring them to use a plain language "summary prospectus". These documents explain key information like fees, investment objectives, and risks in short, understandable sections. Firms that used technical or overly complex disclosures faced fines, reputational harm, and customer complaints, while those adopting plain summaries found that consumers better understood their investments and made fewer claims of mis-selling.

Cost savings

Clarity reduces the need for repeated explanations, customer support interventions, and legal clarifications. Ambiguous or excessively technical language often generates confusion, which in turn may require additional resources to manage.

A customer support team regularly dealing with questions about unclear billing terms might incur operational costs that could be avoided with better drafting. But examples are endless. Think about a software license agreement that says the client can "use the software internally" but doesn't define internal use. This could lead to misuse of the software, thus ushering in the risk of being sued for infringement and breaching the license agreement.

The plain language ISO

The publication of ISO 24495-1:2023[16] represents a defining moment in the broader conversation on clarity in legal and institutional communication. For the first time, an international standard articulates a coherent, applicable framework for plain language, offering not only a shared definition but a set of principles and operational guidelines intended to be adopted across sectors, jurisdictions, and legal traditions. The standard defines plain language as a form of communication in which wording, structure, and design are so clear that readers can effortlessly locate the information they need, grasp its meaning, and use it to make informed decisions. This pivot from readability in the narrow sense to usability in the functional sense marks a conceptual evolution, reframing how professional texts should be planned, drafted, and assessed – not in terms of aesthetic simplicity, but in relation to the reader's capacity to act.

Insight:

ISO 24495-1 offers a concrete framework for plain language, but its emergence did not occur in a vacuum. The standard builds on decades of scholarly, professional, and advocacy work. One of the players worth mentioning is Clarity International,[17] a legal and public communication-focused non-profit organization. Alongside the Center for Plain Language

(US)[18] and PLAIN (Plain Language Association International),[19] Clarity co-founded the International Plain Language Working Federation,[20] which in recent years has encouraged stakeholders around the world to mobilize local support (whether by forming national sub-committees, gathering stakeholder endorsements, or surfacing country-specific needs and considerations).[21] For those interested in the plain movement, I suggest reading the Clarity journal, which has been instrumental in not only reporting on the progress of the standards initiative but contributing key documents.[22, 23, 24]

The standard rests on four interdependent principles – relevance, findability, comprehensibility, and usability. These are not treated as linear stages but as mutually reinforcing elements of a single design objective – to produce written communication that works.

1. *Relevance* addresses the need for documents to respond to the context, expectations, and informational needs of their intended audience.
2. *Findability* concerns the organization of content – its structure, hierarchy, and navigation cues, all essential for readers to orient themselves quickly and locate what matters.
3. *Comprehensibility* relates to language choices, sentence structure, and tone, promoting precision without excess.
4. *Usability*, the final principle, extends across the full document lifecycle and requires continuous testing, revision, and feedback to ensure that the text not only informs but enables action.

What gives this standard particular weight in the legal context is its adaptability to both compliance-focused environments and innovation-driven approaches such as legal design. The integration of ISO 24495-1 into legal departments offers a practical method for improving the quality of both internal and public-facing documents, without compromising the accuracy or formality required by legal institutions. The standard also positions itself within a broader normative and technological framework. Although it does not address digital accessibility directly, its principles align with existing instruments such as the Web Content Accessibility Guidelines and the European standard EN 301 549, both of which are referenced in the European Accessibility Act. In this light, plain language becomes a marker of legal accountability – an instrument through which democratic institutions can express clarity, respect, and fairness.

Pro tip:

The widest use of plain legal language is for governing documents, like legislation and regulations; documents that govern personal or organizational relationships, like financial, housing, and medical agreements; and documents that cover other relationships, like powers of attorney, wills, privacy policies, and terms of use.

To engage with ISO 24495-1 means embracing a broader ethical stance – writing not for the drafter, but for the reader; prioritizing clarity as a tool of inclusion, not an aesthetic preference; and treating transparency as a structural feature of legal communication. While most companies think about ISO certifications in terms of labels, I would rely more on different aspects – the ethical part and the awareness part – using a parameter as a benchmark to evaluate your internal quality.

To date, more than 20 national standard bodies have adopted the ISO, including Australia, Brazil, France, Germany, Italy, and the UK. The standard is also available in more than ten languages, including French, Portuguese, Spanish, Dutch, Finnish, and Norwegian. Where it has not been adopted, some national bodies still offer the international version for purchase. The International Plain Language Federation[25] encourages countries not yet involved to request adoption through their local standards authorities. This broad localization effort underscores the growing global recognition of plain language as a vital tool for inclusive and effective communication.

A world in emojis

Emojis, once confined to light-hearted, personal exchanges, have become a permanent fixture in digital communication. From early typographic smileys like :) to today's expansive set of pictograms, these symbols help compensate for the absence of non-verbal cues in text-based messaging. Their role, however, is no longer limited to informal interactions. As digital conversations expand across personal, professional, and legal domains, emojis have entered legal agreements,[26] negotiations, and even courtrooms,[27] raising questions of intent, interpretation, and evidentiary value.

Their widespread use reflects this transition. According to Unicode, over 92 percent of internet users regularly employ emojis in their messaging, making them one of the most ubiquitous forms of modern communication.[28] Every day we send 23 billion mobile messages[29] whilst 100 billion messages are sent daily on WhatsApp.[30] But their interpretative fragility remains a concern.

While an emoji may convey warmth, sarcasm, or affirmation, these meanings are rarely stable. What appears as a small gesture on one screen may be rendered – and perceived – entirely differently on another.

This issue of inconsistency is compounded by what has been termed "cross-platform depiction diversity".[31] Emojis are rendered according to the design conventions of each platform and operating system. A "grinning face" might appear joyful on one device, awkward on another, or even menacing on a third. Emojipedia attempts to document emoji appearances and intended meanings across platforms, but there is no official or universally recognized reference guide for courts to rely upon.[32] Technological limitations add further risk. Emojis may disappear or be rendered incorrectly if they are not supported on a recipient's device, appearing instead as blank squares or placeholder icons. This may sound trivial, but think about a sarcastic remark followed by a wink emoji 😉. It might convey irony or playfulness, but without the emoji, it risks being read as harsh or literal, potentially leading to miscommunication or legal disagreement.

Courts are already grappling with these complexities. A striking example emerged in Canada, where the Saskatchewan Court ruled that a thumbs-up emoji 👍 could constitute acceptance of contractual terms.[33] In that case, a buyer sent a contract via text message and asked the seller to confirm receipt and agreement. The seller replied with the emoji. The court determined that this symbol satisfied the legal requirements for acceptance, thus rendering the contract binding.[34] The ruling sparked wide debate over the thresholds for intention and clarity in digital communication.

Insight:

In the United States, the role of emojis in legal proceedings has also been contested. During the trial of Ross Ulbricht, founder of the Silk Road marketplace, the court faced the question of whether jurors should be shown the emojis that accompanied his messages.[35] Out of concern for misinterpretation, the final compromise was for lawyers to read the messages aloud, merely stating that an emoji had been used without showing or describing it. This cautious approach illustrates the legal system's difficulty in addressing the ambiguity that emojis introduce, even when the messages themselves are admissible.

The instability of emoji visibility thus raises concerns about their reliability in formal documents or agreements, and cultural variation compounds these interpretive difficulties. Much like language, emoji usage is culturally situated. A gesture that signals friendliness in one country may carry a different or even offensive meaning in another. This cultural relativity makes it difficult to design universally interpretable messages and further complicates the task of embedding emojis in legal instruments without risking misalignment between sender and recipient. I would also add that – as technology evolves – new forms of expression are continuously introduced. Animated emojis, for example, already convey motion and multi-layered emotional states, complicating any attempt to attribute clear intent.[36] Augmented reality (AR) emojis, which enable users to overlay digital expressions onto real-world environments, add another layer of ambiguity.[37] Companies are already offering the possibility of creating your own emojis with AI.[38] As these technologies become more widely adopted in business communication, they will inevitably introduce new interpretive and evidentiary challenges for legal professionals. In anticipation of this evolution, I suggest legal designers remain attentive to emerging technologies, exploring responsible ways to incorporate these expressive tools into legal documents when appropriate.

Pro tip:
Legal professionals can mitigate the risks associated with emoji misinterpretation by combining visual clarity, contextual disclaimers, and explicit drafting choices. One possible approach is to standardize the use of emojis within contracts and formal communications by introducing clear interpretive guidance directly in the document. For instance, a dedicated clause could define the intended meaning of specific emojis commonly used in business exchanges, thereby reducing ambiguity and ensuring consistent interpretation across platforms.

Notes about inclusive language
In recent years, the legal profession has shown growing interest in the use of inclusive language as part of a broader reflection on how legal documents can better reflect the diversity of the individuals they concern. This shift is often framed as both an ethical and a functional matter. Language that risks alienating, misrepresenting, or marginalizing people – whether on the basis of gender, background, ability, or status – can compromise not only the accessibility of legal texts but also the relationships built around them. At the same time, efforts to adopt more inclusive language are not without debate, and

they intersect with a wide range of views shaped by legal tradition, institutional culture, and personal experience. What some may view as an essential gesture of fairness, others may regard as unnecessary or politically loaded. Still, there is an emerging consensus that sensitivity in legal writing can play a constructive role in making documents more respectful, open, and usable.

One area that often draws attention is the treatment of gender in legal language. Historically, legal drafting has defaulted to masculine generics or binary formulations such as "he/she" or "him/her", which may feel outdated or unnecessarily prescriptive to some readers. A variety of alternatives have since gained traction – the singular "they" is increasingly accepted in legal and institutional contexts, and many occupational titles traditionally gendered, such as "chairman" or "foreman", can be replaced with neutral equivalents like "chairperson" or "supervisor". The aim of these changes is not to alter meaning, but to broaden the language's capacity to speak without assumption. Yet, as with all such shifts, what feels inclusive in one context may not be embraced in another, and different audiences may bring differing expectations to the same text.

Inclusion also raises important questions around references to race, ethnicity, and cultural identity. Legal documents that aim to speak to general audiences may need to revisit terminology that, even if not deliberately exclusive, can inadvertently narrow the scope of who is addressed.

Insight:

The word "citizen" may unintentionally exclude those who are nonetheless governed by a particular law or policy. Terms such as "individual", "person", or "resident" may offer broader and more neutral alternatives. Likewise, formulations based on idiomatic expressions or culturally specific metaphors can reduce clarity and, in some cases, risk reinforcing stereotypes. Here too, inclusive language is less about correctness than about care – about being alert to how words may travel across different audiences and contexts.

Another relevant dimension regards disability. Language that implicitly frames disability as a form of deficiency – phrases like "suffering from" or "confined to" – can reinforce negative assumptions. Alternatives that focus on the person and use neutral descriptors, such as "a person with a visual impairment", may be more respectful without being euphemistic.

That said, it is important to acknowledge that there is no universally accepted path when it comes to inclusive language in legal writing. Preferences differ, as do cultural and institutional expectations. Some will prioritize clarity above all; others will emphasize representation. Our view is that inclusive language is best approached not as a checklist but as a process of ongoing attention – one that remains sensitive to context, audience, and purpose. In this sense, the question is not whether to use inclusive language, but how to use it thoughtfully, in ways that serve both the content and the people it is meant to reach.

Insight:

In our practice, we do not align with a single, uniform approach. Instead, we choose to remain attentive to the diversity of preferences and linguistic sensitivities that characterize the environments in which we operate. This means that rather than prescribing a fixed formula, we seek to respond flexibly to the expectations and realities of each context, whether linguistic, institutional, or cultural. Our intention is not to dilute the debate, but to acknowledge that language is a living, evolving tool; one that cannot always be standardized without sacrificing nuance or relevance.

We understand that this position may be viewed by some as cautious or insufficiently assertive. Advocates of more radical reform often empha-size the role of language in reshaping social attitudes and dismantling power asymmetries. Indeed, research suggests that linguistic forms can influence perception and contribute to cultural transformation. At the same time, we observe that within corporate and professional settings, the use of inclusive or non-binary language remains a nuanced issue – frequently shaped by organizational culture, legal frameworks, and varying degrees of public acceptance. What is perceived as progressive in one setting may be viewed as intrusive or unfamiliar in another.

Rather than minimizing the transformative potential of language, our approach seeks to navigate its complexity with attentiveness and respect.

The intercultural factor

The internationalization of legal practice is no longer a projection of what may come. It is a present reality. Contracts, policies, and regulatory docu-ments routinely cross jurisdictions, legal systems, and linguistic boundaries. In this context, moving away from legalese is often a strategic and ethical necessity. Drafting for international contractors and policymakers demands more than translation. It requires rethinking assumptions, reworking struc-tures, and, perhaps most critically, revisiting the language itself.[39] Legal professionals are increasingly expected to produce documents that communicate effectively across cultures and professional domains, while preserving the clarity and enforceability that legal texts require.

Language is never entirely neutral. Legal documents often originate within a specific national tradition, shaped by its idioms, references, and embedded legal concepts. These elements do not always travel well. Phrases such as *"cutting red tape"* may seem innocuous in one jurisdiction, yet risk confusion when read by someone unfamiliar with its bureaucratic metaphors.[40] Similarly, legal terms that carry specific connotations in one jurisdiction, such as *"at-will employment"* or *"fair dealing"*, benefit from clarification when used internationally. Without appropriate context, they may be misunderstood or misapplied, sometimes with tangible legal consequences.

In this environment, plain language can serve as a bridge. It connects civil and common law traditions, local terminology and global relevance, formal drafting and user comprehension. It prompts legal professionals to consider not only what they are writing, but also for whom, and within which legal and linguistic framework. This includes recognizing how legal assumptions vary. A clause that appears essential in a common law contract might seem redundant or confusing in a civil law context, where statutory rules already govern the matter.

Structure plays a role as well. International documents benefit from clear sequencing, concise sections, and meaningful headings that guide the reader. This type of structural clarity reduces ambiguity, improves navigation, and supports consistency in both comprehension and implementation.

Pro tip:
Where key concepts differ across jurisdictions, explanatory notes or a definitions section can be particularly useful. How about including a brief glossary to clarify technical terms and provide a shared frame of reference for readers who may not be familiar with the originating legal system?

References
1   Plain English Foundation, "Plain Language and Human Rights" (Plain English Foundation, 2023) www.plainenglishfoundation.com/plain-language-and-human-rights/
2   Paula Baron and Lillian Corbin, *Legal Writing* (Oxford University Press, 2016) ch 1.
3   Plain Writing Act of 2010, HR 946, 111th Cong (2010) www.congress.gov/bill/111th-congress/house-bill/946

4   Plain English Campaign, "Government Organisations with Crystal Marks" (Plain English Campaign, 2024) www.plainenglish.co.uk/services/crystal-mark/crystal-mark-holders/1353-government-organisations-with-crystal-marks.html

5   European Commission Legal Service, *Joint Practical Guide of the European Parliament, the Council and the Commission for Persons Involved in the Drafting of European Union Legislation* (Publications Office of the European Union, 2015). https://data.europa.eu/doi/10.2880/5575

6   Employment Standards Act, RSBC 1996, c 113. www.bclaws.gov.bc.ca/civix/document/id/complete/statreg/00_96113_01

7   Financial Sector Conduct Authority, *Language Policy*, Version 3, C&L/POL/02/2024-26 (approved 26 March 2024, effective 1 April 2024). www.fsca.co.za

8   Office of Parliamentary Counsel, *Plain English Manual* (Commonwealth of Australia 1993, rev 2013) www.opc.gov.au

9   Income Tax Act 2007 (NZ), Public Act 2007 No. 97, as at 2 February 2025, www.legislation.govt.nz/act/public/2007/0097/latest/DLM1512301.html. Rewrite Advisory Panel, "Process for Resolving Potential Unintended Legislative Changes in the Income Tax Act" (RAP 002, Inland Revenue Department, 2004). www.taxtechnical.ird.govt.nz/general-articles/panel-statement-rap-002-process-for-resolving-potential-unintended-legislative-changes-in-the-income

10   Lawyers as Changemakers, "Rob de Rooy – Comic Contracts" (2023) https://lawyersaschangemakers.com/rob-de-rooy-comic-contracts/

11   Landers & Rogers, "Visual Contracts and the Pitfalls of Employment Agreements" (Landers, 21 November 2022) www.landers.com.au/legal-insights-news/visual-contracts-and-the-pitfalls-of-employment-agreements. N Høegh Madsen, M Stengaard and MJ Schmidt-Kessen, "The Visualized Employment Contract: An Exploratory Study on Contract Visualization in Danish Employment Contracts" (2021) 11(1) *The Comics Grid: Journal of Comics Scholarship*, 5. https://doi.org/10.16995/cg.4353.

12   Nations Online, "Languages of the World" (Nations Online Project, 2024). www.nationsonline.org/oneworld/languages.htm

13   https://go.grammarly.com/2024-state-of-business-communication-report

14   Art. 12(1), GDPR.

15   www.broadridge.com/_assets/pdf/broadridge-am_00306_ss_20-rule-498a-sell-sheet_rel-071320-web.pdf

16   International Organization for Standardization, ISO 24495-1:2023 *Plain Language – Part 1: Governing Principles and Guidelines (1st edn, ISO 2023)*, www.iso.org/standard/78907.html

17   Clarity International, www.clarity-international.org/

18   Center for Plain Language, https://centerforplainlanguage.org/

19   Plain Language Association International, https://plainlanguagenetwork.org/

20   International Plain Language Federation, www.iplfederation.org/

21   Clarity International, "Plain Language Standards" (Clarity, 2024) https://clarity-international.net/plain-language-standards.html

22 Neil James, "Strengthening plain language: public benefit and professional practice" (2010) 64, *Clarity: Journal of the International Association Promoting Plain Legal Language*, 1.

23 Regarding plain language, I would also suggest the work of Rob Waller, www.robwaller.org/who

24 See note 11.

25 International Plain Language Federation, ISO Plain Language Standard (IPLF, 2024) www.iplfederation.org/iso-standard/

26 LexisNexis, "Contracting by Emoji", *LexisNexis Practical Guidance Journal*, 2023 www.lexisnexis.com/community/insights/legal/practical-guidance-journal/b/pa/posts/contracting-by-emoji

27 *Cumberland Trial Journal*, "Emojis and Emoticons in Court: No Laughing Matter", 22 September 2023. https://cumberlandtrialjournal.com/2023/09/22/emojis-and-emoticons-in-court-no-laughing-matter/

28 Unicode Consortium, "Emoji Frequency" (Unicode, 2021) https://home.unicode.org/emoji/emoji-frequency/

29 www.forbes.com/councils/forbestechcouncil/2021/01/06/the-past-present-and-future-of-messaging/

30 Stephen Harrison, "How Emojis Have Invaded the Courtroom", *Slate*, 26 November 2019 https://slate.com/technology/2019/11/emoji-law-court-cases-interpretation.html

31 Eric Goldman, "Emojis and the Law" (2018) 93 *Washington Law Review* 1227 https://ssrn.com/abstract=3133412

32 Emojipedia, https://emojipedia.org/

33 *South West Terminal Ltd v. Achter Land & Cattle Ltd* (2023) SKKB 116 (CanLII, 8 June 2023).

34 CBC News, "Emoji Contract Dispute Heads to Supreme Court of Canada", 8 March 2024. www.cbc.ca/news/canada/saskatchewan/supreme-court-appeal-emoji-contract-1.7464272

35 . *ABA Journal*, "Emoticons Matter, Judge Rules in Silk Road Trial", 8 February 2015. www.abajournal.com/news/article/emoticons_matter_judge_rules_in_silk_road_trial

36 Google Fonts, "Noto Emoji Animation" https://googlefonts.github.io/noto-emoji-animation/

37 Samsung, "How to Use the Emoji Feature on Your Galaxy Phone" www.samsung.com/sg/support/mobile-devices/how-to-use-the-emoji-feature-on-your-galaxy-phone/

38 The most common example is Apple, with its Genmoji on Apple Ios16. For further info: https://support.apple.com/it-it/guide/iphone/iph4e76f5667/ios

39 Regarding culture in international contracting, I mainly refer to two books: Erin Meyer's *The Culture Map* (Public Affairs, 2016), and Richard D. Lewis' *When cultures Collide* (John Murray Press, 2018).

40   Regarding phrases and proverbs, see Andrew White's article, "Pure nonsense – how English speaking lawyers can't resist absurd language", *Modern Lawyer*, July 2024: https://globelawonline.com/article/738/pure-nonsense-how-english-speaking-lawyers-cant-resist-absurd-language

Thoughtful perspective
Michael Doherty

Professor Michael Doherty is associate head of the law school, Lancaster University, UK. He is co-author of Public Law *(3rd edition, Routledge 2023), co-founder of the Connecting Legal Education online community, and former chair of the Association of Law Teachers. His legal design work encompasses education, disciplinarity, and access to justice. He is the founding editor-in-chief of the* Legal Design Journal.

Marco: The first question is the kind one might expect, given your role: tenured professor, first-ever chair in legal design, and editor-in-chief of the Legal Design Journal. *Let's begin with something apparently simple, but not so easy in practice. Close your eyes and imagine it's 2030. What does the legal design community look like?*

Michael: Looking five years ahead, I see the legal design community as broader and more established than it is today. The field has grown consistently, and although we're still relatively young, perhaps a decade old if we consider 2012 as a foundational year, the expansion is undeniable. That year saw the emergence of key infrastructure elements that have supported our field's development.

Since then, the number of people engaged with legal design has steadily increased. I believe that in 2030, the community will not only be larger but more structured. Our field's infrastructure is still in its early stages. Take the *Legal Design Journal*, for example – we're just getting started. But in five years, I expect a far richer body of published work, both more extensive and more intellectually sophisticated.

I also anticipate that one of the central themes in legal design's evolution will be its intersection with generative AI. I see legal design as a cognate discipline within the broader legal innovation ecosystem. It shares space with legal tech, but its strength lies in its distinctive method.

Legal design is valuable because it begins by ensuring that we are solving the right problem before moving to how we solve it. That sequence is fundamental. For me, legal design is an essential tool for legal problem-solving and a key part of any legal thinker's toolkit. The ways in which design thinking and generative AI will intertwine will be among the most compelling developments in the coming years.

Marco: You are the first chair in legal design that I am aware of. What does that role represent, and why is it important for the community?

Michael: My professorship in legal design is both symbolic and practical. On the one hand, it marks a visible milestone in our field. On the other, it represents a deliberate step in building the necessary infrastructure. We cannot assume that legal design will automatically continue to grow and flourish. There are examples of other innovation methods – like lean thinking – that have seen influence but have not matured into fully fledged disciplines.

For legal design to continue its development, it must be supported structurally. We need courses in higher education that train future lawyers in design methods. We need spaces that act as growth engines – the Legal Design Summit in Helsinki is one, and the *Legal Design Journal* is another.

If we want legal design to take root, especially in academic contexts, we need the full apparatus – chairs, books, journals, and conferences. My position contributes to this foundation. It signals to the broader legal community that legal design is not a passing trend, but a maturing field worthy of institutional investment.

Marco: I couldn't agree more. This book only briefly mentions the Legal Design Journal, so I'd like to dive deeper here. Why is this journal important, and what role does it play in the community?

Michael: The *Legal Design Journal* is a sign of our field's growing maturity. When I surveyed the existing literature, I noticed that legal design scholarship was scattered across a wide range of publications, mostly in subfields of law. Those articles often spent a good part of their word count justifying the existence of legal design before even discussing the actual case study or tool. They had to re-establish the same ground over and over again – what legal design is, that it is real, and why it matters.

That's understandable in what I call the evangelical phase of a field, where your first task is to make your field visible and credible. But we've reached a point where we can be more ambitious. We now need a space where scholars and practitioners can talk to one another without having to explain themselves from scratch. A place where the conversation begins from shared understanding, so that we can explore deeper ideas and move forward intellectually.

What makes our journal especially distinctive is how it was created. We approached its development as a design challenge. I don't know of any other journal – legal or design – that started in this way. We conducted user research – surveys, interviews, and questionnaires. We asked people where they currently find information on legal design, what's missing, and what would make them read or contribute to a journal.

This feedback, gathered from around the world, shaped our development. We worked as a global team of around 20 to 25 academics and practitioners. Together, we prototyped various structures, values, and editorial policies. What emerged is a diamond open access journal – free to read and free to publish. We're entirely online and have two core sections. The first is for peer-reviewed academic articles of five to ten thousand words. The second, called the Studio Section, is dedicated to practical case studies. In this way, the journal speaks to the whole legal design community, across both theory and practice.

Marco: Now, a broader question: how can legal design inform and influence public policy-making, especially when it comes to transparency and effectiveness?

Michael: That's a timely topic. I recently worked on a European public policy initiative concerning rights in the digital public space. I'm not a policy specialist, but I noticed that much of the discussion was based on assumptions – or on what I'd call a weak evidence base.

What legal design brings to policy-making is its attention to lived experience. Our methods often rely on qualitative research and storytelling. For example, in debates about misinformation and its effects on European elections, a legal design approach would seek to understand how misinformation impacts ordinary citizens' perceptions of their choices. It would look at how non-experts engage with digital platforms and media.

This kind of perspective is largely absent from current policy-making. Legal design could fill that gap by offering more grounded, people-centered evidence that reflects how policy is actually experienced on the ground.

Marco: What do you see as the most pressing challenges facing the legal design community, and how might they be addressed?

Michael: I'd divide the answer into two main parts. First, there's a persistent cultural resistance – or perhaps a misunderstanding – within parts of the legal community about what design is and why it matters. Legal designers must constantly demonstrate that our work is practical and relevant. Some of the language used in service design or design thinking can be off-putting to legal professionals. We have to navigate that carefully – we must avoid both intimidating people and being dismissed as trivial.

So one ongoing challenge is to show that legal design delivers value – that it works, that it's concrete, and that it contributes meaningfully to legal practice.

The second challenge, looking ahead, is the risk that legal design could be subsumed under legal tech or legal innovation. In the UK, for example, legal design doesn't have high visibility in most innovation teams within major firms. When you look at the public-facing missions of these units, legal design is rarely named. There's a danger that it could be absorbed and diluted.

But legal design has a distinct voice, and that identity needs to be maintained and articulated with care.

Marco: That's an important reflection. Looking back over your career, what inspired your focus on legal design? And how has your perspective changed over time?

Michael: I had already built a fairly successful academic career as a constitutional law scholar and legal educator before I even discovered legal design. When I encountered it, I was probably about 15 years away from retirement. It completely transformed how I saw my work. It gave me a new lease of life.

Let me give you an example. I'd been teaching the rule of law for 25 years, and my favorite theorist was always Joseph Raz, who says the law's purpose is to guide human behavior – and therefore, it must be clear. I'd been repeating that for decades. But it was only after I embraced legal design that I thought, "Wait a minute. Most laws are not understandable to ordinary people. So how can they possibly guide behavior?".

Legal design made me ask questions that had been in front of me all along, but that I'd never really seen.

I'd also spent a lot of time in educational leadership. In Europe, the dominant theme in education over the past 30 years has been student-centered learning. It's official EU policy. It's part of the Bologna Declaration. But in reality, when education is reformed, it's usually a group of professors sitting in a room, perhaps glancing at some feedback, then deciding, based mostly on assumptions, what needs to change.

Design thinking disrupted that completely for me. It made me realize that we cannot address educational challenges without understanding students' lived experiences – how they experience learning, university life, wellbeing, career pressures, and so on. Legal design changed not just how I work, but how I think.

Part II:
Legal Design and...

Introduction to Part II:
Beyond legal design

Legal design is a response to a deeper structural tension – the growing distance between legal systems and the people they are meant to serve. If the first part of this book traced its conceptual cartography, defining legal design's foundations, its vocabulary, and the cultural shift it proposes, this second part moves into the fields where that vocabulary may find common ground.

We begin by confronting an ambiguity that still shapes both research and practice – is legal design merely an offshoot of existing design disciplines, such as service design, information design, and graphic design, or does it stand as a field of its own, defined by its particular constraints, consequences, and normative weight? From this point, the journey continues through a series of thematic chapters that investigate what legal design can generate across contexts, systems, and demands.

We open with sustainability, exploring how legal design supports the principles of the 2030 Agenda. From there, we turn to the emergence of generative artificial intelligence and examine how legal design is positioned to respond to its challenges and opportunities. We then trace the outer edges of the field. We look first at how legal design can counter manipulation in interface architecture, especially in relation to dark patterns. This is followed by a chapter on proactive law – a perspective that invites legal professionals to anticipate friction, prevent breakdowns, and design for continuity and foresight.

Finally, the closing chapter of this section is dedicated to gamification, a practice often misunderstood as a matter of gimmicks or superficial engagement, yet which holds the potential, when thoughtfully applied, to reshape how people experience and interact with law. These chapters offer several scenarios, but they reveal the same recurring tension – the aim is not to make law look better, but to help it live better. The ambition is not to communicate what law is, but to design what it can become.

Chapter 5:
Legal design and other designs

Legal design vs...

One of the main discussions among academics in the legal design field is the following: is legal design "just another type of design", or an entirely new and different field?

The issue is not trivial. If we consider that legal design belongs to the fields of design (like service design, information design, and graphic design), the legal part is just an add-on, or a matter of industry where this design is practiced. If we believe that legal design is "something different", then the legal part may become a critical element. While there are pros and cons in both choices, one thing has to be clear – despite verbal or conceptual differences, legal design is strictly related to the authoritative aspect of the law. A wrong clause will always make a contract void, regardless of the aesthetic beauty of the product.

Insight:

This is also true regarding the design thinking vs legal design thinking debate. While design thinking and legal design thinking share core principles, including empathy, iteration, and user focus, legal design thinking is specifically tailored to the unique challenges of the legal field. Comparative analysis of traditional design thinking frameworks and legal design applications reveals nuanced differences in approach and implementation, highlighting a need for specialized training and awareness among legal professionals engaging in this field. While I believe that the two are ontologically and practically different, I have to clarify that, both at professional and academic level, there are different positions on the matter.

Let's compare legal design with other designs and similar disciplines.

Legal design vs service design

Service design is a discipline concerned with the planning and organization of people, infrastructure, communication flows, and material components in order to improve services. It often looks at entire ecosystems, coordinating multiple touchpoints across different channels, and addressing both front-stage and back-stage experiences. The comparison is relevant because legal design often borrows tools and mindsets from service design, especially in mapping user journeys, designing interactions, and prototyping new solutions. However, the scope is different. Service design usually operates within a broader canvas and is not inherently concerned with normative structures or legal consequences. Legal design, by contrast, works within rights, duties, procedures, and institutional authority. Moreover, its ambition is not only to enhance service interactions but to improve how legal systems (in its broadest possible sense, including contract, policies, documents, etc.) perform their function.

Legal design vs information design

Information design focuses on presenting information clearly and effectively, often through structured layouts, data visualization, and visual hierarchies. It is primarily concerned with clarity, speed of comprehension, and reduction of cognitive load. The connection with legal design is obvious – both fields care about readability, user navigation, and the clarity of content. However, legal design has different aims. First, it does not stop at presenting data well. It intervenes in documents and systems that carry legal weight, affect rights and obligations, and often rely on technical language. Second, legal design seeks not only to make information accessible, but to reshape legal texts, procedures, and tools so they can be used more effectively. Lastly, while information design optimizes for understanding, legal design also integrates this concept with trust, fairness, and the consequences of interpretation and application. All these elements make the scenario more complicated.

Legal design vs product design

Product design focuses on creating tangible or digital goods that are usable, functional, and appealing. The process is usually guided by user needs, market demands, and technological feasibility. Legal design and product design share an iterative approach and an attention to user experience. Yet legal design does not follow market logic in the same way. The users are not consumers, but people navigating legal systems (clients, citizens, employees, judges, lawyers, etc.). Moreover, the outcomes are not always products in a traditional sense, though I do believe legal design often produces products –

they are redesigned documents, toolkits, digital platforms, and frameworks. Finally, there is a difference lying in the type of problems being addressed, which in legal design are often bound to regulation, procedural requirements, or institutional practices.

Legal design vs UX design

UX design is the practice of enhancing user satisfaction by improving the usability and pleasure provided in the interaction with a product, particularly digital ones. It relies on research, testing, and iterative improvements. Legal design draws on many of the same tools (user research, wireframes, prototyping) but operates in a different environment. While UX design is typically tied to apps, platforms, or digital services, legal design extends across both digital and non-digital domains – contracts, policies, procedures, court forms, even signage in public buildings. Moreover, the emotional and relational stakes differ. UX design often engages with satisfaction, ease, or habit formation, while legal design frequently operates in contexts marked by fear, stress, urgency, or suspicion.

Legal design vs graphic or visual design

Visual design is concerned with aesthetics, visual communication, and the use of layout, typography, icons, and color to convey messages. Legal design clearly borrows from visual design, especially when reworking contracts, policies, or explanatory materials. But its aim is not visual appeal for its own sake. Visual elements in legal design serve a function – helping the user to orient, understand, decide, or comply. They are not structural, not necessarily decorative. Moreover, legal design integrates text and visual design in a more interdependent way – it often works on documents where the wording cannot be fully replaced, only clarified or restructured. While graphic design may enjoy more freedom, legal design must remain anchored in the content's normative function.

Legal design vs behavioral design

Behavioral design applies insights from psychology and behavioral economics to influence choices, often using subtle cues or nudges. It aims to shift behavior with minimal friction, relying on cognitive shortcuts, habits, or emotional triggers. Legal design sometimes uses similar techniques, for instance when designing default options, prompts, or warnings. Yet the intention is different. Behavioral design can be used to steer, sometimes without full transparency. Legal design, at its best, avoids manipulation. It seeks to inform and empower, rather than persuade. Still, the boundary is not always clear. When legal design incorporates behavioral insights to improve understanding, compliance, or engagement, the risk of influence arises. That is why I believe transparency must remain a central element in our work as legal designers. Legal choices must be framed clearly, options must be genuine, and persuasion must never override fairness.

Legal design or contract design?

I often see legal design and contract design mistakenly treated as if they were the same thing. To be fair, the distinction is not always straightforward. Legal design has gained visibility through its applications in contract design, and contract design has, in turn, benefited from the broader momentum of legal design. Still, I believe it is important to clarify the boundaries. Legal design reaches far beyond the world of contracts. It can be applied to a variety of challenges, from improving access to justice and simplifying regulatory systems to rethinking legal education and redesigning compliance mechanisms. Contracts are just one of many domains where legal design methods can make a difference. At the same time, I do not consider contract design to be a mere subset of legal design. Despite the strong connections between the two, contract design stands as an independent and recognizable practice, with its own tools, goals, and traditions. Table 1 highlights the differences.

Table 1: Distinctions between contract design and legal design.

Aspect	Contract design	Legal design
Definition	Focuses on improving the structure, clarity, and usability of contracts.	Applies legal design thinking to various legal processes, documents, and systems to provide a better legal experience.
Scope	Primarily concerned with contracts and agreements.	Encompasses a broader range of legal areas, including policies, regulations, compliance, and user interactions.
Objective	To make contracts more understandable, actionable, and user-friendly.	To enhance legal accessibility, efficiency, and user experience across legal processes.
End users	Contract stakeholders such as clients, suppliers, and employees.	A wider audience, including legal professionals, businesses, regulators, and end-users.
Focus areas	Contract lifecycle, negotiation, drafting, execution, and management.	Legal service delivery, access to justice, compliance, dispute resolution.

Chapter 6:
Legal design and sustainability

Legal design and the United Nations 2030 Agenda

The 2024 Report of the Secretary General on Progress towards the Sustainable Development Goals leaves little room for optimism.[1] Fewer than one in five targets are on track to be achieved by 2030.[2] Nearly half are advancing slowly, and more than a third are stagnating or regressing.[3] Yet the most critical issue lies not only in individual delays, but in the dense interdependence that connects the Goals to one another. A 2017 study[4] had already demonstrated how progress in one area, such as poverty eradication (SDG 1),[5] is deeply influenced by others, including health (SDG 3),[6] education (SDG 4),[7] gender equality (SDG 5),[8] and access to clean water and sanitation (SDG 6).[9]

Insight:

The SDGs should not be seen as a checklist, but as a system. Without shared infrastructure, shared principles, and shared language, this system cannot function. Legal design offers a way to help build that infrastructure, because it proposes an approach in which the law is not only formally correct, but actually usable.[10]

Sustainable Development Goal 16,[11] which concerns peace, justice and strong institutions, is perhaps the most explicit convergence point. It calls for legal frameworks that are accessible, accountable, and inclusive. Likewise, SDG 12,[12] on responsible consumption and production, depends on regulatory clarity. Businesses find that it is hard to fulfil environmental or social obligations if the rules they are expected to follow are incomprehensible or impractical. The same logic applies across the Agenda. SDG 3[13] on good health and well-being often fails not for lack of intention, but because consent forms, patient rights materials, and privacy notices remain unreadable. In education (SDG 4),[14] legal design may support civic literacy, particularly in contexts where students are expected to understand rights and responsibilities with little or no guidance. In the realm of gender equality (SDG 5),[15] legal design has the potential to uncover and reframe structural biases, starting with the way legal texts are written, interpreted, and enforced. Regarding employment and labor relations (SDG 8)[16] we can intervene proactively so that employment contracts, digital platform policies, and grievance mechanisms avoid excluding low-income or precarious workers. SDG 10,[17] focused on reducing inequalities, finds in legal design a framework that questions who is excluded and why. Finally, concerning climate action (SDG 13),[18] legal design may help reframe technical directives as user-facing materials, whether for municipalities, companies, or citizens.

Legal design and the SDGs share a mission – to turn declarations into action, rights into tools, and obligations into shared understanding. What the 2030 Agenda demands in breadth, legal design helps to deliver in structure. And if global ambition continues to outpace delivery, the need for this kind of infrastructure will only grow.

Enhancing accessibility

While the SDGs define ambitious goals, the question of how people engage with the legal and institutional systems that underpin them remains unresolved. One of the hardest challenges in that sense is managing accessibility – the ability to understand, navigate, use, and experience the law.

Let's start with the norms. Frameworks such as the UN Convention on the Rights of Persons with Disabilities (CRPD)[19] codify access to legal information and justice as essential components of equal participation. Similarly, the European Accessibility Act,[20] entered into force in 2025, reinforces this shift. By mandating that digital legal interfaces meet standards such as the Web Content Accessibility Guidelines (WCAG),[21] the Act imposes a new baseline – legal information must be perceivable, operable, understandable, and robust.

Example:

Legal design helps translate these criteria into practice in many ways – structured layouts, alt-text, keyboard navigation, modular content – ensuring that information is actually usable by people with cognitive, motor, sensory, or linguistic differences.

Strictly related to physical accessibility is the concept of digital parity. How can we account for digital poverty and support multi-channel delivery, ensuring accessibility offline, via print, phone, or in-person services? We can also go further and think about communities historically excluded from legal participation, due to language, education, geography, or status. Can we provide toolkits, community-driven interfaces, multilingual formats, or simplified templates that allow these systems to become more porous, responsive, and open to co-creation?

True accessibility requires an intersectional lens, attuned to how race, disability, gender, migration status, and economic precarity compound legal exclusion. This is where the principles of legal design meet their ethical test – the space in which we discover whether law is merely published, or genuinely shareable.

About clear communication as a human right

The recognition of communication as a fundamental human right was first established in Article 19 of the Universal Declaration of Human Rights,[22] which affirms the right to freedom of opinion and expression, including the right to seek, receive, and share information and ideas through any medium, across all borders. This principle has since been echoed in several key international legal instruments, including the International Covenant on Civil and Political Rights[23] and the International Convention on the Elimination of All Forms of Racial Discrimination,[24] reaffirming the central role of communication in safeguarding dignity, equality, and participation. Yet while these texts assert the right to communicate, they rarely interrogate the quality or effectiveness of that communication. As early as 1976, UNESCO drew attention to this gap by calling for the active involvement of all people in the communication process, linking access to communication resources with broader social rights such as education, democratic participation, and development.[25, 26] Since then, international bodies have frequently underlined the importance of effective communication as a means of fostering dialogue, reducing conflict, and supporting social cohesion. Communication has been described as a bridge – between institutions and individuals, between cultures, between communities and their futures.

However, the question of clarity – arguably the very heart of meaningful communication – has remained largely peripheral in global legal and policy discourse. Structural barriers such as linguistic variation, cultural fragmentation, unequal access to education, and social disadvantage continue to obscure messages that are legally or politically relevant. The result is a persistent disconnection between those who draft rules and those who must live by them. Declaring communication as a right is not enough if the content of that communication remains inaccessible or unintelligible. If people are not able to understand the information that affects their rights, obligations, and opportunities, the right itself is hollow. Upholding the right to communicate, then, must include an explicit commitment to clarity.

Insight:
Is this a trivial issue? Not for us. Clear communication enables individuals to navigate public services, exercise legal rights, and take part in collective decisions. It empowers rather than excludes. It reduces dependency and opens space for self-determination.[27] While the emergence of ISO standards and the plain language movement (see Chapter 4) suggest that a cultural shift may be underway, much remains to be done.

In this context, the proposal to introduce a global initiative under the name "Communication for All", inspired by the structure and ambition of the Sustainable Development Goals, becomes more than a symbolic gesture. It reflects the growing awareness that clear, inclusive communication is not secondary to development, but central to its success. Recognizing communication as a structural right – anchored not only in access, but in understanding – would provide the normative foundation for more just, participatory, and sustainable legal and institutional systems. Only by ensuring that people are communicated with clearly, and that they can communicate back with equal clarity, can we claim to honor the full scope of this right.

Legal design and neurodiversity, part one – designing for a neurodiverse audience

Legal design, when applied with rigor and attention, offers a concrete way to start addressing one of the most underestimated issues in terms of legal communication – neurodiversity. In this group we include people whose neurological profiles – such as autism, ADHD, dyslexia, dyspraxia, dysgraphia, color blindness, or Tourette syndrome – differ from what is commonly considered "neurotypical".

Insight:
The term neurodiversity, coined by sociologist Judy Singer in the late 1990s, refers to the idea that neurological differences are part of the normal variation of the human genome.[28] Singer's core idea is that neurodiversity should be viewed in a similar way to biodiversity, a natural

variation that confers social and evolutionary advantages. When we look at it as a human variation that demands accommodation, not correction, we shift the legal system's duty from management to inclusion. It is worth mentioning that – while mostly used interchangeably – the concept of neurodiversity and neurodivergence[29] are related but have different meanings. Neurodiversity is mostly used when we aim to promote inclusion and equality, pushing back against the idea that these differences should be viewed as problems or stigmatized. Neurodivergence, on the other hand, specifically refers to an individual person whose brain functions differently from what society considers typical or "neurotypical". In other words, neurodiversity is about broader societal acceptance and inclusion, while neurodivergence is centered on the individual's personal perspective and autonomy.[30]

Not surprisingly, research suggests that neurodivergent individuals often face substantial barriers in accessing justice.[31] These include difficulty in processing dense legal language, understanding procedural norms, dealing with overstimulating environments like courtrooms, and navigating adversarial communication styles.[32]

Example:
For instance, someone with dyslexia may struggle with the volume and formatting of standard legal documentation, while a person with ADHD may find it challenging to sustain attention during prolonged legal processes or hearings. Not to mention reading contracts of 100 plus pages. Individuals on the autism spectrum may experience sensory overload or communication barriers when expected to interpret vague language, unspoken social norms, or emotional cues.

Legal design reframes these challenges as design opportunities. How about using our methodology to help remove cognitive, sensory, and emotional barriers?[33] Contracts presented in modular formats with visual guides, icons, and short video explainers could dramatically improve comprehension for users with dyslexia or ADHD. Court orientation materials offered in multiple formats (written, audio, visual) could reduce anxiety and uncertainty for people with autism or social processing differences. Interactive tools like guided digital forms or clickable visual timelines could support better navigation of legal procedures.

There are, of course, ethical and practical challenges. How do we balance universal design with specific accommodations?[34] How do we ensure we are not creating parallel systems that unintentionally stigmatize? How do we handle the collection of sensitive data about neurodivergence? And then, we should take into account that 1,000 people with 1,000 dyslexia diagnoses may all look at the same document in 1,000 different ways.

These are complex issues, but not unsolvable ones. They require a commitment to ongoing dialogue, transparency, and inclusive ethics – something the design world is increasingly learning to navigate.

Legal design is not a magic wand, but it is a lever. When applied thoughtfully, it can help shift legal systems from being exclusionary by default to inclusive by design. Designing for neurodiverse users is about dignity, autonomy, and agency. By making space for different ways of thinking, feeling, and processing information, we don't just improve usability – we help redefine justice itself.[35]

Pro tip:
Sometimes, small actions can have a big outcome. One of our go-to tools is the color blindness simulator. It's a simple yet eye-opening way to test how your design appears to users with different types of color vision.[36]

Legal design and neurodiversity, part two – when the legal designer is neurodivergent

Neurodiversity shapes not only how legal systems are experienced – it also informs how they are designed. When neurodivergent individuals contribute to legal design as facilitators, researchers, or creative leads, they bring cognitive approaches that challenge traditional thinking and expand the boundaries of innovation. People with neurological profiles such as autism, ADHD, or dyslexia often possess heightened skills in pattern recognition, systems thinking, creative ideation, or detailed analysis. These ways of thinking align naturally with legal design, which thrives on multidimensional reasoning, iterative experimentation, and user-focused approaches.

Example:
A designer with ADHD might bring rapid, associative thinking during the ideation phase, generating a wide range of unconventional solutions. Someone on the autism spectrum may offer a precise, methodical lens for mapping intricate legal processes with clarity and rigor. A person with

dyscalculia could propose alternative ways to express payment terms in a sales contract, revealing formulations that are clearer for everyone.

I see these characteristics as strengths to be recognized more than necessities to accommodate.

Yet, the design environment itself can become exclusionary when it is structured around neurotypical norms. Fast-paced brainstorming sessions, loosely defined group dynamics, heavy reliance on verbal interaction, or overstimulating physical spaces can all limit the participation of neurodivergent contributors. This is why I stress the necessity of reconsidering how collaboration unfolds. The strategies may be different – providing written agendas in advance, offering asynchronous methods of contribution, using visual tools instead of purely verbal debriefings, and managing cognitive and sensory load are some of the practices for inclusive co-creation.

This shift is not merely about fairness. Embracing neurodiversity within legal design teams expands the discipline's creative range and ethical depth. In my experience, when neurodivergent perspectives are not only included but placed at the center of innovation, the outcomes are more grounded, more nuanced, and more resonant with real users. It is also true that doing so is harder than it seems, because it requires a shift from uniform productivity and fast delivery towards values such as psychological safety, adaptive rhythm, and cognitive flexibility.

Just as legal design invites us to move from institutional logic to user experience, it must also move from narrow definitions of professional conduct to broader understandings of collaboration. Recognizing neurodivergence not as deviation but as dimension allows legal design to evolve from a tool for inclusion to a method born of it. In doing so, it brings us closer to legal systems shaped by the richness of human difference, rather than distorted by its denial. At the end of the day, a truly human-centered process must begin with the humans in the room.

Redesigning governance towards transparency

Just as inclusivity reshapes the act of designing law, it also reshapes how institutions communicate legal and policy commitment. Transparent governance and sustainability reporting are areas where legal design can demonstrate its full potential. Think about the European Union's Corporate Sustainability Reporting Directive,[37] or India's Business Responsibility and Sustainability Reporting standards,[38] where organizations face growing pressure to communicate their conduct not only to regulators but also to clients, citizens, and wider stakeholder communities. Companies and public bodies are already rethinking the way they present reports, policy dashboards, and compliance documentation, transforming them from technical appendices into coherent, navigable, and engaging tools. Can we support them in adopting a legal design thinking methodology?

Example:

This shift is already visible in initiatives that embrace participatory design in public governance, such as the European Union Policy Lab[39] or New York's environmental review process (SEQR),[40] where platforms are built not only to inform, but also to involve. These approaches create spaces in which citizens, including those traditionally marginalized, can understand, interact with, and influence legal and policy outcomes.

However, there is one point we should reflect on, which has come about several times in my career, both in the corporate and institutional environment. We assume that transparency is always a virtue, something inherently positive. But in practice, the picture is more complex. Many of the lawyers we work with use ambiguity not out of carelessness, but deliberately and strategically. Whether in the wording of a clause or the overall structure of a contract, ambiguity can serve a function – leaving space for negotiation, softening rigid positions, or postponing conflict. It is more than hiding information; sometimes it is about preserving flexibility.

Recognizing this does not mean abandoning the goal of clarity. It means acknowledging that the legal profession has long developed a refined way of navigating between precision and vagueness, and that transparency is not always neutral. It has effects. It sets expectations, removes buffers, and reduces interpretative margins. In legal design, while promoting transparency, we need to be honest about this tension. Pushing for clarity is essential, but it should not come at the cost of ignoring how and why ambiguity is sometimes used with intent and skill.

References

1   United Nations, *The Sustainable Development Goals Report 2024* (UN 2024) https://unstats.un.org/sdgs/report/2024/
2   *Ibid.*
3   *Ibid.*
4   Yao Wei, Fanglei Zhong, Xiaoyu Song, and Chunlin Huang, "Exploring the Impact of Poverty on the Sustainable Development Goals: Inhibiting Synergies and

Magnifying Trade-Offs" (2022) *Sustainable Cities and Society,* 104367, https://doi.org/10.1016/j.scs.2022.104367

5   United Nations, "Sustainable Development Goal 1: No Poverty" (UN Sustainable Development Goals, 2024) https://sdgs.un.org/goals/goal1

6   United Nations, "Sustainable Development Goal 3: Good Health and WellBeing" (UN Sustainable Development Goals, 2024) https://sdgs.un.org/goals/goal3

7   United Nations, "Sustainable Development Goal 4: Quality Education" (UN Sustainable Development Goals, 2024) https://sdgs.un.org/goals/goal4

8   United Nations, "Sustainable Development Goal 5: Achieve Gender Equality and Empower All Women and Girls" (UN Sustainable Development Goals, 2024) https://sdgs.un.org/goals/goal5

9   United Nations, "Sustainable Development Goal 6: Ensure Availability and Sustainable Management of Water and Sanitation for All" (UN Sustainable Development Goals, 2024) https://sdgs.un.org/goals/goal6

10   UNGA Res 70/1, "Transforming Our World: the 2030 Agenda for Sustainable Development" (21 October 2015) UN Doc A/RES/70/1 www.un.org/sustainabledevelopment/development-agenda/

11   United Nations, "Sustainable Development Goal 16: Promote Peaceful and Inclusive Societies for Sustainable Development, Provide Access to Justice for All and Build Effective, Accountable and Inclusive Institutions at All Levels" (UN Sustainable Development Goals, 2024) https://sdgs.un.org/goals/goal16

12   United Nations, "Sustainable Development Goal 12: Ensure Sustainable Consumption and Production Patterns" (UN Sustainable Development Goals, 2024) https://sdgs.un.org/goals/goal12

13   See endnote 6.

14   See endnote 7.

15   See endnote 8.

16   United Nations, "Sustainable Development Goal 8: Promote Sustained, Inclusive and Sustainable Economic Growth, Full and Productive Employment and Decent Work for All" (UN Sustainable Development Goals, 2024) https://sdgs.un.org/goals/goal8

17   United Nations, "Sustainable Development Goal 10: Reduce Inequality Within and Among Countries" (UN Sustainable Development Goals, 2024) https://sdgs.un.org/goals/goal10

18   United Nations, "Sustainable Development Goal 13: Take Urgent Action to Combat Climate Change and Its Impacts" (UN Sustainable Development Goals, 2024) https://sdgs.un.org/goals/goal13

19   https://social.desa.un.org/issues/disability/crpd/convention-on-the-rights-of-persons-with-disabilities-crpd

20   Directive (EU) 2019/882 of the European Parliament and of the Council of 17 April 2019 on the accessibility requirements for products and services (2019) OJ L151/70

21   World Wide Web Consortium (W3C), *Web Content Accessibility Guidelines (WCAG) 2.1,* W3C Recommendation, 12 December 2024 www.w3.org/TR/2024/REC-WCAG21-20241212/

22 Universal Declaration of Human Rights, adopted 10 December 1948, UNGA Res 217 A(III), Art. 19.

23 International Covenant on Civil and Political Rights (adopted 16 December 1966, entered into force 23 March 1976) 999 UNTS 171, Art. 19(2).

24 International Convention on the Elimination of All Forms of Racial Discrimination (adopted 21 December 1965, entered into force 4 January 1969) 660 UNTS 195, Art. 5(d)(viii).

25 UNESCO, *Report on Means of Enabling Active Participation in the Communication Process and Analysis of the Right to Communicate*, 19th Session of the General Conference, 19 C/93 (1976).

26 Among the reports advocating for the need for participatory, inclusive, and clear communication, I would share MacBride's 1980 Report. This foundational UNESCO report introduced the idea of the "right to communicate" as more than just access. It also helped launch decades of policy debates around communication equity. https://archive.ccrvoices.org/articles/the-macbride-report.html

27 Amartya Sen's notion of development as the expansion of freedoms implies that individuals must be able to understand and act upon the information that shapes their choices. Communication, in this context, is capability-enhancing only if it is comprehensible. Particularly intriguing is how Sen frames development as a process of expanding people's capabilities to live the lives they value. Communication, particularly accessible, understandable communication, would be therefore crucial for exercising agency and making informed choices. Sen, A. (1999). *Development as Freedom*. Oxford University Press.

28 Nicole Baumer and Julia Frueh, "What Is Neurodiversity?" (Harvard Health Publishing, 23 November 2021) www.health.harvard.edu/blog/what-is-neurodiversity-202111232645

29 Introduced by autistic activist Kassiane Asasumasu, neurodivergence highlights personal identity and individual experiences, allowing people to define their own cognitive experiences. Those who identify as neurodivergent might have conditions such as autism, ADHD, or dyslexia, each with its own unique lived experiences. Mixing these terms up can unintentionally erase the specific experiences and identities of neurodivergent individuals.

30 www.theswaddle.com/why-neurodiversity-and-neurodivergence-shouldn-t-be-used-interchangeably

31 Family Justice Council, *Guidance on Neurodiversity in the Family Justice System for Practitioners* (January 2025) www.judiciary.uk/guidance-and-resources/

32 B Clasby, B Mirfin-Veitch, R Blackett, S Kedge and E Whitehead, "Responding to Neurodiversity in the Courtroom: A Brief Evaluation of Environmental Accommodations to Increase Procedural Fairness" (2022) 32(3) *Criminal Behaviour and Mental Health* 197, https://doi.org/10.1002/cbm.2239

33 From this perspective, legal design shares similar principles with Universal Design Principles (originated by Ron Mace) and Universal Design for Learning (CAST Framework), foundational design principles that emphasize flexibility, multiple

modes of representation, and anticipatory design rather than reactive accommodation. They push for being used by the widest range of people, including those with cognitive, sensory, and physical differences.

34 It is interesting to see the work of thinkers like Lennard Davis, Tom Shakespeare, and Garland-Thomson in terms of Critical Disability Theory and Social model of Disability. Their work reminds us that disability arises not from individual impairment, but from systemic barriers. Legal design, in this view, becomes a method of dismantling those barriers.

35 The Law Society actively supports neurodivergent individuals in the legal profession through raising awareness, providing guidance and resources with detailed advice on how employers can create a more inclusive environment (adjustments are not special treatment, but rather, they equalize opportunities), and educational and career support for students. Among other publications, it has published a guide to disability terminology and language (www.lawsociety.org.uk/topics/disabled-solicitors/a-guide-to-disability-terminology-and-language), guidance to support disabled people in the workplace (https://www.lawsociety.org.uk/contact-or-visit-us/press-office/press-releases/law-society-publishes-guidance-to-support-disabled-people-in-the-workplace), and guidance to support disabled students (https://www.lawsociety.org.uk/contact-or-visit-us/press-office/press-releases/law-society-publishes-guidance-to-support-disabled-students). Through its Disabled Solicitors Network, the Law Society connects neurodivergent and disabled solicitors, offering mutual support, visibility, and opportunities to advocate for change. It also emphasizes using accurate, respectful terms and avoiding assumptions or stereotypes.

36 www.color-blindness.com/coblis-color-blindness-simulator/

37 Directive (EU) 2022/2464 of the European Parliament and of the Council of 14 December 2022 amending Regulation (EU) No 537/2014, Directive 2004/109/EC, Directive 2006/43/EC and Directive 2013/34/EU, as regards corporate sustainability reporting (2022) OJ L322/15.

38 Securities and Exchange Board of India (SEBI), *Business Responsibility and Sustainability Reporting by Listed Entities: Annexure I* (SEBI 2021), www.sebi.gov.in/legal/regulations/jul-2021/sebi-listing-obligations-and-disclosure-requirements-amendment-regulations-2021_51290.html

39 European Union Policy Lab, https://ec.europa.eu/knowledge4policy/organisation/eu-policy-lab_en

40 New York State Department of Environmental Conservation, "Stepping Through the SEQR Process" (DEC, 2024) https://dec.ny.gov/regulatory/permits-licenses/seqr/stepping-through-process

Chapter 7:
Legal design and artificial intelligence

The evolution of legal design with generative AI

With the arrival of generative artificial intelligence, the reimagination of legal documents took on new urgency, and new complexity. Generative AI is not simply accelerating existing workflows. It is reshaping how legal documents are conceived, created, maintained, and experienced. Tools such as ChatGPT and its domain-specific counterparts can now produce, revise, and contextualize contractual language with extraordinary fluency. Because of their vast training on contracts, statutes, and commercial precedents, they can assist us in generating tailored content at scale – adjusted for tone, sector, or jurisdiction. What was once the domain of slow, layered human review is now compressed into real-time suggestion and iteration. Moreover, the promise of these tools extends beyond the drafting phase – they offer functionality across the contract life cycle, from clause monitoring and performance tracking to compliance alerts and suggested renegotiation triggers.

But if this is the promise, it comes with its own set of complications. Unlike traditional rule-based systems – where logic trees, conditionals, and structured scripts allowed for full control – generative AI introduces a degree of unpredictability. Designing for this environment no longer means scripting each user interaction. It means defining roles, goals, knowledge domains, and constraints. It requires what has been described as a shift from micro-management to macro-management. In this new paradigm, the legal designer's role becomes curatorial and strategic – training the model on the right content, defining its scope, and placing reasonable guardrails on its outputs.

This shift is not trivial. The risk of misuse or miscommunication is real. Misaligned prompts, overly general training data, or ambiguous user queries can produce results that are not just inaccurate but potentially harmful. Here, the work of the legal designer becomes less about interface and more about architecture – designing moderation layers, embedding retrieval-augmented generation techniques, and anticipating the clever ways users might subvert or misuse the system.

> **Example:**
> Consider, for instance, a procurement team using an AI-enabled platform to draft NDAs in multiple jurisdictions. The system dynamically adjusts the governing law clause, dispute resolution venue, and confidentiality scope based on user input, contract history, and risk thresholds – automating what would have taken hours of manual tailoring. Or think of a compliance department that monitors ongoing obligations in real time, relying on AI to flag deviations from payment terms or alert the team when a counterparty breaches a clause linked to sanctions.

And yet, these challenges should not deter us. They are part of working responsibly in an environment shaped by generative systems. The task is to bring the values of legal design into conversation with the affordances of AI. Done well, generative tools can help legal documents become more adaptive, more conversational, and more responsive to the needs of real users, because they shift the legal product from static output to interactive service.[1] However, doing this well demands new skillsets, deeper reflection, and a design mindset that understands both the potential and the pitfalls of these emerging technologies.

From design thinking to emergent thinking

Design thinking,[2] long celebrated as a method for solving problems creatively and collaboratively, is undergoing a profound transformation. At the center of this shift is the rise of artificial intelligence – not only as a tool to assist with tasks but as a force that reshapes how we conceive, explore, and generate ideas. Increasingly, what we refer to as design thinking is giving way to something more fluid, more decentralized, and more dynamic – emergent thinking.

The term "emergence" finds its roots in the Latin *emergere* – to arise, to come forth. In science, it has traditionally described how complex patterns or behaviors arise from simple interactions, like how consciousness arises from networks of neurons or how collective behavior emerges in ecosystems. In our context, it may point to something similar – a shift from predefined frameworks to outcomes that evolve through interaction, iteration, and systemic responsiveness. Where classical design thinking follows staged sequences such as empathize > define > ideate > prototype > test, emergent thinking embraces continuous transformation, less as a process to manage than as a space to inhabit.

This shift is way more than conceptual if we think about how AI systems may intervene in the design process. They do not merely assist – they anticipate, iterate, and increasingly suggest. AI can surface insights from complex datasets, propose directions, test assumptions, and even generate early prototypes. As a result, the burden of mapping and connecting information no longer falls entirely on the human side. What changes is the role of human input – from analytical effort to creative direction, from synthesis to vision, from prototyping to prompting. This reallocation of mental energy opens up space for new kinds of thinking – more intuitive, more exploratory, and more deeply adaptive.

Insight:
Emerging thinking thrives in environments where control is distributed, feedback loops are alive, and outcomes are not fixed in advance. It requires letting go of certainty and embracing ambiguity. In bureaucratic or hierarchical settings, this can be unsettling. Yet the alternative is a form of stagnation – solutions that remain static in a world that is in constant motion. What if we think of the world not as a puzzle to be solved but as a system in perpetual becoming? Can we reward curiosity more than prediction? Can we promote responsiveness over rigidity?

For legal design, this transformation is especially relevant. The classical image of legal design thinking as a sequence of steps may no longer fit a context in which tools like generative AI can perform real-time sensemaking, co-draft legal content, simulate variations, and respond to user feedback in ways that mimic human creativity. On a positive note, these tools also come with their own constraints and unpredictability, making the designer's role not one of orchestration alone, but of negotiation – setting boundaries, interpreting results, and allowing for a degree of emergence without losing direction. In this new landscape, legal design is no longer about imposing structure onto the world. It is about enabling the conditions through which something useful, usable, and often unexpected can arise. AI doesn't replace design thinking, it repositions it. And what emerges is not only a new set of tools, but a new way of thinking altogether.

How about AI as final user?
In the near future – and in many cases already today – the primary user of legal documents will not be human. Or, more precisely, not only human.

Legal texts are increasingly parsed, interpreted, and operationalized by non-human agents – algorithms, smart systems, machine learning models, and AI-driven assistants. These systems are already embedded within services, powering decision-making, automating compliance, triggering contractual events, and interfacing with users on behalf of legal institutions. If legal design is to remain relevant, we must recognize that these systems are no longer passive processors of information. They are readers, actors, and – in certain contexts – users.

Some may call this anthropomorphism. And to a degree, it is. But it is also a strategic necessity. Treating AI as a user shifts our approach to design – from seeing AI as a neutral conduit to understanding it as an agent with specific interpretive logic, interaction modes, and limitations. AI does not read like we do. It does not infer context, intention, or emotional subtext in the way a lawyer might. It extracts patterns, follows syntax, and applies statistical correlations based on training data. What looks to a human like a beautifully designed, navigable contract might appear to a machine as a jumbled surface – lacking metadata, semantic clarity, or structure.

This introduces what we might call a paradox. The very features that make a legal document more readable for humans – typographic variation, color, spatial hierarchy – often render it harder to interpret computationally. We are writing in two languages at once – one visual, rhetorical, and context-rich; the other syntactic, rule-based, and data-sensitive. Bridging this divide is the next frontier of legal design.

So, what does this mean in practical terms? It means suggesting a new architecture – legal documents conceived not as monoliths, but as layered artefacts, each layer serving a different audience. Think about a machine-readable layer, stripped of ambiguity and optimized for processing, sitting beneath a contextual layer rich with relational logic. Above these, a human interface layer that communicates with empathy, clarity, and visual coherence. This modular design would acknowledge both human and machine needs, without sacrificing either. It would mean co-readership – contracts that can be interpreted by AI without excluding the people they bind.

And yet, this is more than a formatting challenge. It is a conceptual shift in how we understand the purpose of legal texts. For centuries, law has been written with the assumption that its reader is a human – legally literate, perhaps even trained in jurisprudence. In the last few years, legal design and the plain language movement asked us to focus on the final user – client, citizen, consumer. But in today's digital infrastructure, AI systems are not just parsing legal texts, they are executing them. They extract obligations, monitor deadlines, enforce performance, and generate alerts. They act. And therefore, they must understand.

This duality presents several tensions. First, we have a responsibility to maintain human-centeredness. Legal documents are still instruments through which rights are claimed, agency is exercised, and trust is built. Over-formalization in the name of computational readability risks alienating the very people the law is meant to serve. Second, we should be aware that failing to design for AI risks obsolescence. If documents cannot be parsed by the systems that now mediate decisions, they lose efficacy, regardless of how beautifully they are written. The question, therefore, is no longer whether a contract is readable, but for whom, under what circumstances, and with what consequences.

Legal designers have the skills to operate within this tension. However, the shift requires more than accessible language or clearer layouts. It calls for a design practice that integrates ethics, machine logic, interface sensibility, and legal rigor. It demands fluency not only in words, but in metadata, APIs, and interoperability standards. Above all, it asks us to accept that the most human-centric approach may be, paradoxically, one that takes machines seriously as readers.

Designing for AI as a user is not a departure from legal design – it is its natural evolution. It ensures that documents remain functional, that the law continues to be actionable, and that rights stay visible and understandable within ecosystems where human and artificial agency coexist. I do not view this evolution as a substitution of human needs with machine logic. Rather, I see it as the design of legal documents capable of performing effectively across both domains, preserving the intelligence of the law while maintaining its deeply human character.

Thinking before building

Before introducing artificial intelligence into a legal design context, it is essential to pause. Not to slow progress, but to think deliberately. AI, like any tool with transformative potential, brings opportunities that are both real and tangible. Yet these are always accompanied by equally real and tangible risks. In our profession, risks are not theoretical constructs. They are reputational consequences, breaches of confidentiality, regulatory exposure. They are the very matters we are trained to prevent. For this reason, I often advocate for a considered and responsible approach to AI. One that avoids rushing towards efficiency without a parallel concern for ethics. One that prioritizes clarity over novelty, and consequence over enthusiasm. A mindful legal designer does not simply automate. She interprets. She examines. She stays in charge.

The most immediate and perhaps most underestimated principle is also the simplest – AI outputs should never be accepted without scrutiny. Whether drafting a clause, generating a summary, or suggesting a layout, what AI provides may sound fluent, look elegant, and appear precise. But that appearance is often misleading. Fluency does not guarantee legal accuracy. I have seen generative systems confidently offer flawed descriptions of data protection frameworks, miscategorize liability clauses, or soften binding language into something that alters its legal effect. The risk is not merely in the words, but in the trust they seem to invite. Legal professionals must therefore treat AI-generated content as a sketch, not a final draft. AI may speed up certain phases, but it cannot and must not substitute legal judgement. The responsibility remains ours, and that accountability cannot be delegated to a machine (at least for now).

Another area requiring careful attention is data handling. Most generative AI models operate on cloud infrastructures. Depending on the provider and the configuration, any input, be it a policy draft, a clause, or internal analysis, may be stored, logged, or even reused to train future versions. This is unacceptable when dealing with confidential material.

Pro tip:
During one of our workshops, we explored how to work with anonymized and intentionally altered content, ensuring the experimentation did not compromise sensitive data. This may become a default approach.

Legal teams must coordinate closely with IT departments and data protection officers before introducing AI at scale. Without this coordination, exposure is almost inevitable. Beyond internal collaboration, it is essential to verify that the tools employed are compliant with applicable legislation, whether national, regional, or sector-specific.

There is also a deeper, often unspoken matter of professional posture. This is not about resisting AI, nor about surrendering to it. It is about understanding its role. Caution must not turn into paralysis, but curiosity should not be mistaken for abdication. Our work is about nuance. It is about implications, strategy, the invisible threads between interests and intent. AI cannot grasp this. It does not understand internal politics, institutional memory, or reputational tone. It cannot distinguish between compliance and alignment. It does not know whether a particular clause serves your client's values or undermines them. That remains our responsibility. The most constructive use of AI, in my experience, happens when it is treated not as a drafter, but as a counterpart. Not as a decision-maker, but as a tool for reflection. When used well, AI does not remove the need to think. It reminds us how much thinking is still required. But that only works if we remain in command of the thinking process.

Pro tip:

Before integrating AI into a legal design workflow, I suggest developing a personal or organizational checklist. Ask:

- Who owns the data?
- Who verifies the results?
- Where is the model hosted?
- How is bias identified and reduced?
- How transparent is the logic behind a recommendation?
- Who is accountable for errors, omissions, or misinterpretations?
- How frequently is the model updated, and with what type of data?
- Can the system explain its suggestions in a way that a non-technical stakeholder would understand?
- Are outputs tested with real users before they are implemented?
- Does the AI accommodate accessibility needs, such as those of neurodivergent or low-literacy users?
- What safeguards are in place to prevent overreliance on automated content?
- Is the system aligned with the organization's ethical posture, legal obligations, and communication culture?

These questions are architectural elements. Considering that legal design is a field built on trust, precision, and user awareness, they are foundational.

Ethical considerations and challenges

If we look at ethical perspectives from a practical point of view, the following are the core considerations.

- *Data privacy and security.* AI systems inevitably process large volumes of potentially sensitive or confidential data. Legal designers must ensure that AI tools are compliant with the relevant data protection frameworks, whether GDPR, national legislation, or internal protocols. Consent must be obtained clearly, transparently, and in language the user can understand. Confidentiality cannot be presumed.

- *Mitigating bias.* No dataset is entirely neutral. AI inherits the biases of its training material, and legal systems are already embedded with historical and structural imbalances. If not actively corrected, these biases can reinforce existing inequalities and produce outcomes that are discriminatory or misleading. We need to use inclusive, representative datasets, and to carry out regular reviews to identify distorted patterns in output.

- *Ensuring transparency.* Legal processes demand traceability. In contexts where decisions carry weight, stakeholders must be able to understand and explain how AI has arrived at a given conclusion. This means opting for systems that allow for explainability and auditability, rather than those operating as black boxes.

- *Maintaining human oversight.* So far, legal judgment cannot be automated. AI can inform, accelerate, or support a decision, but it cannot replace the reflective capacity of a trained legal mind. Any AI-generated suggestion must remain open to human verification, context-aware adaptation, and override. Delegating critical assessments to an algorithm is not innovation. It is abdication.

- *Preserving professional accountability.* As AI becomes more embedded in the production of legal texts, questions of authorship and responsibility will arise. Who is liable when an AI-generated clause misrepresents a legal obligation? So far, the answer cannot be the tool. It must be the professional (or the company for which she works). Legal designers and lawyers remain ultimately accountable for the content they choose to validate, circulate, or submit.

- *Safeguarding user dignity.* In legal design, we do not only serve clients. We also serve users. These users may be citizens, consumers, employees, or vulnerable parties. The increasing automation of communication cannot come at the cost of empathy or accessibility. AI should not depersonalize, but support clarity and inclusion. Legal design has a duty to preserve the dignity of its audience, even when speed and scale are within reach.

Beyond ethical considerations, we are also beginning to confront a number of structural and technological challenges that will shape how AI and legal design evolve in tandem. The following are the ones I see most relevant at this moment.

- *Directing AI-assisted contract design.* As AI becomes more integrated into legal workflows, it will inevitably influence contract drafting and structure. The challenge lies in using this influence to improve clarity, accessibility, and fairness, rather than replicating convoluted legalese under the guise of modernity. Will we be curators or facilitators?

- *Advancing predictive capabilities.* With the maturation of predictive analytics, AI tools will increasingly be able to forecast areas of legal friction. This could include identifying clauses that frequently trigger disputes, flagging terms with low enforceability, or modelling the likelihood of renegotiation. Can we shift from reactive lawyering to preventive structuring?

- *Integrating AI with emerging technologies.* The convergence of AI with technologies such as blockchain or smart contracts offers new terrain for legal design. This integration has the potential to create living contracts – agreements that are drafted, executed, monitored, and even updated through automated systems. While this promises efficiency, it also introduces complex questions about control, enforceability, and transparency. Not to mention IT literacy and confidence with APIs.

- *Augmenting decision-making.* In the context of negotiation or legal advice, AI can serve as a support system for real-time analysis, presenting risks, benchmarks, or alternatives that might otherwise go unnoticed. Can we supplement intuition and experience with scalable foresight?

- *Personalizing legal services.* AI will increasingly be used to provide tailored legal content, adjusted to individual users, sectors, or scenarios. While this personalization has the potential to expand access, it also raises concerns about consistency, oversimplification, and legal soundness. A tailored clause may feel intuitive but still fail to meet legal thresholds. Balancing usability with rigor may be harder than it seems.

- *Ensuring accessibility across languages and literacies.* AI is often presented as a tool that increases access to law. But true accessibility means more than translation or simplification. It requires testing across linguistic registers, reading levels, and cultural contexts. Legal designers must ensure that AI-generated content does not merely mimic legal drafting in another language, but actually serves the needs of diverse users.

- *Managing AI literacy within legal teams.* Finally, the challenge is also internal. Legal professionals and designers need a shared vocabulary and baseline understanding of what AI can and cannot do. Without this, expectations will diverge, misuse will proliferate, and risks will compound. Investment in internal education, therefore, becomes part of the infrastructure of responsible use.

References

1   Anthony Novaes, "Legal Design, Artificial Intelligence and Insurance" (2023) 29, *Computer and Telecommunications Law Review*, 29, https://ssrn.com/abstract=4461223
2   While this book is focused on legal design thinking and design thinking for the legal field, this paragraph is more focused on design thinking in general.

Chapter 8:
Legal design and dark patterns

What is a dark pattern?

The expression "dark patterns" refers to a set of interface design choices deliberately constructed to mislead, deceive, or pressure individuals into behaviors they might not otherwise choose. While they may be seen as examples of poor design or technical carelessness, they are most of the time calculated strategies that rely on our cognitive shortcuts, behavioral habits, and moments of distraction.[1] Their purpose is clear – to push users in a direction that serves the interest of the designer or the organization behind the product, often at the cost of the user's clarity, freedom, or welfare. In legal contexts, the presence of such deceptive structures threatens to distort the very conditions under which choices are made. Whether by hiding opt-outs, pre-selecting acceptance boxes, or framing decisions in ways that mislead, dark patterns compromise the integrity of legal communication and contractual exchange.

The term itself was coined in 2010 by Harry Brignull,[2] who began documenting these practices on a public website dedicated to identifying and categorizing recurring deceptive techniques.[3] Since then, academic interest and institutional awareness have both grown considerably. What started as a niche critique of interface design has evolved into a broader reflection on the ethics of interaction, particularly in contexts such as consumer protection, online contracts, and data regulation. Instruments like the General Data Protection Regulation (GDPR)[4] have introduced stricter requirements for consent, mandating that it be informed, unambiguous, and freely given. Nonetheless, enforcement remains complex, especially as digital environments grow more sophisticated and manipulative techniques become harder to detect at a glance.

Example:

In Woodrow Hartzog's *Privacy's Blueprint: The Battle to Control the Design of New Technologies*,[5] Hartzog argues that privacy and user autonomy cannot be protected by laws alone but must be embedded in the design of technologies themselves. He explicitly discusses dark patterns as a failure of ethical design and regulatory oversight.

This growing awareness has gone beyond scholarly circles and begun reshaping legislative language across various sectors of European law. The Digital Services Act,[6] in particular, addresses the use of manipulative interface structures by explicitly prohibiting design choices that deceive or distort the user's autonomy. Article 25 calls on providers of online platforms to refrain from using presentation or structure to nudge users in directions that do not reflect their genuine intention.[7] This marks a significant development, shifting regulatory focus from the accuracy of information alone to the modalities through which that information is conveyed and acted upon. In parallel, the AI Act introduces, under Article 5, a prohibition on AI systems that manipulate human behavior by exploiting psychological or situational vulnerabilities.[8] Although formulated in relation to autonomous systems, the logic behind this rule mirrors many of the concerns surrounding dark patterns, as both rely on asymmetries of knowledge and power to interfere with decision-making.[9] Consumer protection law, specifically Directive 2005/29/EC on unfair commercial practices,[10] offers a complementary perspective, prohibiting practices that materially distort the economic behavior of the average consumer, a criterion under which many dark patterns clearly fall. From drip pricing to misleading opt-outs and obscured terms, the manipulation of perception for commercial gain is increasingly being recognized as a breach of fairness, regardless of whether it occurs through printed contracts or digital interfaces.

Dark patterns often operate below the threshold of conscious awareness. They exploit imbalances of information and power, presenting users with choices that appear neutral but are subtly engineered to favor a particular outcome. From a legal and regulatory perspective, this asymmetry is problematic because it misleads the individual user and undermines the structural fairness of the system as a whole.[11] What looks like user agency may, in fact, be little more than a scripted performance in which outcomes are largely predetermined. The problem extends when companies manage subtle interplays of language, color, spacing, and interface architecture in order to skew decision-making without the user realizing it.

Insight:

Over time, the diffusion of dark patterns has also affected public perception of digital services. Persistent exposure to ambiguous or manipulative experiences can create a climate of suspicion.[12] Instead of fostering trust, digital environments become places where vigilance replaces ease, and every interaction demands skepticism. This loss of confidence started challenging the credibility of digital infrastructures and the legitimacy of legal instruments that rely on digital consent mechanisms.

That said, the distinction between manipulation and mere persuasion is not always easy to trace, and the line between aggressive persuasion and design that violates the autonomy of the individual is often blurred. Some design choices may be ambiguous, questionable, or even misguided without being intentionally harmful. Others, however, cross a more serious threshold, where the intention to interfere with the user's freedom becomes evident. I would also stress that this is a dynamic debate. As technology evolves, so too do the mechanisms for steering user behavior. The rise of behavioral insights, predictive analytics, persuasive computing, and generative intelligence introduced new layers of complexity into the equation. What might once have been labelled as merely "bad design" today requires a more refined vocabulary, capable of addressing the interplay between intention, structure, and consequence. For legal professionals and designers alike, it means committing to a continuous process of reflection, learning, and recalibration. The challenge is more than simply identifying what is wrong. We need proposing frameworks that protect users while preserving the legitimacy of digital legal communication.[13]

Dark patterns in practice

Examples of dark patterns are numerous and varied, reflecting the creativity and sophistication with which manipulative strategies are developed. The following list outlines key categories of dark patterns, presented in an academic format to support clarity and conceptual precision:

- *Deceptive advertising.* Instances where promotional messages exaggerate benefits or conceal essential information, leading users to form incorrect expectations or assumptions.
- *Confirm shaming.* The use of language designed to guilt-trip users into certain choices by portraying alternative decisions as foolish or irresponsible, thereby exploiting emotional vulnerabilities.
- *Disguised advertisements.* Advertisements presented in the form of editorial content or neutral information, obscuring their commercial intent and limiting the user's ability to distinguish between impartial advice and persuasion.
- *Subscription traps.* Mechanisms that facilitate easy sign-ups while

creating significant obstacles to cancellation, relying on user inertia and procedural confusion to prolong financial commitments.

- *Friendly spam*. Repeated promotional communications crafted to appear personalized or benevolent, but primarily aimed at pressuring users into further engagement or consumption.
- *Drip pricing*. The practice of presenting a deceptively low initial price and revealing additional fees or charges only at later stages in the transaction, leveraging psychological commitment to encourage continued purchasing.
- *Preselected options*. Defaults set in favor of actions advantageous to the provider, such as automatic subscriptions or additional purchases, which exploit user inattention and hurried decision-making.
- *So-called free rewards*. Offerings presented as complimentary but conditional upon further purchases or subscriptions, enticing users through the illusion of gratuitous benefit while obscuring the true cost.

Why legal design is important for dark patterns (and potential related risks)

Legal design and dark patterns mark the two ends of a moral continuum in interface and communication design. The former aspires to enable under-standing, participation, and trust; the latter seeks to obscure, coerce, or manipulate. If dark patterns exploit the weaknesses of human cognition to favor institutional or commercial interests, legal design begins with an oppo-site assumption – that people are entitled to access, comprehend, and respond to legal information without distortion or interference.[14]

There is also a deeper ethical dimension. Legal design aligns with core principles of democratic legal systems – transparency, dignity, participation. By resisting the logic of trickery, it protects the conditions under which deci-sions acquire legitimacy. Where dark patterns reduce the act of consent to a click devoid of context or comprehension, legal design restores its meaning, requiring that agreement be traceable, intentional, and understood. Lastly, it is a matter of legal validity. As highlighted in the regulatory reports by Noyb,[15] banners and interfaces that fail to present symmetrical options for acceptance and refusal violate the very standards of free consent required under European data protection law.

That said, and beyond the immediate interface, legal design contributes to broader institutional trust. In a digital ecosystem where suspicion and confusion are often the default user response, clear legal communication represents a form of reputational capital. It demonstrates respect for users' time, attention, and autonomy. Rather than relying on legal disclaimers and defensive strategies, legal designers enable proactivity, building agreements, disclosures, and interactions that anticipate scrutiny and pass it with coherence.

Ultimately, we do not merely aim offer an alternative to dark patterns. We aim to disrupt their premises, refusing to see opacity as a design solution and treating comprehension as a design requirement, not a by-product. It is precisely because legal language is complex, and because legal processes are often high-stake, that the case for legal design becomes necessary. We need to restore legal communication to its proper role – enabling informed action in a world where not being misled should be a baseline more than a luxury.

References

1   Justin Hurwitz, "Designing a Pattern, Darkly" (2020), 22 *North Carolina Journal of Law & Technology*, 57 https://scholarship.law.unc.edu/ncjolt/vol22/iss1/3.

2   Harry Brignull, "Dark Patterns: Dirty Tricks Designers Use to Make People Do Stuff" (8 July 2010), www.90percentofeverything.com/2010/07/08/dark-patterns-dirty-tricks-designers-use-to-make-people-do-stuff/

3   Brignull, H., Leiser, M., Santos, C. & Doshi, K., "Deceptive Design" (2023) www.deceptive.design/

4   Regulation (EU) 2016/679 of the European Parliament and of the Council of 27 April 2016 on the protection of natural persons with regard to the processing of personal data and on the free movement of such data, and repealing Directive 95/46/EC (General Data Protection Regulation) (2016) OJ L119/1

5   Woodrow Hartzog, *Privacy's Blueprint: The Battle to Control the Design of New Technologies*, Harvard University Press (2018)

6   Regulation (EU) 2022/2065 of the European Parliament and of the Council of 19 October 2022 on a Single Market for Digital Services and amending Directive 2000/31/EC (Digital Services Act) (2022) OJ L277/1.

7   Regulation (EU) 2022/2065 of the European Parliament and of the Council of 19 October 2022 on a Single Market for Digital Services and amending Directive 2000/31/EC (Digital Services Act) (2022) OJ L277/1, Art. 25.

8   Regulation (EU) 2024/1689 of the European Parliament and of the Council of 13 March 2024 laying down harmonised rules on artificial intelligence and amending certain Union legislative acts (Artificial Intelligence Act) (2024) OJ L 168, 1.

9   T. Naheyan and K. Oyibo, "The Effect of Dark Patterns and User Knowledge on User Experience and Decision-Making" in N. Baghaei, R. Ali, K. Win and K. Oyibo (eds), *Persuasive Technology*. PERSUASIVE 2024, Lecture Notes in Computer Science, vol. 14636 (Springer 2024) https://doi.org/10.1007/978-3-031-58226-4_15

10   Directive 2005/29/EC of the European Parliament and of the Council of 11 May 2005 concerning unfair business-to-consumer commercial practices in the internal market (Unfair Commercial Practices Directive) (2005) OJ L149/22.

11   Mark Leiser, "Illuminating Manipulative Design: From 'Dark Patterns' to Information Asymmetry and the Repression of Free Choice Under the Unfair Commercial Practices Directive" (2022) 34(3) *Loyola Consumer Law Review* 484, 505.

12   Colin M. Gray and others, "End User Accounts of Dark Patterns as Felt Manipulation" (2020) arXiv:2010.11046 https://arxiv.org/abs/2010.11046

13   On this level, I would like to share the work of Fair Patterns, which is not only a company working in the field, but also a research center on the matter. www.fairpatterns.com

14   Katri Nousiainen and Catalina Perdomo Ortega, "Dark Patterns in Law and Economics Framework" (2024), *Loyola Consumer Law Review* 90.

15   Noyb, *Consent Banner Report: Overview of EU and National Guidelines on Dark Patterns* (noyb.eu, November 2023), https://noyb.eu/sites/default/files/2024-07/noyb_Cookie_Report_2024.pdf.

Chapter 9:
Legal design and proactive law

What is proactive law? Evolution and significance

According to the *Oxford Learner's Dictionaries*, to be proactive means "controlling a situation by making things happen rather than waiting for things to happen and then reacting to them".[1] When applied to the legal domain, this mindset marks a decisive shift from the traditional reactive approach, focused on addressing problems post-factum, towards an anticipatory, enabling role for law and legal professionals. The proactive law approach proposes that law should not only respond to conflict and non-compliance but also prevent undesirable outcomes and promote conditions for success.[2]

This shift is not a recent invention but rather a contemporary reconfiguration of long-standing legal sensibilities, building upon the preventive law movement initiated by Louis M. Brown in the mid-20th century.[3] Brown envisioned lawyers as anticipators of human behavior rather than merely interpreters of judicial outcomes. From this foundation, proactive law emerged in the late 1990s and early 2000s in Finland and the wider Nordic region, particularly through the work of Helena Haapio and the Nordic School of Proactive Law, which was formally launched in 2004.[4, 5]

In her seminal work, *Introduction to Proactive Law: A Business Lawyer's View*,[6] Haapio compares proactive legal practice to preventive medicine. Just as vaccinations reduce the likelihood of illness, proactive legal thinking seeks to reduce the likelihood of disputes, litigation, and regulatory failure. The idea, more than providing an abstract ideal, was a call for embedding legal awareness into the daily processes of business and governance (design, procurement, marketing, service delivery), not just in boardrooms or courtrooms.

Building upon this foundation, Haapio and George J. Siedel introduced a twofold structure of proactive law – preventive and promotive.[7] The preventive aspect echoes Brown's legacy, emphasizing early identification and reduction of legal risk. The promotive aspect, however, reflects a more generative legal function, which contributes positively to value creation, collaboration, and strategic outcomes. This evolution aligns with broader interdisciplinary trends, where law intersects with business strategy, human-centered design, and technology.[8]

In this light, the role of the lawyer transforms. Rather than acting only in crisis or in defense, the legal professional becomes a co-designer of processes, contracts, and relationships. However, this reconceptualization demands a wider skillset – empathy, strategic literacy, communication, and the ability to collaborate across disciplines.

Insight:

The theoretical grounding of proactive law also resonates with Regulatory Focus Theory, developed by psychologist Tory Higgins,[9] which distinguishes between promotion-focused and prevention-focused orientations. Proactive law does not choose between them but seeks to hold both – reducing risk while fostering opportunity. This dual focus adds conceptual maturity to the legal function, positioning law as both a guardian and an enabler.

What emerges is not merely a new methodology, but a new legal mindset. Proactive law repositions legal professionals from being last-resort responders to strategic contributors involved from the beginning – before contracts are signed, before policies are finalized, before products are launched. This shift requires not just different tools, but different incentives, metrics, and forms of education.

However, this transition is not without friction. Legal education, hierarchical structures, and billing models often reinforce reactive postures. Despite these barriers, the case for proactivity grows stronger. In a world defined by speed, complexity, and interdependence, legal functions that intervene too late are, by definition, ineffective. Proactive law shifts this dynamic, aiming to create value and reframing law as a positive force. A generator of clarity, sustainability, and trust.

Benefits of proactive law

The adoption of proactive law brings a wide array of advantages for businesses. Among the various benefits we can find the following.

Establishing a partner-like relationship between businesses and legal teams

Legal counsel is often consulted only once problems have materialized, reinforcing a perception of law as a costly and defensive tool. Many business leaders, particularly in small and medium-sized enterprises, hesitate to involve legal professionals early on, either due to concerns over cost or because they underestimate the strategic value of legal input. Proactive law seeks to overturn this mindset, aiming to develop a new kind of relationship in which legal professionals are brought into the process from the outset, contributing to policy formulation, risk assessment, and strategic planning. Inevitably, this approach also requires a transparent discussion around legal fees and scope, ensuring clients trust that legal advice is proportionate, clear, and tailored to their business goals.

Promoting positive relationships with stakeholders

Traditional legal services are often designed to protect against worst-case scenarios, but proactive law moves beyond defensive logic. It sees contracts and legal documents as frameworks for cooperation. This shift leads to agreements that encourage performance, reduce ambiguity, and anticipate change. A proactive contract is designed to be understood, followed, and adapted. It reflects relational intention more than legal protection. By incorporating language that supports clarity and mutual understanding, proactive contracts become instruments of trust, reducing the chances of conflict and making it easier to resolve disagreements when they do occur. This strengthens the long-term quality of the business relationship, not just compliance.

Enhancing legal literacy

One of the most overlooked benefits of proactive law is its capacity to democratize legal knowledge within organizations. Rather than isolating legal competence within a single department or figure, this approach encourages shared understanding and cross-functional awareness. When business leaders are involved in proactive legal discussions, they become more attuned to potential risks, more fluent in legal reasoning, and better equipped to use legal tools as part of their strategic toolkit. At the same time, legal professionals gain a deeper understanding of the organization's operational realities and risk appetite. This mutual learning creates a culture where legal conversations become part of business conversations.

Effective risk management aligned with business objectives
For many entrepreneurs, risk is a prerequisite for growth. The challenge lies in managing risk in a way that supports ambition without courting avoidable losses. Traditional legal advice often errs on the side of caution, recommending overly restrictive measures that can stifle innovation. Proactive law, by contrast, seeks balance. It starts with an understanding of the business' goals, its financial context, and its strategic priorities. From this basis, it proposes legal strategies that support calculated risk-taking. The legal team becomes a compass more than an anchor – helping the business navigate uncertainty with confidence, without suppressing initiative.

Minimizing uncertainty through preparedness for conflict
Even in the most well-managed organizations, disputes will occur. The difference lies in how they are handled. A reactive legal team responds only once conflict has already disrupted operations. A proactive legal team, by contrast, prepares for the possibility of conflict well in advance. By understanding the client's values, objectives, and reputation, proactive lawyers can anticipate areas of friction and put in place procedures for early resolution. These might include internal escalation paths, clearly defined roles and responsibilities in contracts, or pre-agreed mediation mechanisms. The result is a more coherent, less damaging scenario. Businesses equipped with such foresight are better able to absorb shocks, protect relationships, and maintain operational continuity.

Facilitating internal alignment and decision-making
In complex organizations, misalignment between departments often generates friction, inefficiency, and legal exposure. Proactive law helps bridge these internal gaps by involving legal professionals in cross-functional discussions and framing decisions with a fuller understanding of risk, compliance, and regulatory strategy. This anticipatory presence prevents contradictory choices, clarifies responsibilities, and enables quicker, more consistent decision-making across the organization.

Building a culture of accountability and transparency
Proactive legal thinking fosters a cultural shift, encouraging individuals across the organization to take responsibility for their actions and decisions. Rather than treating law as a distant or specialized concern, this approach integrates legal awareness into daily routines. It strengthens internal gover-

nance and reinforces ethical behavior, reducing the risk of misconduct and reputational damage. When employees at all levels know what is expected and why, accountability becomes less of a burden and more of a shared norm.

Reducing operational friction and administrative waste

Legal ambiguity is a hidden cost. It generates hesitation, slows down approvals, and invites over-cautious behavior. Proactive law addresses this by clarifying rules, roles, and processes before misunderstandings emerge. When contracts are clearly drafted, when procedures are designed with the user in mind, and when legal guidance is accessible in real time, operations become smoother and less prone to delay. This legal streamlining increases efficiency across departments. It frees up time, attention, and energy to be invested in strategic priorities, rather than in solving avoidable legal problems.

Strengthening reputational resilience and external trust

In a world where reputation is one of the most fragile and valuable assets, organizations must be perceived as acting with responsibility, fairness, and foresight. Proactive law supports this by ensuring that communication with clients, partners, regulators, and the public is clear, coherent, and trustworthy. Whether it involves transparent contract terms, fair dispute resolution mechanisms, or accessible privacy policies, every proactive legal touchpoint reinforces credibility. This trust, once built, becomes a competitive advantage, attracting customers, retaining partners, and sustaining long-term relationships even under pressure.

The five main barriers to proactive law and potential pathways to success[10]

Proactive law offers a renewed and compelling vision for legal practice – one that prioritizes prevention over reaction, collaboration over isolation, and long-term value over short-term fixes. For this reason, it resonates strongly in today's context, shaped by accelerated change, growing regulatory demands, and heightened stakeholder scrutiny. Yet, despite its solid theoretical grounding and its clear alignment with contemporary organizational needs, proactive law remains underused. The reasons are rarely technical. They lie deeper – in entrenched habits, cultural inertia, and institutional design.

Among the reasons why proactive law still struggles to find its way in the legal field, I see the following five:

1. *The weight of the reactive mindset.* Legal practice has long been governed by a reactive logic. Legal work is typically triggered by disputes, regulatory non-compliance, or contractual breakdowns. This logic shapes how lawyers are trained, how legal departments operate, and how success is measured – by cases won, penalties avoided, or conflicts settled. Law schools still focus largely on adversarial thinking, doctrinal precision, and retrospective interpretation. Little attention is given to the preventive potential of law, or to its capacity to shape decisions before problems emerge. This approach influences not only legal professionals but also the organizations they support. In many companies, the legal department is consulted only once something has gone wrong. Without an immediate crisis to handle, the legal function is often seen as non-essential. This leads to a cycle of underinvestment, where early risk-mapping and proactive dialogue are sidelined in favor of reactive firefighting. The legal profession's own conservatism reinforces this. Change is not only seen as difficult, but risky. Preventive action may not produce visible results, and in a culture steeped in precedent and cautious by design, many professionals find comfort in tradition. Even thoughtful evolution is met with resistance when systems reward stability over experimentation.

2. *The silo trap – structural barriers to integration.* Even when legal teams aspire to a more proactive posture, organizational structures often work against them. Most companies remain divided into vertical silos, where each function operates with limited visibility into others. Legal, product, operations, and marketing often run in parallel, not in concert. As a result, legal input arrives late – after decisions have been made, campaigns launched, contracts signed. When issues aren't flagged, however, there may be no mechanism for constructive escalation or collaboration. Communication falters. Responsibilities are blurred. Opportunities to address risks before they materialize are lost. A proactive legal function needs a different model. It must be embedded, and this means more than assigning legal staff to cross-functional teams – it calls for a redefinition of legal work itself. Think about shared platforms, early-stage workflows, or basic legal fluency across departments. Leadership plays a decisive role as well. Without visible commitment from top management, proactive law lacks the institutional leverage to take root. Management must model openness, early involvement, and mutual accountability across business and legal roles.

3. *The measurement dilemma.* In organizations driven by metrics, what cannot be counted is often dismissed. This is perhaps the most subtle but most damaging obstacle to proactive law – it is hard to measure what does not happen. Success in a proactive legal model is often invisible – a dispute avoided, a fine not imposed, a delay prevented. These absences, while meaningful, are difficult to convert into the kind of performance indicators that dominate corporate reporting. Traditional legal metrics such as hours billed, claims resolved, and contracts closed are backward-looking by nature. Preventive legal work resists this framing. Yet its value is real – in fewer legal crises, smoother compliance, stronger internal governance, and reduced friction across the business. If we need indicators, we might include the number of issues resolved at draft stage, early interventions initiated, or levels of legal literacy in non-legal teams. Surveys capturing business leaders' trust in legal input or the clarity of legal documents can also offer insights. But none of this will matter if the organization fails to see prevention as excellence.

4. *Budget aversion and the logic of short-termism.* Funding proactive legal work remains a challenge, largely due to cost-justification models that demand rapid, measurable returns. Legal departments are often treated as cost centers, expected to do more with less. Requests for investment in training, document redesign, or compliance infrastructure are frequently denied because they do not promise immediate savings. External legal providers, still bound to the billable hour, have little incentive to reduce problems upfront when they could instead be paid to resolve them later. This logic distorts priorities. To counter it, I suggest legal teams rethink their narrative. Instead of framing proactive law as a way to reduce costs, it should be presented as a route to operational agility, reputational stability, and strategic clarity. Business cases must speak in terms that resonate across departments – efficiency gains, decision-making confidence, and time saved. Success stories and pilot programs can help make this case. So too can innovative budgeting – how about earmarking funds for legal design within transformation budgets, allocating cross-functional resources, or testing cost-sharing models for upstream initiatives?

5. *The global complexity problem.* The final obstacle is structural and systemic. Proactive law depends on foresight, but foresight becomes difficult in a legal environment characterized by overlapping

jurisdictions, regulatory volatility, and fragmented enforcement. Multinational companies must navigate a maze of national and sector-specific rules – from GDPR to local content regulations, from labor legislation to AI governance. This level of variability makes it hard to anticipate legal consequences across geographies and business units. For small and medium enterprises, the challenge is often one of capacity. For large organizations, it is one of coordination. In both cases, the answer is not to build ever-larger legal teams, but to build systems – regulatory intelligence tools, shared compliance dashboards, and workflows capable of responding to change without paralysis. Legal professionals must also broaden their competence, shifting from doctrinal knowledge to strategic fluency. How about training professionals not just in black-letter law, but in interpretation, communication, and business framing? Still, this is not only a question of skill. It is a matter of culture. Proactive law can only thrive in organizations that value anticipation over improvisation, collaboration over control, and learning over repetition.

Legal design and proactive law

While legal design and proactive law originate from different disciplinary traditions and maintain distinct theoretical frameworks, they share a common ambition – to reshape the role of law from a reactive, isolated function into a strategic contributor to business, institutional, and societal goals. Both disciplines question the prevailing paradigms that often define legal culture – namely, an overreliance on rigidity, formalism, and ex post intervention. Instead, they promote a vision of law as an enabler of collaboration, a designer of relationships, and a structured yet flexible tool for anticipating and managing complexity. In doing so, they redefine the role of the legal professional – not as a guardian of rules imposed from above, but as a partner in co-creation, someone who helps shape systems, conversations, and agreements that work in practice, not just in theory.

At their intersection lies a shared commitment to transparency, measurability, and inclusiveness. Both legal design and proactive law challenge the opacity of traditional legal work. They advocate for legal tools that are understandable, usable, and capable of producing outcomes that can be monitored, evaluated, and improved. Whether through metrics that track early intervention, or through design-led processes that test and refine contractual clarity, both disciplines push law toward a more deliberate, intelligible, and responsive practice. This convergence is particularly evident in their shared emphasis on shifting from a lawyer-centric to a user-aware perspective, where the needs of clients, partners, and non-lawyer stakeholders are given priority in shaping legal outputs.

I see legal design as one of the most pragmatic methodologies to realize the ambitions of proactive law. It is not the only path, but it offers a structured and tested process grounded in empathy, iterative framing, and solution-building. Through its attention to clarity, plain language, and visual thinking, legal design enables the creation of contracts and systems that are not only legally robust but also functionally intelligible. This improves the quality of relationships, supports mutual understanding, and reduces friction long before disputes arise. It also fosters adaptability, allowing agreements to evolve with the needs of the business and the expectations of stakeholders.

Proactive law's focus on prevention, strategic alignment, and long-term value finds a natural complement in legal design thinking. Design methodologies offer legal professionals the tools to translate that mindset into process – mapping user journeys, running co-creation sessions, testing prototypes, and refining materials based on feedback. This integration produces legal documents and systems that are both context-aware and forward-looking, transforming the contract from a static repository of clauses into a dynamic artefact that supports behavior, collaboration, and innovation.

Yet this integration is not automatic. It requires a recalibration of legal education, professional identity, and organizational structures. Legal professionals must acquire new skills, invest in interdisciplinary collaboration and rethinking workflows, team compositions, and decision-making processes. Only by following these steps will we be able to see meaningful client engagement, better alignment between legal function and business strategy, and a renewed relevance for law in a rapidly shifting world.

References

1   *Oxford Learner's Dictionaries*, "Proactive", www.oxfordlearnersdictionaries.com/
    definition/american_english/proactive
2   Helena Haapio, "Business Success and Problem Prevention Through Proactive
    Contracting" in Peter Wahlgren (ed.), *A Proactive Approach*, Scandinavian Studies in
    Law, vol 49 (Stockholm Institute for Scandinavian Law, 2006) 149 https://ssrn.com/
    abstract=2624979, George J. Siedel and Helena Haapio, "Using Proactive Law for
    Competitive Advantage" (2010) 47, *American Business Law Journal*, 641.

3   Louis M. Brown, *Manual of Preventive Law* (Prentice-Hall, 1950).?

4   Seppo Pohjonen, "Proactive Law in the Field of Law" in Peter Wahlgren (ed.), *A Proactive Approach*, Scandinavian Studies in Law, vol 49 (Stockholm Institute for Scandinavian Law, 2006) 54.

5   Recognition of proactive law has expanded beyond the private sector. In 2008, the European Economic and Social Committee (EESC) explicitly called for a proactive legal approach in its opinion, "The Proactive Law Approach: A Further Step Towards Better Regulation at EU Level". The Committee urged a shift from reactive legal mechanisms to frameworks capable of anticipating social needs, improving regulatory clarity, and supporting trust and collaboration. It describes proactive law as a tool for making regulation more understandable and effective – "a living structure" rather than a static set of constraints.

6   Haapio, Helena, "Introduction to Proactive Law: A Business Lawyer's View" (2006). Peter Wahlgren (Ed.): *A Proactive Approach*, Scandinavian Studies in Law, Vol. 49, Stockholm Institute for Scandinavian Law, 2006, pp. 21-34., https://ssrn.com/abstract=2691940

7   See endnote 29 in chapter 6.

8   Gerlinde Berger-Walliser, "The Past and Future of Proactive Law: An Overview of the Development of the Proactive Law Movement" in Gerlinde Berger-Walliser and Kim Østergaard (eds), *Proactive Law in a Business Environment* (DJØF Publishing, 2012) 13 https://ssrn.com/abstract=2576761

9   J. V. Cavallo, "Regulatory Focus Theory" in V. Zeigler-Hill and T. Shackelford (eds), *Encyclopaedia of Personality and Individual Differences* (Springer, 2017) https://doi.org/10.1007/978-3-319-28099-8_1152-1

10 These arguments have been developed in my article, "Proactive Law in Contemporary Legal Landscape: Five Main Barriers and Potential Pathways to Success", published in *Taltech Journal of European Law Studies*, 1/2025 https://sciendo.com/article/10.2478/bjes-2025-0015.

Chapter 10:
Legal design and gamification

A brief introduction to gamification

Gamification, at its core, refers to the practice of introducing game-like mechanisms, such as points, progress bars, levels, rewards, and challenges, into contexts that are not games in themselves.[1] The objective is to encourage sustained participation and motivation, tapping into psychological triggers such as curiosity, a sense of achievement, and the desire for progression. While the term may evoke video games, its presence has become pervasive across a wide range of digital platforms. From e-commerce to fitness trackers, from language learning applications to employee training systems, gamified elements shape and guide how users interact with content and processes. In these contexts, gamification builds engagement loops that reinforce behavior and sustain attention over time.

At the heart of gamification lies the intent to generate active involvement and user retention. How do gamification strategists achieve it? First, they pay close attention to users' motivations, behaviors, and limits. Second, they make interactions less burdensome and more enjoyable, encouraging users to return. Another key element is behavioral reinforcement. Immediate feedback, visual progress, and symbolic rewards provide positive reinforcement that nudges users toward specific actions. Lastly, they adjust to the user. Through personalized pathways, adaptive levels of difficulty, and content that responds to individual preferences, gamification creates a dynamic system in which users feel recognized and supported in their journey.

In the legal context, this approach presents both opportunities and tensions. On the one hand, the legal field is marked by a demand for precision, neutrality, and often a high degree of formality. The credibility of the system and the necessity to maintain a top-notch reputation represent key issues for legal professionals. On the other hand, the potential of gamification is undeniable. Imagine a compliance training system that rewards completion in ways that encourage sustained attention to detail, or a contract review platform that integrates progress tracking, goal-setting, and immediate feedback to encourage users to reflect more attentively on the legal implications of their actions. The real challenge, therefore, is not understanding the benefits of gamification. It is exploring how far gamification can go in helping lawyers and users engaging with legal processes without diluting their seriousness, nor trivializing their content.[2]

Insight:

If you want to understand better the gamification realm, I suggest grounding the discussion in established psychological theories that explain why game mechanics effectively drive user engagement and behavior.[3] Two pivotal frameworks in this domain are the Self-Determination Theory (SDT) by E. Deci and R. Ryan,[4] and the Flow Theory by M. Csikszentmihalyi.[5] These theories provide valuable foundations for understanding how gamification can support motivation, learning, and sustained interaction in a legal context.

Self-determination theory (SDT) posits that human motivation is governed by the fulfilment of three fundamental psychological needs – autonomy, competence, and relatedness. Autonomy is about feeling in control of one's actions and decisions. Competence refers to the experience of mastery and progress. Finally, relatedness concerns the human desire to feel connected with others. These three dimensions, when harmonized, generate intrinsic motivation – arguably the most enduring form of engagement.

Flow Theory offers a complementary perspective.[6] It describes a mental state in which individuals are fully absorbed in what they are doing, often losing awareness of time and external distractions. Flow arises when there is a clear goal, immediate feedback, and a perceived balance between the difficulty of the task and the individual's skill (technically it's more complex than that – but this is a good starting point). What if a legal user becomes immersed in bureaucratic and tedious tasks like a teenager playing his favorite video game?

Gamification in the legal field – strategies and applications

Gamification in the legal field can take on numerous forms, each catering to a different aspect of user interaction with legal content. Whether the goal is regulatory compliance, contract negotiation, or legal education, applying these theories thoughtfully allows for a richer, more human-centered approach.

Progress tracking and achievement systems

Progress bars, achievement levels, and badges may be effective to provide users with visual indicators of advancement, helping them navigate lengthy legal documents, compliance training, or onboarding processes.

Example:

Imagine a contract review platform where users move from basic clauses to complex negotiation points only after demonstrating understanding through interactive checkpoints. Rather than displaying the entire contract at once, the platform could gradually reveal new sections as users complete key review tasks in the current part.

Interactive experiences

Unlockable content creates a sense of progression and accomplishment while ensuring that users engage with information in a structured, digestible format. Legal documents, contracts, and policies can be designed to reveal sections only after users complete comprehension checks or interactive summaries.

Example:

A corporate legal department might implement interactive contracts that require users to answer short scenario-based questions correctly before advancing to the next section. This method would likely encourage reading and comprehension. Similarly, in a litigation or due diligence environment, a dynamic checklist could display all preparation tasks (document collection, witness preparation, timeline building). Items could automatically check off as the user uploads required documents or completes tasks.

Simulations and role-playing scenarios

Legal scenarios frequently involve intricate decision-making processes with significant real-world consequences. Integrating interactive simulations or role-playing elements could allow users to immerse themselves in hypothetical (or even real) legal situations, fostering experiential learning in a controlled and risk-free environment. This method can be particularly effective for training new employees or trainees, or educating clients on complex legal protocols.

Example:

A corporate legal department might develop an interactive role-playing simulation in which employees must navigate a simulated data breach, making time-sensitive decisions that influence the outcome. The game would help build practical problem-solving skills, increase awareness of compliance obligations, and support legal risk management. This could lead to a videogame resumé, where a custom adventure storyline tracks an employee's progress from trainee to global counsel.

Challenges and quests

Framing legal training or document review as a series of structured "challenges" or "quests" is another strategy to significantly enhance user engagement. This approach transforms passive information consumption into an interactive, goal-oriented experience. Quests can be designed to guide users through complex legal processes in incremental stages, reinforcing comprehension while rewarding progress.

Example:

A law firm may challenge its associates to re-think a specific contract, changing its clauses, altering the information architecture, or targeting it for a neurodiverse audience. How about pitting one team against another? Lawyers love competing. We can also create a "faulty contract challenge", where a slightly broken agreement needs to be debugged. Instead of passive reading, the players become investigators – finding hidden logical errors, conflicting clauses, missing regulatory obligations, and so on.

Feedback loops

In the context of gamification, immediate and constructive feedback can clarify user decisions, correct misunderstandings, and reinforce accurate legal knowledge. Prompt feedback may help users taking informed decisions and strengthening their strategies.

Example:

Think about a GDPR compliance module that offers real-time corrective feedback when users mishandle data classification tasks. This would reinforce best practices and reduce the likelihood of future errors. Similarly, we could use reverse-engineered feedback. After making an error and seeing the consequence, users may enter a mini-quest. "Reverse engineer the mistake: What clues should you have seen? How would you prevent it earlier?" This would allow users to undertake a root-cause analysis and deliberately learn from mistakes.

Reward systems

One of the key elements of gamification is the presence of rewards once we achieve a specific target. Digital badges, certificates, and icons may be used to acknowledge progress and professional growth. Legal professionals could unlock exclusive resources, gain access to advanced legal tools, or receive certification credits after completing complex legal tasks or training modules.

Example:

How about implementing a reward system, allowing users to accumulate points for completing legal readings, participating in simulations, or solving compliance challenges, which could then be redeemed for tangible professional benefits? Similarly, law firms may trade challenge points for sponsorship of conferences, advanced certifications, and innovation project funding. This could also democratize opportunity creation.

Gentle friction and motivated correction

Among the most delicate tools in the gamification toolbox are gentle deterrents – subtle mechanisms that introduce friction when users deviate from a desired path. Rather than resorting to punitive or shaming strategies, which would be ethically questionable and counterproductive in legal contexts, these forms of negative feedback can be thoughtfully calibrated to encourage reflection, attentiveness, and behavioral course correction. In practice, this may involve temporary pauses, locked pathways, or the temporary unavailability of certain functionalities when key learning steps are skipped or misunderstood. The aim is not to punish but to promote active engagement by requiring users to take responsibility for their choices within a low-risk environment.

Example:

In a legal training platform, a user who fails to correctly answer a scenario-based question might be guided back to a previous module as an opportunity to strengthen their understanding on a specific topic before moving forward. Similarly, a contract negotiation simulator could momentarily restrict access to specific clauses if a user has not yet grasped the foundational legal concepts. Another option could be blocking access to specific internal platforms if lawyers don't undertake generative AI training (I personally know a law firm that really did it – but I won't mention the name and the platform!).

Challenges and ethical considerations of gamification in the legal field

As legal designers, we must ensure that interactive elements serve the primary goal of improving understanding and accessibility, not entertainment. To navigate these challenges effectively, I suggest improving the following strategies:

- *Maintaining professionalism.* Gamification must be carefully designed to uphold the gravity of legal contexts. Visual design, tone of voice, and interactive elements should reflect the professionalism expected in legal communications. This ensures that the engaging aspects of gamification support, rather than undermine, the credibility and seriousness of legal content.
- *Avoiding user manipulation.* Gamified systems should prioritize user comprehension and informed decision-making over superficial engagement. Reward systems must not exploit psychological triggers in ways that distract users from understanding important legal information. Transparency in how game mechanics influence user behavior may help preserve trust.
- *Balancing complexity and accessibility.* Legal content is inherently complex and simplifying it for the sake of engagement may result in the loss of critical information. Gamification should be used to break down complex concepts into manageable parts without distorting legal meaning. Go for legal clarity – it's our North Star!
- *Ensuring data privacy and security.* Gamified legal tools often require user interaction and data collection. Law firms and legal departments experimenting with gamification strategies have to comply with data protection laws and implement robust security measures for safeguarding sensitive information. This means clear communication about data usage and inclusion of user consent mechanisms.
- *Promoting inclusivity and accessibility.* Gamification in legal contexts should be designed to welcome all users, regardless of their background, abilities, or familiarity with digital environments. This means

offering alternative navigation modes for users with disabilities, creating introductory paths for legal professionals who are unfamiliar with gaming conventions, and ensuring smooth functionality across different devices and platforms. At the end of the day, the aim is not to reward digital fluency, but to support meaningful engagement for everyone.

- *Being aware of the risks of dark gamification.* Gamification may create pressure, dependency, or even addictive behaviors. When the mechanisms we introduce push users to act without reflection, impose artificial urgency, or exploit social comparison to induce anxiety, we are no longer supporting legal comprehension. We are distorting it. Our aim is to promote user autonomy, not erode it. Every point, every badge, every visual choice must serve this principle. When in doubt, prioritize clarity over persuasion, depth over metrics, and empowerment over performance. Gamification is a tool. How we choose to use it defines the ethical boundaries of our work.

A virtual legal experience

Although virtual reality (VR) and the Metaverse have not traditionally been linked to legal design, they offer increasingly concrete opportunities to reimagine legal education, training, and client interaction. These immersive technologies create interactive environments where complex legal notions and procedures can be experienced directly, rather than merely described. By simulating real-world legal dynamics, VR and Metaverse applications can allow users to build practical skills and gain a more intuitive understanding of legal mechanisms within safe, controlled settings.

One of the most promising use cases is the development of virtual courtrooms. Within these spaces, lawyers, judges, and law students can rehearse courtroom procedures, sharpen advocacy techniques, and familiarize themselves with judicial workflows without the consequences of real litigation. Simulations can reproduce a range of scenarios, from criminal trials to arbitration sessions, enabling practice in delivering oral arguments, questioning witnesses, or presenting evidence. These environments also allow for real-time feedback, performance analysis, and iterative improvement, which in turn supports the development of legal reasoning, rhetorical clarity, and confidence under pressure. Importantly, they also offer a direct, embodied understanding of procedural rules, courtroom etiquette, and professional roles – elements often overlooked in traditional education.

The Metaverse, for its part, introduces a further dimension to how legal services can be delivered and experienced. Virtual legal offices could offer clients accessible, engaging spaces for consultation, contract review, or dispute resolution. Legal professionals could host workshops, seminars, or even entire proceedings in digital venues, enabling international collaboration and lowering the barriers of physical access. In this scenario, geography becomes secondary and interaction can take place in real time across jurisdictions.

Example:

In legal education, these tools could fundamentally change how students approach learning. Instead of passively absorbing information through static materials, students could engage in immersive moot courts, explore interactive 3D models of legal systems, or conduct research in virtual libraries designed around thematic areas. This experiential approach has the potential to deepen engagement, foster problem-solving, and transform abstract legal concepts into tangible, lived experiences – one of the main weak points of the law school experience.

Legal design and gamification

Incorporating gamification into legal design signals a broader cultural and methodological shift toward legal systems that place the user at the center. Far from being a superficial layer of interaction, gamification may really become a tool capable of transforming legal complexity into structured, engaging, and meaningful experiences.

At the same time, this remains a developing area, rich in potential but still lacking in extensive research. Many open questions remain. What is the long-term behavioral effect of engaging with gamified legal tools? Do users retain knowledge more effectively? Are they more likely to act in compliance with legal norms, or to challenge them more confidently? Can legal training modules incorporating gamification genuinely improve decision-making under pressure, or foster greater ethical awareness?

Equally pressing is the question of balance – how far can personalization and interactivity be taken without running afoul of regulatory constraints or professional codes of conduct? What level of transparency should be required in gamified legal tools to ensure users understand when they are being guided or influenced? Can legal gamification accommodate different levels of literacy, cognitive styles, or cultural background without reinforcing exclusion or bias?

In highly regulated contexts, especially in areas like financial services, data protection, or health law, the integration of gamified elements must be both deliberate and auditable. Future developments will likely require close collaboration between legal designers, behavioral scientists, developers, and regulatory bodies to ensure that innovation does not come at the cost of accountability.

We can engage with the law in ways that were once unthinkable. As these technologies mature, they may amplify the potential of gamification in ways we are only beginning to grasp. But this means rethinking not just how we communicate the law, but how we structure participation, understanding, and trust. As with many of the aspects of this book, this is easier said than done.

References

1   For an academic definition of gamification, I suggest that of Deterding et al. (2011), who define gamification as "the application of game elements in non-game contexts for purposes other than entertainment".
    https://link.springer.com/article/10.1007/s11528-024-00968-9#

2   A longer-term goal of many gamification efforts is to create lasting habits – to have users continue the desired behavior even after the gamified incentives are removed. Habit Formation Theory provides insight into how repetitive behaviors become automatic. A common model for habit formation is the habit loop popularized by Charles Duhigg (2012) and very much aligned with behaviorist principles: it consists of a Cue – Routine – Reward cycle. Also see B. J. Fogg, *Fogg Behavior Model* (2025), www.bjfogg.com/fogg-behavior-model

3   Gamification's use of points, badges, levels, and rewards draws heavily from behaviorist psychology, especially B. F. Skinner's theory of operant conditioning. Operant conditioning is the process by which behaviors are learned (or extinguished) through rewards and punishments (for more info on Skinnerian Behaviorism, see "Skinner's Behaviourism" (*New Learning Online*, 2025), https://newlearningonline.com/new-learning/chapter-6/supporting-material/skinners-behaviourism

4   Edward L. Deci and Richard M. Ryan, *Intrinsic Motivation and Self-Determination in Human Behavior* (1st edition, Springer, 1985) https://doi.org/10.1007/978-1-4899-2271-7

5   Mihály Csíkszentmihályi, *Flow: The Psychology of Optimal Experience* (Harper & Row, 1990).

6   Jane McGonigal, a game designer and author of *Reality is Broken* (2011) and *SuperBetter* (2015), is one of the main gamification advocates regarding game principles and its application to improve real lives and solve real problems. According to her perspective, reality often fails to engage us, while games are designed to maximize happiness and can be used to enhance real-life experiences.

Thoughtful perspective
Ashleigh Ruggles and Maclen Stanley

Ashleigh Ruggles and Maclen Stanley are Harvard Law School graduates and practicing attorneys. Ashleigh's practice focuses on entertainment, sports, and music transactions, whereas Maclen specializes in business law and litigation. Maclen's book, The Law Says What: Stuff You Didn't Know About the Law (but Really Should!) *was published in 2021. Geared towards non-lawyers, the book offers a crash course on some of the most bizarre, infuriating, and vitally important legal topics of today.*
It also served as inspiration for their social media channel, "The Law Says What", which breaks down legal concepts for their ~1.5 million followers.

Marco: Maclen and Ashleigh, you both have an amazing talent for making legal content not just clear, but genuinely fun. What sparked the idea to start sharing law through platforms like TikTok, YouTube, and Instagram?

Maclen and Ashleigh: Ironically enough, the initial idea arose as a way to market Maclen's book, which focuses on introducing interesting legal topics to non-lawyers. The plan was to tease interesting legal topics in short form content online, then pitch the actual book at the end of the videos. But we quickly found there was a voracious appetite for legal education content online, specifically when we started tying the content to contemporary news events. Candidly, we were surprised at the interest from laypersons in the law, but it turns out that people want to know more about the legal topics that they see every day in the news or in their personal lives (landlord–tenant / police / employment, etc.). Our social media channels just took off from there by themselves.

Marco: Legal language often gets a bad rap for being overly complicated. Do you think humor can help make legal concepts more understandable? And if so, how do you find the balance between simplifying and oversimplifying?

Maclen and Ashleigh: We 100 percent agree that humor is useful in making the law less boring and more accessible. Good lawyers make their clients feel comfortable (not condescended to) and allow them to fully understand what is taking place. Humor is a great bridge to make our viewers feel more comfortable when topics get dense. As silly as it sounds, we try to intersperse low-brow humor (think: fart jokes!) in areas where topics are overly complex. It lightens the whole vibe of the video.

We're also staunch proponents of simplifying legal language. We have yet to find an example of the law being necessarily written in a complex manner. Complex legal jargon is almost always a result of pretentious pedantic pomposity (see, like that). The law is a human construct, not quantum physics – it doesn't need to be so hard.

Our concerns with oversimplifying most often arise with the facts or details of a certain topic, not the law itself. It's quite challenging to give a full and objective recounting of all facts at issue in a short-form video capped at 90 seconds.

Marco: What kind of feedback do you hear most often from your audience? Is there a recurring theme or question that says something about how people feel about the legal system today?

Maclen and Ashleigh: We constantly hear that our viewers have lost trust in the legal system. This applies to both sides of the political aisle. For example, Conservatives believe that prosecutors in liberal cities refuse to put anyone in jail anymore. Liberals believe that the Supreme Court is a new arm of an authoritarian right-wing government. The political rift and overall distrust of the law seems to only be growing. That said, we think all of the contention surrounding the legal system has simultaneously made people want to learn more about it and educate themselves more than before.

Marco: How has your work as creators and influencers shaped the way you approach your legal career?

Maclen and Ashleigh: We have definitely noticed a real benefit in our own legal work as a result of our content. Particularly with our client interactions. Having focused for years now on explaining and simplifying the law to our viewers, we've developed a real expertise in explaining legal issues to clients. Demystifying the law has also influenced our actual legal work to some extent. For example, Maclen just finished negotiating a purchase agreement in a small-scale transaction. The document ended up getting cut down in size by half from where it started and the language was simplified so that his client fully understood each provision, while still benefiting from full protections. Opposing counsel kept saying that the simplifications were "not market". It's important to exercise caution here, but just because something is standard doesn't necessarily mean that it is the best!

Marco: You've built a brand around being approachable and real – which isn't always easy in the legal world. What have you learned from your community about trust and engagement that you think more lawyers and legal institutions should pay attention to?

Maclen and Ashleigh: We think it's important to stick to the identity and reputation you've built. Our niche has always been unbiased and objective legal education. In today's political climate, it can be very challenging to avoid introducing our own personal opinions in videos. But our particular audience wants objectivity, so that they can learn and form their own opinions, and that's what we always strive to deliver.

Marco: How do you see the future of legal education, especially with the rise of new media and digital-native learners?

Maclen and Ashleigh: All education is about to experience a paradigm shift with online content readily accessible and AI tools getting better and better. Lawyers' jobs – and law professors' jobs – will necessarily have to adapt. To us, that means becoming a better communicator and synthesizer of information. It will be critical to take available content, condense it, and present it in a manner that is more engaging than what students can find online.

Marco: Finally, what's one piece of advice you'd give to legal professionals who want to communicate better – not just for marketing, but to build clarity, accessibility, and human connection into their work?

Maclen and Ashleigh: As simple as it sounds, talk to your clients and colleagues like you're having a human-to-human conversation.

Part III:
From Theory to Practice

Introduction to Part III:
Law and IKEA Instructions

In the preceding chapters, we laid the theoretical groundwork of legal design, exploring its definitions and mapping its relationship with neighboring disciplines. As we now turn to its practical application, the focus shifts from conceptual framing to concrete interventions. This part of the book is designed to support that transition, helping the reader navigate the space between abstraction and implementation.

When I think about legal design, I often return to a familiar analogy – assembling IKEA furniture. Why do people across languages, geographies, and skill levels manage to complete the task with relative ease? Because the instructions are visual, sequential, and deliberately intuitive. They guide the user step by step, removing ambiguity and building confidence. What might initially seem complex becomes approachable through design.

Legal information, like a flat-pack wardrobe, often appears daunting in its raw form. But when reorganized into manageable steps, supported by visual cues and clear sequencing, it becomes usable. We provide the scaffolding for this shift, restructuring rights, obligations, and decisions in ways that align with how the human brain handles complexity – incrementally and visually. However, I have to stress that legal design is not merely about producing legal instruction manuals. The true challenge lies in execution – ensuring that documents are not only intelligible, but actively used, integrated into processes, and evaluated over time.

This is where practice begins to deliver on promise. When we observe how documents perform in real settings – collecting data on user interaction, friction points, and outcome – we move beyond aesthetics and into functionality. We democratize access to legal information and reframe value in terms of performance indicators and measurable outcomes.

This section of the book is organized to support this shift. Chapter 11 sets the stage, then chapter 12 presents the core elements of the legal design toolbox. Chapter 13 examines the primary challenges that emerge in applied contexts, whilst chapter 14 gathers a selection of what we might describe as practical insights – small, often unspoken details that shape success. Chapter

15 explores the most common mistakes of legal design practitioners. Chapter 16 addresses the contribution of generative AI to legal design and its current uses in practice before, finally, chapter 17 looks at how to leverage from the experience.

Together, these chapters form a pathway from theoretical reflection to tangible change.

Chapter 11:
Setting the stage for our legal design project

Choosing the format, part one – online, in-person, or hybrid?

The format of a legal design project – whether virtual, in-person, or hybrid – shapes the experience in ways that go far beyond logistics, influencing how people collaborate, how ideas emerge, how accessible the process is, and even how trust is built within the team. No format is inherently better than another – each brings its own logic, benefits, and drawbacks. Each invites different rhythms and relationships.

It's worth pausing to weigh the trade-offs before jumping into design, because this choice is strategic, not just technical. What matters is choosing the one that best suits your project's aims, your team's composition, and the context in which you're operating. Whatever format you choose, the key lies in intentionality – know why you're choosing it and design the experience accordingly.

Online

Running a legal design project fully online allows people from different cities and time zones to collaborate without the constraints of geography. Tools like Miro enable real-time interaction and shared whiteboards, making it possible to move through the design phases with structure and speed. The format is cost-efficient, reduces logistical friction, and is often more inclusive for those with demanding work or family schedules. That said, virtual sessions tend to flatten energy. Spontaneous idea-sharing becomes harder, small signals get lost, and the collective atmosphere risks slipping into passivity. Moreover, not everyone is equally comfortable navigating digital tools, and some might disengage behind their muted microphones or switched-off cameras.

Pros: Cost-effective, geographically inclusive, accessible for flexible schedules, easier recording.

Cons: Weaker group dynamics, "Zoom fatigue", lower fluency with platforms, reduced immediacy.

In-person

In-person sessions bring a very different dynamic. Ideas move faster, feedback loops are tighter, and participants are more likely to stay present, engaged, and invested. The energy in the room is tangible, and non-verbal communication – so essential in moments of uncertainty or conflict – flows naturally. This format often suits early-phase workshops where trust, speed, and co-creation matter most. But the trade-off is clear – it requires more planning, often more budget, and more physical availability. Moreover, it can be exclusionary for dispersed teams, and scheduling is rarely simple.
Pros: Stronger bonding, faster feedback, richer interactions.
Cons: Higher costs, geographic limitations, logistical constraints.

Pro tip:

For live sessions, an effective strategy to try is to print the original contract at full scale (or, even better, in bigger scale) and display it on the wall. There's something undeniably powerful about confronting the entire document in its raw form – page after page of dense, disjointed, or impenetrable text. It becomes immediately clear why change is needed. The visual impact alone often provokes a mix of disbelief and motivation. Beyond its symbolic value, this wall-sized contract becomes a practical anchor throughout the session. It serves as a visual benchmark of progress – with each redesigned section, each simplification, and each insight, the transformation becomes tangible. Whenever energy dips or discouragement sets in, a glance at that wall reminds everyone just how far the work has come.

Hybrid

The hybrid model promises the best of both worlds – physical energy and digital reach. In theory, it's the most inclusive option, giving participants a choice of how to attend while keeping the benefits of in-person interaction. In practice, however, it can be complex to manage. Balancing attention between remote and on-site participants is not trivial. Engagement can be uneven, and unless managed carefully, those online often become spectators rather than contributors. Tech hiccups, time zone gaps, and unclear roles can erode the very inclusivity the format hopes to deliver.
Pros: Flexible, potentially inclusive, adaptable to different needs.
Cons: Coordination-heavy, unequal participation risks, technical demands.

So, which to choose? In most cases, go fully in or fully out. Either embrace the depth and immediacy of in-person work or commit to the flexibility and reach of digital collaboration. Hybrid formats can work but are a second choice. We've found that they tend to become a compromise that satisfies no one.

Ultimately, the choice should be shaped by your project's objectives, your team's geographical spread, your budget, and the digital confidence of the people involved. That said, the vibe of sticky notes on a wall – so colorful, chaotic, and collaborative – is still hard to replicate online.

Choosing the format, part two – hackathons, jams, and periodic sessions

Choosing the right format for collaboration is another important choice. Among the most widely used approaches are intensive formats – such as hackathons and design jams – and longer, recurring sessions that unfold over time. Each offers distinct rhythms, energies, and outcomes. While both aim to foster creativity, co-design, and problem-solving, their structures differ significantly. One prioritizes speed and boldness; the other, depth and reflection.

As with our previous reflections, we believe it is useful to explore all available options, weighing their respective strengths and limitations – not in search of a universal solution, but to help each team find the right format for their goals, constraints, and context.

Hackathons and jams[1]

Whether virtual or in-person, hackathons and design jams are short, high-energy events designed to catalyze creativity and accelerate problem-solving. Their compressed format pushes participants to concentrate quickly, make rapid decisions, and take bold, sometimes unconventional, design risks. They are especially effective at energizing teams and unlocking fresh ideas under time pressure.

Though often used interchangeably, the two formats differ in intent, structure, and atmosphere. A hackathon is typically more structured and competitive. These events usually span 24 to 48 hours and involve teams working intensively to tackle a defined legal challenge. The goal is often the development of a prototype or a tangible solution, which is then presented to a panel of judges. Prizes or recognition are usually involved, and the mood tends to be goal-oriented and time-driven. It aims for concrete outputs and thrives on time constraints and competition.

A design jam, by contrast, is a more informal, collaborative, and non-competitive gathering. Rather than aiming for a finished product, jams prioritize ideation, collective exploration, and creative freedom. They are ideal for brainstorming, testing concepts, and introducing participants to legal design principles. Typically lasting a half-day or full day, jams encourage experimentation without the pressure of performance. They tend to be more exploratory, favoring learning, discussion, and early-stage ideation.

Pros: Rapid prototyping and idea generation by compressing time and removing overthinking. Their intensity can stimulate risk-taking and unlock unexpected solutions. Their multidisciplinary nature attracts varied expertise, often creating rich intersections between law, design, and technology.

Cons: Time constraints can limit deeper reflection and ideas may remain underdeveloped. Participants might leave energized, but, without sufficient follow-up, insights risk being lost before they can mature.

Periodic and recurring sessions

Unlike short-form events, periodic sessions unfold over weeks or months, creating a framework that supports more gradual development. This format is well-suited to complex or sensitive projects that require research, multiple iterations, and sustained feedback. The space between sessions allows teams to implement learning, adjust direction, and refine outcomes in a way that is difficult to achieve during a single sprint.

Pros: They encourage depth. Ideas have time to breathe, evolve, and stabilize. They support better integration of feedback, and help teams build continuity and cohesion over time. This is especially valuable for long-term or strategic legal design initiatives.

Cons: The longer format runs the risk of losing momentum between sessions. Energy dissipates and responsibilities are often delayed or forgotten. Keeping focus and accountability over time may be hard.

Insight:

How about workshops? The term itself is not as clear-cut as it may seem. It does not sit neatly at one end of the spectrum or the other. Sometimes we call something a workshop when it is a single, guided session with a clear objective. Other times, the same word is used to describe a series of recurring meetings aimed at gradual co-creation or iteration. The boundaries are blurred, and that is not necessarily a problem. What matters is less the label and more the experience it delivers – are people working together, exploring possibilities, and making progress? Then it probably qualifies as a workshop.

Which to choose? Both formats can be highly effective, but for different purposes. Hackathons and jams are ideal for generating momentum, producing quick prototypes, and kicking off a project with intensity. Recurring sessions, on the other hand, offer the time and structure needed for robust development and meaningful transformation. Teams may also benefit from using both – starting with a high-energy jam or hackathon to spark ideas, then following up with a series of periodic sessions to develop and implement them.

Pro tip:

If you're feeling adventurous, have you thought of a legal design retreat? We sometimes propose them to law firms and corporate legal departments. Instead of cooking classes or sport challenges, participants spend a weekend reworking a contract together. It's hands-on, immersive, and surprisingly enjoyable. The rules are simple – leave the office, bring the document, and redesign the way you work.

Choosing the format, part three – parallel, serial, or both?

In legal design projects, work can unfold either in parallel, with multiple activities running simultaneously, or in a serial manner, with tasks following a defined sequence. Each approach brings distinct strengths, but also specific constraints, and understanding when and how to apply them can make a substantial difference in both process and outcomes.

At first glance, the distinction between parallel and serial might appear straightforward, but it can be misleading. As mentioned earlier, legal design is not a linear discipline. It does not follow the logic of a Gantt chart. Instead, it invites iteration, movement across phases, and moments of deliberate backtracking. Insights that arise during prototyping may send you back to research; feedback from a test may reshape your framing. For this reason, what I call "serial vs parallel" is not a fixed opposition, but more a way of describing the dynamic rhythms a project might follow.

Parallel approach

This can be particularly effective in large-scale initiatives or multidisciplinary teams. Different workstreams, such as language revision, visual prototyping, and legal risk assessment, can progress simultaneously, provided there is strong coordination. For instance, it is often possible to begin revising the language of a document while a separate team explores user journeys or creates visual mock-ups. This approach can accelerate delivery, distribute workload, and maintain momentum. Needless to say, it requires a clear structure and regular alignment to avoid fragmentation or misalignment.

Serial approach

This offers more clarity and cohesion. Each step builds logically on the one before, making it well-suited for smaller teams or projects with a more linear scope. This method ensures that decisions are made with the benefit of prior insights, and that participants stay focused on one problem at a time. Sometimes, because of the participation of the whole group, it can result in deeper thinking.

Which to choose? In this case, there is more flexibility than in previous examples. While hackathons or session formats often require early structural decisions, the rhythm of parallel and serial work can adapt as the project unfolds. Moreover, while the choice of parallel vs serial may seem clear-cut, it's highly likely you'll end up combining both in different phases of the project. It really depends on the "vibe" of the team (or the teams), the resources available, and the nature of the challenge. The key is not to rigidly choose one path from the outset, but to remain aware of which mode you're operating in and be ready to shift when needed.

Preparing a legal design project

To borrow a Latin expression, a legal design project should be approached *cum grano salis* – with a grain of salt. In practice, this means exercising thoughtful judgment and acknowledging the particular dynamics of the place you're in, especially considering how legal professionals work and approach problems. Working in a design-led, informal, non-hierarchical, prototype-driven, and feedback-heavy environment can feel unfamiliar (if not uncomfortable) for those trained in precision, precedent, and control. This is especially true in law firms, where time is not just a constraint but a currency. Every minute spent in a workshop or exploratory session could be spent billing. For this reason, we should be purpose-driven and clearly open to communicate the value of our work.

Before engaging in the substance of the work, I suggest investing time in creating shared understanding. Produce a slide set introducing the fundamentals – what legal design is, why it matters, and how it differs from traditional legal work. Clarify the goals, address doubts, and, crucially, manage expectations. You might also share information about the tools that will be used, whether digital platforms or facilitation methods. Structure the agenda thoughtfully and choose a facilitation style that suits the group.

Pro tip:
Not every team will be ready for full immersion from the start, and that's fine. Meeting them where they are, and guiding them with clarity and respect, often proves more effective than insisting on methods that feel too foreign, too fast.

Great sessions don't just happen. They are built. They rely on careful preparation, an inclusive mindset, and a sincere commitment to collaboration. When these elements are in place, even the most skeptical participants begin to engage. Not because they have to, but because they start to see how legal design speaks to challenges they face every day, in a language that is both accessible and actionable.

Involving the right players and creating an inclusive environment
Legal design thrives on collaboration and creativity. However, to truly harness its transformative potential, we need to build teams that not only participate actively but are also deeply committed to the process and capable of making a realistic impact within their organizations. Ideally, these teams should also be encouraged to share their experiences and outcomes both internally and externally, fostering a culture of innovation that extends beyond the immediate project.

In my experience, the most successful legal design initiatives emerge in environments that prioritize diverse points of view and inclusivity. Different points of view bring together unique perspectives, foster richer collaboration, and produce solutions that are more responsive to the needs of users and stakeholders.

In order to maximize the impact of legal design, and to cultivate an environment where all voices are heard, valued, and empowered to contribute, these are my suggestions:

- *Assemble a diverse team.* Assemble teams with a diverse mix of backgrounds, including legal professionals, designers, technologists, and business strategists. Different experiences and perspectives help identify blind spots and lead to more innovative and comprehensive solutions. When I'm asked by clients a question such as, *"Can the marketing team participate?"* or, *"Can the AML expert attend?"* my answer is always, *"Yes, they should!"*.

- *Be sure that the same people will attend all the meetings and be present.* It's better to have five committed people than a group of 12 constantly changing. It seems obvious, but it's one of the hardest things to manage.
- *Leverage neurodiverse talent.* As seen in the second part of this book, neurodiverse individuals – such as those with ADHD, dyslexia, or autism – bring unique strengths to legal design projects. Additionally, their involvement can help ensure that solutions are accessible to a wider audience, especially when testing documents and processes designed for neurodiverse users.
- *Adopt inclusive facilitation techniques.* Effective facilitation ensures that all team members have the opportunity to contribute meaning-fully. Techniques such as brain writing, anonymous idea submissions, and breakout groups can help quieter participants feel more comfort-able sharing ideas.
- *Respect different working rhythms.* Not all team members contribute in the same way, or on the same timeline. Some think aloud, others need space before speaking. Some prefer walking and speaking out loud, other will sit and be silent all the time. Some work best in short bursts, others need deep focus time. Designing the rhythm of the project to accommodate different cognitive and work styles can dramatically improve both the quality of collaboration and the expe-rience of participation.
- *Rely on feedback loops and safe spaces.* Foster a culture in which constructive feedback is welcomed and mistakes are viewed as learning opportunities. Create a safe space where participants feel comfortable sharing insights, concerns, and unconventional ideas, which leads to more robust and innovative solutions.

Developing a preliminary checklist

One of the most underestimated yet consistently effective tools for managing complex projects is the checklist. Often dismissed as a mere administrative aid, a checklist, when used thoughtfully, becomes a strategic framework that promotes consistency, focus, and accountability. As bril-liantly explained by Atul Gawande in *The Checklist Manifesto*,[2] the power of this simple tool lies in its ability to bring structure without rigidity. From aviation to surgery, engineering to emergency response, checklists have repeatedly proven their worth by helping professionals navigate complexity and reduce human error.

Insight:

Why are checklists so powerful? There are several compelling reasons:

- *They are non-hierarchical.* Relying on the checklist may lead a secretary to contradict a partner or a trainee his senior. Something that rarely happens in the legal field.
- *They foster shared responsibility.* When reviewed together or used as a group touchpoint, checklists shift accountability from the individual to the team. If you read them aloud, they also encourage collective ownership.
- *They reduce complexity to clarity.* Checklists break down broad ambitions into manageable, actionable steps, keeping the focus on what matters most. They act as cognitive offloading tools, freeing up mental space for creative thinking and user engagement.
- *They prevent avoidable mistakes.* No matter how experienced the team, when juggling multiple inputs, deadlines, and iterations, it's easy to overlook something fundamental or to miss a crucial step. A checklist serves as a quiet reminder. Unassuming, but effective in safeguarding against omissions.
- *They strengthen communication.* A clear checklist helps everyone understand who is doing what, when, and why. It demystifies the process and creates transparency, especially in cross-functional teams where legal professionals, designers, and stakeholders may not share the same jargon or working habits.
- *They evolve with the project.* Unlike static plans, checklists are living documents. They can be refined, adapted, and improved over time. This dynamic quality encourages reflection, iteration, and continuous improvement, making them particularly suited to legal design's feedback-oriented ethos.
- *They support quality assurance.* By embedding checkpoints throughout the process, checklists help uphold the standard of each deliverable. They ensure that quality is not only achieved but maintained from one stage to the next.

In the context of legal design, a checklist is more than a project management tool – it is a compass. It ensures alignment from the outset, helps track each critical element of the design process, and anchors the team when navigating ambiguity. Structured yet adaptable, it reduces risk, enhances clarity, and keeps the focus squarely where it belongs – on the users and the quality of their legal experience.

Some legal design players use also checklists to share the entire trajectory of a legal design project. Doing so has both advantages and potential drawbacks. In some contexts, offering a complete roadmap from the start can support transparency, align expectations, and foster a shared sense of direction. It helps people understand not just what is happening now, but where it is leading. In other situations, revealing the process gradually, one step at a time, can keep the group focused and engaged, preserve flexibility, and allow space for shifts as the work unfolds. As for many legal design questions, there is no single right answer. The choice often depends on your facilitation style, the group's rhythm, and the demands of the project.

Pro tip:

Most of our checklists are related to things we should do. But how about reversing the narrative and creating a "not to do" checklist? The possibilities are endless. We can make it principles-based (not being hierarchical, not being afraid to fail, not looking backward, etc.), or more practical (not moving forward without having listened to everyone, not making decisions without having validated our assumptions, etc.)

Creating common knowledge

Every team operates differently, but one consistent recommendation is to establish a shared knowledge base or a central document repository. This space should serve as a single source of truth where all relevant materials (platform links, session notes, video recordings, prototypes, iterations, etc.) are easily accessible. A well-curated knowledge base sustains institutional memory and enables new team members to familiarize themselves with the project's trajectory. Moreover, it allows ongoing participants to revisit ideas and decisions without starting from scratch each time.

Beyond storing materials, I also suggest creating a concise summary of key learnings at the end of each phase or session. This document should capture what worked, what didn't, and any insights that emerged unexpectedly. Such recaps are invaluable when planning future legal design sessions, allowing teams to avoid repeating mistakes and to refine their methods over time. It's a lightweight but strategic tool for growing internal competence and design maturity.

Pro tip:

One particularly delicate area concerns access to the collaboration boards and the mock-ups. Should clients or team members be allowed to edit the board between sessions? Can they contribute asynchronously? Once again, there is no universal answer. What I suggest is articulating some clear, agreed-upon rules. Define who can edit, when, and how. Decide what is exploratory and what is final. Transparency and shared expectations help prevent confusion, maintain the integrity of the process, and ensure that collaboration remains constructive rather than chaotic.

References

1   Among the main examples of Legal Design Jam, the ones created by Stefania Passera, arguably the first in the field, are worth a mention. https://stefaniapassera.com/portfolio/legaldesignjam/

2   Atul Gawande, *The Checklist Manifesto: How to Get Things Right*, Metropolitan Books (2010).

Chapter 12:
The legal design toolbox

The platforms

Platforms in legal design are the structural backbone of any project. They influence how information is shaped, presented, and experienced from the very beginning. Their role is never limited to execution – they frame the project's logic, govern the collaboration between stakeholders, and ultimately define how legal content is absorbed, interpreted, and acted upon. Some platforms support linear, text-based outputs; others allow for visual navigation, interactivity, and iterative co-creation. Choosing one over another is never a neutral act – it reflects the nature of the legal content, the ambitions of the project, the skillset of the team, and above all, the needs of its users.

Before we dive into the platforms themselves, it is useful to clarify three points. First, success does not depend on the platform alone, but on how it is used. A thoughtful legal design project can be implemented with Word or PowerPoint just as it can with InDesign or Miro. The same tool can serve a conservative purpose or open the door to experimentation. Second, the choice of platform depends on the type of legal design work being done. If the outcome needs to be frequently revised (think of a contract or a policy) then flexibility and editability matter more than aesthetic refinement. If, instead, the goal is to create a visually compelling structure or a communicative journey, then design-oriented tools offer better support. Third, the list I propose is not exhaustive. The surge of generative AI and no-code interfaces has introduced a constant flow of new platforms, many still too recent to be reliably integrated into legal work. What follows, therefore, is not a definitive catalogue, but a curated selection based on our actual practice and the tools most commonly recognized in the field.

Word

Often underestimated in legal design discussions, Word remains one of the most widely adopted platforms in the legal field. There is a reason for this. Lawyers know Word better than anything else, therefore they can focus on substance without the friction of learning a new tool. I would also highlight that, if used well, Word supports a range of typographic structures, permits the embedding of tables, symbols, and graphics, and can accommodate layered formatting that goes far beyond the default black-and-white aesthetic. Last but not least, when documents must remain editable, traceable, and easy to circulate within legal teams, Word is always a fast and safe choice.

Pro tip:
Some teams decide to go a step further, embedding specific widgets into Word to create interactive experiences. From clause toggles to checkboxes, from fonts to grammar check, the possibilities are endless. Have you already thought about ways to improve your Word experience?

Miro

Miro has gained remarkable popularity in the legal design world, particularly for remote collaboration and system thinking exercises. Its interface, based on infinite canvases, tables, and modular blocks, lends itself naturally to mapping legal processes, exploring interdependencies, and making sense of abstract legal flows. Miro's strength lies in enabling structure without imposing form, which is precisely what many legal design processes require in their early stages. Its structure, while problematic at first glance, may become intuitive after a few sessions.

Pro tip:
While most lawyers may not be familiar with the tool at the outset, they tend to respond positively once introduced, especially when the experience is guided and time bound. A short introductory session of 15-30 minutes is often enough to unlock intuitive interaction and share the basics (how to use post-its, graphs, tables, sticky-pads, etc.).

PowerPoint

PowerPoint, although generally associated with corporate presentations, deserves a second look in the context of legal design, because it offers a unique combination of structure, layout control, and accessibility. On paper, many of its features can be repurposed to create legal deliverables that are both visual and structured. Moreover, its compatibility with other Microsoft Office tools can ensure consistency across different document formats. In our experience it's hardly used, but it may be useful as a middle ground when we need to allow for increased visual expression while staying within the comfort zone of most legal users.

Pro tip:
We usually think about PowerPoint for final presentations, but have you thought about using a presentation during a legal design process, to see the direction you're going in and the result you'd like to achieve?

Canva and InDesign

When the goal is to move towards highly designed, publication-ready outputs, Canva and InDesign emerge as preferred tools. Canva is particularly effective for professionals without a design background who still wish to introduce visual language into legal documentation. Its drag-and-drop interface, rich template library, and accessible sharing options make it ideal for short-form visual content such as infographics, one-pagers, or user-friendly guides. InDesign, by contrast, is more suitable for long-form documents that require precise typographic control, consistent layout, and professional quality. In terms of precision in spacing, alignment, and page architecture, it's the go-to choice. Moreover, it offers great depth for those familiar with design grammar.

Pro tip:
In my experience, lawyers prefer using Canva while designers prefer InDesign. But I've seen (very rarely) designers working with Canva and lawyers working with InDesign. Mix it up!

Figma and XD

Traditionally associated with digital product design, Figma and XD are increasingly being used in legal design, especially when the output requires interactivity, modularity, or a strong visual logic. These platforms are particularly suited for prototyping – an essential phase in many legal design projects. With Figma, designers can simulate interfaces, test different layout versions, or even create clickable experiences that mimic the final outcome, whether digital or print-based. Its web-based structure enables real-time collaboration, commenting, and versioning, making it ideal for team projects and iterative cycles. XD follows a similar logic, though with a slightly different interface and structure.

These tools are not for everyone (there is a learning curve, after all) but they are proving particularly useful when legal design intersects with product design, user journeys, or legal tech interfaces.

Pro tip:
If you choose a specific platform, don't underestimate the way it interacts with other digital platforms. Having platforms collaborating is surely one of the added values in complex legal design projects.

Sticky pads, pins, markers, boards

Live legal design sessions are grounded in interaction. They rely on a combination of spatial tools and tactile elements to encourage participation, focus attention, and unlock creative energy. Among the many tools available, the most effective are often the simplest – sticky pads, markers, pins, and sticky boards. These objects, seemingly modest in appearance, play a pivotal role in shaping the cognitive and collaborative dimension of any co-creation process. They offer a shared visual language, a structure for dialogue, and a flexible canvas for collective reasoning. More importantly, they make abstract legal concepts tangible, while levelling the playing field between participants of different backgrounds and hierarchical role.

Sticky pads

Sticky pads remain the quintessential tool of legal design thinking. They allow participants to externalize thoughts quickly and move them around to test associations, sequences, or clusters. This ability to manipulate physical tokens of ideas introduces a form of embodied cognition that enhances both pattern recognition and strategic thinking. Reorganizing post-its on a wall is still my favorite way of organizing thought, building consensus, and surfacing contradictions. It invites redefinition without judgment. I have to say I use them to structure my own thoughts as well. What you see in this book is the outcome of many reflections about content, structure, and hierarchy.

Pro tip:
When working with sticky pads, take into account color choice. Color should not be random, ornamental, or excessive. One of my tricks is linking every hue to a category, a priority, a stage, or a type of user.

Pins

Pins can be used to introduce a decision-making layer into the workshop. They make it easy to prioritize options, select features, or eliminate ideas. The act of pinning or removing a card from a board is immediate, visible, and symbolically strong. It introduces a form of voting without words, often helping groups reach convergence without needing to verbalize every choice. Pins signal selection and exclusion in a way that is quick and clean.

Pro tip:

If you need to prioritize but don't have pins around, don't be discouraged. Change the position of your sticky pads to represent hierarchy!

Sticky boards

Another favorite. Unlike static whiteboards, they are designed to accommodate change. Their dynamic structure reflects the iterative rhythm of legal design and invites a more forgiving mindset – not everything must be perfect on the first try. Participants are encouraged to share incomplete thoughts, test hypotheses, and challenge assumptions, knowing that nothing is permanent. If an idea does not work, the board can simply be removed. There is a subtle liberation in this gesture, one that reduces fear of being wrong and reinforces the idea that failure is part of the process, not its opposite.

Pro tip:

How about using the removal feature as an asset? For example, you can decide that only the third or the fifth mock-up will be the right one. This forces us to experiment and go beyond the laziness that makes us believe that our first effort is surely the best one.

Markers

A must in legal design live projects. Try to carry out legal design projects without markers and you'll immediately feel empty. They serve as tools for annotation, connection, and emphasis. Moreover, they help structure collective reasoning and create a visible trace of discussion, turning ephemeral thoughts into a shared map of the group's thinking. With markers, participants can underline a constraint, circle a key concept, or draw links between ideas. Furthermore, as with sticky pads, color matters – different markers can signify urgency, complexity, or user perspective.

Pro tip:

Take into account that while the advantages of these kinds of tools are evident, their effectiveness depends on how the session is structured and facilitated. Without clear moderation, the use of sticky pads, boards, and markers can descend into chaos, leading to repetitive ideas, fragmented outputs, or an overabundance of unprocessed information. That is why every session should be guided by someone with experience in legal design – someone who can frame the problem, manage time, surface tensions, and synthesize findings into something usable. In the end, tools are only as powerful as the structure they are embedded in, and structure only works if someone is holding the frame.

Common visual tools

The integration of visual elements into contracts marks an important shift in the way legal information is communicated. Visual cues can reshape how contracts are read, interpreted, and applied. They help reduce ambiguity, increase clarity, support negotiation, encourage engagement, and reinforce compliance. They bring order and readability to what would otherwise remain abstract or overly technical. When used carefully, these tools allow legal professionals to simplify procedures, clarify obligations, and guide users through each step without overwhelming them with dense legal language. Rather than replacing text, they work alongside it, creating a more balanced, accessible, and intelligible contract experience.

Pro tip:

One of the main challenges in legal design projects emerges when changes are requested after a deliverable has been completed. When visual cues are involved, this becomes particularly complex. Think about it – unlike plain text, which can often be adjusted with relative ease, diagrams, icons, layouts, and information flows are interdependent. In a visual contract, editing a single element often means revisiting the entire structure. In this case, I suggest treating the project as a new iteration – not a patch – reassessing the visual and textual elements as part of a new design cycle.

Infographics

Infographics bring together visual clarity and informational density, blending concise text, numbers, icons, and layout design. Within legal design, they serve as a powerful tool to highlight essential points, illustrate legal processes, or provide comparisons across options, jurisdictions, or timelines. Their strength lies in making information visible and immediate, without requiring the reader to navigate through pages of narrative explanation. Whether used in contracts, policy documents, or internal communications, infographics help reduce cognitive load and support comprehension across different levels of legal literacy. They are particularly effective in client-facing materials and executive summaries, where clarity and speed of understanding are paramount.

Insight:

One of our favorite examples of practical and easily implementable legal design is what we call "panini contract". This name comes from the similarity with the layers of a sandwich, or "panino" as it is called in Italy. The main features of the contract remind us of the sandwich structure. Rather than redesigning the entire agreement, we add an introductory infographic that visually summarizes the key points of the contract. It acts as a cover or preview and is very much liked by non-legal figures. On paper, it is quicker to implement, efficient to use, and reassuring for lawyers because the original text remains untouched. However, reaching full consistency between the infographic and the underlying document may be harder than it seems (and it may also require a review of the long document).

Flowcharts

Flowcharts are visual tools that map out step-by-step processes, illustrating how individual decisions or actions lead to specific outcomes. In legal contexts, they are particularly effective in areas such as contract execution, compliance procedures, and dispute resolution pathways, where each step may trigger a distinct legal consequence. By visually representing conditional logic and procedural sequences, flowcharts help users reduce the risk of misinterpretation and guide the reader through otherwise opaque legal mechanisms.

Insight:

In my experience, flowcharts are particularly appreciated by M&A professionals when they need to represent a transaction in a clear and accessible manner, or even to clarify their own thinking. Their visual immediacy and linear logic often help simplify what would otherwise be a tangled web of steps, actors, and conditional paths. Yet their usefulness goes well beyond deal representation. Flowcharts can be employed to prepare a presentation, structure an argument, or support internal communication within a team or towards a client. As with most legal design tools, the possibilities are endless.

Tables

Tables offer a structured and accessible way to organize legal information, especially when we need comparisons, classifications, or lists of terms. They allow users to grasp similarities, differences, and hierarchies at a glance, without having to decode lengthy textual explanations. In legal design, tables are particularly useful for presenting obligations across parties, timelines of events, clauses across jurisdictions, or definitions within a contract. Their format naturally invites clarity and precision, making them an effective bridge between technical detail and user comprehension. Another added value is that they help reduce repetition and avoid ambiguity, giving structure to information that would otherwise be buried in paragraphs.

Pro tip:
Have you thought about using tables to represent different degrees of risk? In a complex compliance scenario, this is a practical, useful, and generally appreciated way of visualizing complex scenarios.

Graphs

Graphs are particularly suited for quantitative legal content. They translate numbers into visual stories, making it easier to interpret trends, proportions, and relationships within data. In the legal field, graphs can be used to show patterns in litigation outcomes, compliance levels across departments, risk exposure over time, or evolution of regulatory frameworks. They tend to be used not only as tools for communication, but also as an instrument for reflection, helping teams spot inconsistencies or areas for improvement. When used responsibly and with proper context, graphs can make legal documents more transparent and persuasive, especially when addressing non-expert audiences or decision-makers.

Pro tip:
A column chart on incident reporting trends can present the number and type of incidents (e.g., data breaches, discrimination claims) reported each

quarter. This allows legal and HR teams to prioritize areas that show persistent issues.

Timelines

Timelines are powerful visual tools for representing sequences of events, deadlines, or procedural stages in a linear and accessible format. In legal documents, they are particularly effective when we need clarity around chronology (such as in contract performance, litigation steps, or regulatory reporting obligations). By laying out information along a vertical or horizontal axis, timelines help users understand not only what happens, but when and in what order. They reduce confusion around overlapping dates, dependencies, and critical milestones, making them especially useful in complex scenarios involving multiple actors or jurisdictions.

Example:

For a large public procurement procedure, we created a timeline mapping each submission deadline, review period, and appeal window. The legal team said it saved them from two missed deadlines in a row.

Mind maps

A mind map is a diagram used to display information, with the main accent on how this information is organized. Information is put into a hierarchy, showing relationships among pieces of the whole. The most common representation is an image in the center of a blank page, to which other ideas such as images, words, and parts of words are added. Some ideas are connected directly to the center image, while others are connected indirectly. Mind maps offer a visual overview of how different elements within a legal document relate to each other. They are particularly effective in illustrating the connections between clauses, parties, obligations, and conditions, but I've also seen them used to manage a team or a specific project. In legal design, they can be used during both drafting and negotiation phases to clarify roles, responsibilities, and dependencies across a contract or legal process. Their intuitive format supports strategic thinking and enhances communication, especially in multidisciplinary settings where legal, technical, and business perspectives intersect.

Emojis

Emojis can be used sparingly and strategically to support tone, indicate actions, or highlight specific parts of a legal text. While they may seem informal, their presence in contracts and legal communication is increasingly recognized, particularly in digital environments and consumer-facing materials. When used with care, emojis can reinforce meaning, guide attention, and humanize content without compromising legal clarity. For example, a checkmark can signal confirmation, a clock can point to a deadline, or a warning symbol can flag important obligations. However, their interpretation can vary depending on context, culture, and platform, which means they should always be tested and framed with clarity.

Pro tip:
Have you thought about creating your own emojis? While it may appear like a crazy idea, it is way easier than you may think. Google genmoji, then play with it on your own!

Content boxes
Content boxes are one of my favorite tools for reinforcing clarity and ensuring that visual elements are properly anchored in meaning. They provide short, focused explanations that complement diagrams, icons, or charts, helping users interpret the information accurately and in context. Whether used to summarize a process, define a legal term, or explain an exception, they support comprehension without overwhelming the layout. I see them as interpretative anchors, guiding the reader through the logic of the visual while avoiding ambiguity.

Insight:
A lawyer friend of mine once adopted a rather unconventional technique in her litigation documents. Rather than relying on the traditional arsenal of bold, underline, or italic formatting to emphasize key points, she chose to work exclusively with content boxes. Every important argument, every strategic element she wished to highlight, was neatly enclosed within its own visual frame. At first, I found the choice surprising, almost too radical compared to the norms of legal writing. Yet observing the results she achieved, and the clarity with which her submissions were received, I must admit that the approach proved remarkably effective.

Territorial maps
Territorial maps offer a distinctive way to present legal information, partic-

ularly when geographical elements play a central role. Whether used to represent jurisdictions, highlight regional compliance requirements, or illustrate the reach of a regulation, maps help translate spatial complexity into visual clarity. For instance, a visualization of the areas affected by a new piece of legislation can help identify compliant zones, regions requiring further alignment, and those awaiting interpretation. Once barely used, they are becoming a standard for law firms involved in international matters, cross-border litigation, or global policy implementation.

Example:
When helping a logistics company navigate international customs laws, we used a custom map to highlight country-specific declarations. While it did not replace ten pages of text, it became the most used page of the entire document.

Icons

Icons play a pivotal role in legal design by acting as navigational aids that enhance the readability and accessibility of legal documents, providing a universally understood visual language that complements or, in some instances, replaces text. This visual representation facilitates rapid comprehension, engages users, and reduces cognitive load, thereby assisting users in navigating legal documents more efficiently.

Pro tip:
Incorporating a calendar icon next to a date can immediately signify a deadline, as can a gavel icon to denote a legal judgment or decision. These simple visual cues help readers quickly identify and understand critical information without solely relying on textual explanations.

The selection and implementation of icons must adhere to principles of clarity, consistency, and contextual relevance. Icons should be instantly recognizable and harmonized with the document's overall visual structure. Moreover, their use should be deliberate and restrained to prevent visual clutter and ensure they enhance rather than distract from the text. Are we adding icons to highlight critical sections of a document, drawing attention to essential provisions such as deadlines, deliverables, or payment terms, or just for the sake of it? It is also worth stressing that well-designed icons play a crucial role in improving accessibility, particularly for individuals with limited literacy or proficiency in the document's primary language. In such cases, well-designed icons function as cognitive anchors, facilitating comprehension and engagement across diverse user groups.

Pro tip:
Platforms such as The Noun Project,[1] Iconfinder,[2] and Flaticon[3] offer extensive libraries of customizable icons suitable for legal documents. Additionally, Microsoft's icon library, accessible within its Office applications, provides a convenient option when working on its platform.[4]

To maintain consistency and effectiveness in the application of icons within legal documents, the following are the guidelines we follow and indicate to our clients:[5]

- *Minimalism.* The principle of "less is more" should guide icon usage, ensuring that visual elements serve a clear functional purpose rather than acting as decorative additions.
- *Alignment with text.* Icons should directly relate to the content they accompany, reinforcing meaning rather than introducing ambiguity.
- *Corner and edge uniformity.* Maintaining consistent curvature and terminal shapes across all icons ensures a cohesive visual structure within the document.
- *Brand cohesion.* The design of icons should reflect the organization's visual identity, achieving a balance between professionalism and user-friendliness while maintaining uniformity in abstraction or realism.
- *Grid consistency.* Icons should be aligned to both pixel and optical grids to ensure proportional accuracy and smooth integration across digital and print formats.
- *Proportional scaling.* Icons should follow a predefined scaling system, commonly based on an 8px or 10px grid, with recommended sizes such as 16px, 24px, and 32px. Initial designs should be created at the largest scale and refined for smaller versions.
- *Line weight and fill consistency.* We should maintain uniform stroke thickness and fill style (whether outlined or solid) across all icons to help achieve a visually cohesive and professional appearance.
- *Iterative evaluation of icon usage.* Initially, identify elements that can be effectively represented by icons. During the final revision, critically assess the necessity and utility of each icon, ensuring that every visual element contributes meaningfully to the document's clarity and user experience.

Pattern libraries

In the field of legal design, we have a secret weapon – pattern libraries. They serve as curated collections of best practices and standardized solutions aimed at addressing recurring challenges in the creation and presentation of legal documents. These libraries provide frameworks that enhance clarity, usability, and user engagement, ensuring that legal materials are both effective and comprehensible. Not surprisingly, the development and utilization of pattern libraries in legal design reflect a broader movement towards standardization and user-centricity in legal communications.

A prominent example is the World Commerce & Contracting Contract Design Pattern Library.[6] This resource offers a collection of contract design patterns that are effective, repeatable solutions to commonly occurring usability and understandability problems in contracts.[7] Beyond the WCC initiative, other endeavors have sought to establish legal design pattern libraries. For instance, the Legal Design Toolbox, featured by the Observatory of Public Sector Innovation,[8] includes a Legal Communication Design Toolbox, a Legal Design Pattern Library, and a Legal Product Typology. Similarly, the Open Law Lab has explored the concept of defining a library of legal design patterns, focusing on visuals, interfaces, and tools that can be utilized for consumer-facing legal tasks.[9]

Pro tip:

Users tend to use pattern libraries and benefit from them. But how about reversing the narrative and contribute with our own ideas, or creating a new one? This would strengthen the libraries and reinforce the community and the standardization of international contracting.

Tools for law firms

In the constantly shifting terrain of legal technology, a number of specialized platforms have emerged to support the legal profession in handling complexity with greater clarity and control – whether structuring or automating intricate legal arrangements.

The first that comes to mind is Juristic,[10] a company offering a platform that combines visual modelling, document automation, and real-time integration with company registers. Its goal is to turn complex legal and organizational data into structured, navigable, and actionable content, supporting both legal analysis and client engagement through a visual logic that simplifies what would otherwise remain opaque.

StructureFlow also deserves mention in this space.[11] Designed to visualize and communicate complex legal structures, it offers a clear and flexible interface for representing corporate, financial, and transactional arrangements. Used by law firms, in-house teams, and financial institutions, the platform helps map relationships between entities, illustrate deal structures, and provide a bird's eye view of interdependencies across a transaction.

Another is VisiRule, which focuses on the design and deployment of rule-based legal systems.[12] Developed by Logic Programming Associates,[13] the tool allows users to construct visual decision trees that replicate the reasoning processes typically followed by legal experts. These visual diagrams can then be turned into interactive expert systems, enabling the delivery of tailored advice without requiring the end user to navigate dense legal texts.

It is also worth noting that many platforms often associated with automation or legal operations, such as Bryter,[14] Neota Logic,[15] ClauseBase,[16] and Tabled,[17] employ strong visual interfaces. These tools allow users to build workflows, assemble modular contracts, and manage legal tasks through intuitive, often graphical dashboards. However, while their visual structure plays a key role in improving usability and user experience, they do not necessarily fall under the domain of legal design. Their focus remains on process efficiency, standardization, and automation, rather than on rethinking the legal content itself from a user-centered or communication-driven perspective. For this reason, it is correct to acknowledge their relevance, but we should consider them adjacent, rather than integral, to the field of legal design.

Readability tests and software

Readability tests represent a valuable, though often underused, component of legal design. Their purpose is to assess whether the language and structure of a legal document are accessible to its intended audience. In order to do that, they offer a method for identifying excessive complexity, convoluted syntax, and jargon-laden phrasing. Various tools exist to perform these assessments, ranging from the Flesch-Kincaid Grade Level[18] and Gunning Fog Index[19] to more recent digital solutions such as Hemingway Editor,[20] Readable,[21] or the Microsoft Word readability statistics[22] feature. While these tools differ in their methodology, their function is broadly similar – they calculate the estimated education level or reading age required to understand a given piece of text. This information can be used to revise and streamline content, ensuring that legal documents are not only technically accurate but also cognitively accessible.

In legal design, the use of readability tests should not be seen as a mechanical exercise or an afterthought, but integrated into the drafting and revision process, particularly when the target audience includes individuals unfamiliar with legal terminology. For instance, a privacy policy intended for consumers should ideally aim for a reading level equivalent to secondary education or lower.

Insight:

In our team, we use readability tests at two key moments. At the start, to offer a diagnostic snapshot of the current state of a document. This helps us identify overly complex language, convoluted sentence structures, and potential barriers to understanding before any redesign begins. They set a baseline that is both measurable and actionable. At the end, once the redesign has been completed, we apply the same tests again. This allows us to compare results, track improvements, and ensure that the changes made have had a real and measurable effect on clarity.

It is worth noticing that readability tests have their limitations. They do not account for visual design, layout, tone, or user context. A sentence may be short and grammatically simple, yet still unclear due to poor structure or ambiguous terminology. They are not reliable in terms of information hierarchy. I suggest considering readability scores as indicators rather than final judgments. They are most effective when used alongside user testing, feedback loops, and iterative revisions.

An always evolving scenario

The list of tools and platforms relevant to legal design is never fixed. On the contrary, it is constantly evolving, shaped by the rapid pace of technological innovation and the daily emergence of new solutions. Every day, a new application is launched, a feature is updated, or an integration is introduced that may reshape the way we draft, visualize, test, or share legal content. This dynamism means that no inventory can claim to be complete. What matters, therefore, is developing the ability to assess and adopt new ones as they appear. As legal designers, we should remain curious, critical, and adaptable – able to distinguish what genuinely enhances clarity, usability, and collaboration from what is merely a passing trend. In this sense, the best toolbox is not the one with the most items, but the one that remains open to change. At the end of the day, their true value lies not only in what they produce, but in how they challenge our assumptions about what legal content can look like, and how it can be created.

Among the more recent additions to this ever-shifting landscape are tools such as Sketchwow,[23] which allows rapid creation of hand-drawn-style diagrams and visual flows that can help communicate legal journeys or processes with immediacy and informality, Gamma[24] for AI-driven presentations, and the OpenAI Image Generator,[25] a versatile content creation engine capable of producing structured text, idea frameworks, and even visual elements when integrated with plug-ins. But the list is endless, especially when we think about the shift towards faster, more interactive, and increasingly AI-enhanced design environments.

References

1   The Noun Project, https://thenounproject.com/
2   Iconfinder, www.iconfinder.com/
3   Flaticon, www.flaticon.com/
4   AudioEye, www.audioeye.com/ab/home-alt/
5   See also: Jon Hicks, *The Icon Handbook*, Five Simple Steps (2011).
6   World Commerce & Contracting Foundation, Contract Design Pattern Library, https://contract-design.worldcc.foundation/
7   World Commerce & Contracting Foundation, https://contract-design.worldcc.foundation/usability
8   OECD Observatory of Public Sector Innovation, Legal Design Toolbox, https://oecd-opsi.org/toolkits/legal-design-toolbox/
9   Open Law Lab, www.openlawlab.com/
10   Juristic, www.juristic.io/
11   StructureFlow, www.structureflow.co/
12   VisiRule, www.visirule.co.uk/
13   VisiRule, www.visirule.co.uk/contact-lpa/about-lpa
14   Bryter, https://bryter.com/
15   Neota, https://neota.com/
16   ClauseBase, www.clausebase.com/
17   Tabled, https://tabled.io/main/
18   J. P. Kincaid, R. P. Fishburne, R. L. Rogers, and B. S. Chissom, *Derivation of New Readability Formulas (Automated Readability Index, Fog Count, and Flesch Reading Ease Formula) for Navy Enlisted Personnel* (Research Branch Report 8–75, Chief of Naval Technical Training, Naval Air Station Memphis 1975) https://apps.dtic.mil/sti/pdfs/ADA006655.pdf
19   William H. DuBay, "Judges Scold Lawyers for Bad Writing" (23 March 2004) (8) *Plain Language at Work Newsletter*, Impact Information.
20   Hemingway Editor, https://hemingwayapp.com/

21 Readable, https://readable.com/

22 Microsoft, "Get Your Document's Readability and Level Statistics", https://support.microsoft.com/en-us/office/get-your-document-s-readability-and-level-statistics-85b4969e-e80a-4777-8dd3-f7fc3c8b3fd2

23 SketchWow, www.sketchwow.com/

24 https://gamma.app

25 OpenAI, "Introducing 4o Image Generation", https://openai.com/index/introducing-4o-image-generation

Chapter 13:
12 challenges of a legal design process (and tips to overcome them)

Challenge 1: Is this thing valid?

Among the most frequently asked questions during legal design workshops or consultancy projects is, "Are these redesigned clauses legally valid?" "Will they hold up in Court?" "How would a judge interpret them – particularly in civil law systems, where the primacy of written language often reigns supreme?" "Are these contracts binding? Is the approach legally safe?" These concerns are legitimate. The truth is – it depends. It depends on how the project is structured, who is involved, and the degree of rigor applied throughout the process. There is always a margin of risk when innovating within established systems, but that margin can be managed.

When legal design is carried out properly – by professionals who combine legal experience with design competence and a sensitivity to language – legally designed documents tend to be sound from a legal standpoint. They may look different, they may read more naturally, but their legal structure can remain fully intact. What changes is not the enforceability of the document, but the way it communicates.

And that transformation is anything but cosmetic. Behind every clarified clause, behind every restructured line or unnecessary redundancy removed, lies a careful, often time-intensive process. It requires not only advanced legal drafting skills but also an understanding of how people read, interpret, and act on legal information. The more skilled and experienced the team, the more refined the outcome, and the lower the likelihood of critical issues emerging.

Insight:

One key insight from our experience is that many companies believe their contracts are legally sound and well-structured – until they undertake a legal design project. It is often during this process that underlying complexities, redundancies, and inefficiencies begin to surface. What initially appears to be a coherent document frequently reveals itself as a collection of mismatched parts, accumulated over time without a clear logic or user focus. A common example is the habit of copying clauses from counterparties because they seem effective, or inserting sentences based on a local authority's opinion without properly integrating it into the overall structure of the contract. These additions may seem harmless in isolation, but over time they create documents that are fragmented, inconsistent, and difficult to interpret.

In our team, we refer to these as "Frankenstein contracts" – documents stitched together from disparate clauses, borrowed phrases, and regulatory cut-outs. While they may meet formal compliance standards, they often lack internal coherence. They are legally valid but operationally confusing, difficult to read, hard to navigate, and even harder to explain.

Suggestions:
- Start working with clauses, policies, and contracts less likely to be litigated.
- Start small and sense the reaction of internal departments and relevant stakeholders before doing more complex projects.

Challenge 2: Budget

Legal design is, without question, an investment, and often a costly one. The expense goes far beyond hiring a legal design agency or a skilled independent practitioner. It involves assembling a multidisciplinary team, dedicating time to multiple iterations, and conducting user testing that is both methodologically sound and sufficiently representative. It also requires significant time investment from internal stakeholders – something that, in both law firms and legal departments, carries a direct economic cost. And since legal design projects often begin without a clearly defined outcome, the sense of financial risk can feel even more pronounced.

Example:

Consider, for instance, a project involving 25 hours of collaborative work with a team of ten professionals drawn from legal, compliance, operations, and communications, plus the involvement of external consultants. Add to that the time and resources needed for user interviews, surveys, and impact assessments. All of this might all be for the redesign of a single document.

The challenge of budget management in legal design stems largely from its dual nature – it requires both flexibility and long-term commitment. Budgeting cannot be approached in the same way as a traditional procurement or delivery contract. It demands careful scoping, realistic resource allocation, and an understanding that legal design may be subject to iterations, discovery, and redefinition as it unfolds. This does not mean that legal design is inherently inefficient or financially unsound. But it does mean that its value should not be judged solely in terms of immediate output. A well-executed legal design project often leads to fewer misunderstandings, reduced negotiation time, greater user engagement, and enhanced contractual performance. These gains, though harder to quantify upfront, represent long-term value. Budgeting for legal design, then, is less about controlling every variable from the start and more about structuring a process that allows creativity, rigor, and strategic thinking to co-exist within realistic financial boundaries.

Suggestions:
- Leverage existing resources. Internal designers, marketing, and communications teams can help reduce costs.
- Reallocate budgets. Legal design costs should not always fall solely on legal teams. Consider funding from sustainability, R&D, marketing, or training.

Challenge 3: Internal selling
Promoting legal design within an organization – whether or not you are the one leading the design work – can be one of the most challenging steps in the entire process. Many decision-makers still perceive it as a nice to have or a superficial exercise – a set of polished visuals, simplified language, or aesthetically pleasing templates. What is often missed is the deeper transformation legal design enables. In organizations where legal design has already been seen in action, or where there is at least some awareness of its potential, the path is slightly smoother. Yet even in these contexts, gaining internal buy-in remains demanding. Successfully "selling" legal design requires a clear and credible explanation of its value. This means articulating how it improves user experience, reduces friction, enhances compliance, and ultimately saves time and resources. It means framing legal design not as a creative indulgence, but as a strategic decision.

Suggestions:

- Showcase success stories. Use case studies and testimonials to illustrate tangible benefits. Don't have a success story? Call us!
- Show before/after examples. Visual transformations often speak louder than words.
- Align legal design projects with business goals. Present legal design as a strategic enabler, not just as a training session.

Challenge 4: Managing time constraints

Legal design takes time – often considerably more than traditional legal work. As most lawyers already know, clarity and brevity are anything but quick. Crafting a clear clause often demands more effort than drafting a complex one, and that's just the language. Once you add visual elements, information architecture, user testing, feedback loops, and multiple iterations, the process becomes even more time-intensive. For organizations accustomed to rapid legal turnarounds, this can be disorienting. The pace may feel slow, even inefficient, especially when measured against conventional legal productivity metrics.

In legal design, however, speed must often yield to usability and precision. And time, in this context, is a condition for quality. In order to manage time constraints, I suggest aligning the project timeline with the broader strategic goals of the organization, ensuring that the work remains relevant, supported, and appropriately resourced. Without this alignment, legal design risks becoming a marginal exercise, disconnected from core priorities and easily sidelined.

That said, balancing a realistic timeline with the demand for quality is not always easy. There are many variables involved. Experience, discipline, and clear communication with stakeholders may not be sufficient. However, when this balance is struck, the results speak for themselves. We produce legal products that are not only compliant, but coherent. Built not just to be signed, but to be understood.

Suggestions:

- Set realistic expectations. Educate stakeholders on the time investment required for quality outcomes.
- Strengthen leadership commitment. The more leadership is committed, the more the process is likely to succeed.

Challenge 5: Quantifying benefits – measuring what's often hidden

Legal design offers meaningful, often transformative benefits, but capturing its full value remains a complex and nuanced challenge. This difficulty in measurement is one of the reasons we developed a three-level framework, with its highest tier focused entirely on impact. While improvements in comprehension, user engagement, and process clarity are frequently observed, they are not always easy to quantify – especially within legal departments where success is traditionally framed in terms of compliance, risk mitigation, and legal precision.

Even more elusive are the secondary benefits that legal design often trigger – stronger team cohesion, better collaboration across departments, or the surfacing of hidden inefficiencies during co-design sessions. These outcomes, while essential to long-term cultural and operational shifts, rarely fit neatly into traditional performance indicators. They develop over time, embedded in changes to mindset, communication, and internal alignment. Their value is real, but indirect, therefore at risk of being overlooked.

Unlike financial metrics, which offer immediate and visible returns, the outcomes of legal design tend to emerge gradually, often through indirect evidence. You may notice fewer internal disputes, more constructive engagement with stakeholders, or clearer alignment across business units. There may be a rise in positive feedback about legal documents or a noticeable drop in misunderstandings linked to key terms. All these may seem small effects, but they represent genuine progress. Without a strategy for observing and documenting them, they risk going unrecognized.

Suggestions:
- Benchmark performance. Compare pre- and post-implementation results to demonstrate improvements.
- Create a story. Use compelling narratives to showcase the human impact of legal design.
- Look for validation and impact.

Challenge 6: Avoid deviating from the original project

Long legal design sessions often lead to outcomes that go well beyond the original scope of the project. What begins as a review of a document frequently becomes a window into broader organizational challenges. The contract or policy under analysis is rarely the whole story – more often, it reveals deeper issues such as misaligned workflows, communication gaps, or structural inefficiencies that have gone unaddressed for years. These insights typically emerge early in the process, sometimes within the first sessions. When they do, the instinctive response is to address them immediately – especially when the team feels a sense of clarity and momentum. Yet it's important to recognize that resolving these systemic issues often requires more time, resources, and cross-functional involvement than the legal design project initially anticipated. At the same time, leadership and stakeholders may still expect concrete, document-related results within the agreed timeline.

This is not an argument for ignoring those broader issues. On the contrary, one of the most powerful contributions of legal design is precisely its ability to expose and articulate underlying problems that have long remained hidden or unspoken. However, attempting to tackle everything at once risks diluting the focus of the project. There is a fine line between ambition and overreach.

The key lies in managing that tension deliberately. Acknowledge the wider insights, document them carefully, and, if and where appropriate, suggest follow-up initiatives. But maintain clarity about the original goals. Legal design can be a catalyst for transformation, but it must also remain grounded. Balancing strategic curiosity with disciplined execution ensures that the project delivers tangible results while planting the seeds for deeper, long-term change.

Suggestions:
- Create a "parking lot" for structural issues. A dedicated space – physical or digital – may act as storage for systemic problems. Share this with management at project milestones, showing that these issues have been captured without derailing the current deliverables.
- Communicate progress with dual messaging. Update stakeholders by highlighting both short-term legal design outcomes and long-term insights into process improvements. This reinforces the project's value while managing expectations about what can realistically be addressed in the current phase.

Challenge 7: The Tetris agenda – balancing competing priorities
Legal professionals and designers often work under constant pressure, juggling multiple projects and competing deadlines. Within our team, we call this the "Tetris agenda" – a calendar so packed that every task needs to fit

perfectly, or the whole system risks collapse. I often say that, in our legal design projects, the most difficult challenge is not creativity or collaboration, but simply finding the time. It may sound like an exaggeration, but it is remarkably close to reality. When everyone is already stretched thin, carving out space for co-creation, workshops, or iterative review becomes a daily negotiation. And yet, without that time, the process cannot deliver its full value.

Suggestions:
- Think about B-plans. If a key person is missing, can you go on without? Can someone enter the session later or leave earlier? Recognize who are the material players (maybe all of them) and act accordingly.
- Aim for shorter sessions. While selecting three- or four-hour blocks can be hard, one hour is usually less impactful on each one's agenda.
- Use the retreat card. How about doing one or two four-hour sessions during winter or summer retreats?
- For law firms, consider legal design time as billable time.

Challenge 8: Navigating interdisciplinary teamwork
Legal design is, by nature, a collaborative endeavor that brings together professionals from a wide range of backgrounds – lawyers, designers, IT specialists, and sometimes psychologists, linguists, and economists. Each contributes unique expertise and perspectives, enriching the process and expanding the scope of possible solutions. Yet this richness also brings complexity. Workflows, terminologies, and expectations differ across disciplines, and navigating those differences requires time, care, and mutual respect. What one person sees as iteration, another might see as delay. What a lawyer considers a precise formulation might, to a designer, appear overly rigid or inaccessible.

In our experience, the more interdisciplinary the team, the greater the challenge in finding common ground. Interdisciplinarity is a double-edged sword – it fosters creativity, encourages broader thinking, and reveals blind spots, but it also demands more time for alignment and shared understanding. It means negotiating not only the content of a project, but the very language, pace, and rhythm in which that project unfolds. Achieving fluency across disciplines is not automatic. It requires dialogue, patience, and a willingness to suspend assumptions.

Example:

Consider, for instance, how the notion of time plays out differently. For a designer, time is often elastic, measured in cycles of testing and refinement. For a lawyer billing by the hour, it is tracked, finite, and intimately linked to value. Or think about words – a term that must carry precise legal weight for one person may need to be reworked for tone, clarity, or emotional resonance by another. Then there is the question of method – where a designer embraces prototyping and iteration, a lawyer may lean instinctively towards completeness, accuracy, and minimization of risk.

Balancing these logics is not easy, but it is precisely this tension that makes legal design so valuable. The process is not about choosing between perspectives but about constructing a shared space where those perspectives can work together without losing their depth. When it succeeds, the result is more than a compromise – it's a legal product that is robust, usable, and genuinely informed by a diversity of minds.

Suggestions:

- Respect different working styles. Recognize the diverse approaches of legal professionals, designers, and project managers.
- Create a shared language. Develop glossaries or guidelines to bridge professional jargon gaps.
- Maintain an open and informal approach. Generally, designers have difficulties in very formal environments.

Challenge 9: Establishing a structured framework

Legal design, still a relatively young field, often operates without standardized processes. This absence of shared structures can lead to confusion, fragmented efforts, and inefficiencies – especially for newbies in legal design and teams unfamiliar with the iterative, non-linear nature of design work. While each project will inevitably require a tailored approach, working within a general framework and using internal checklists can provide much-needed orientation. A clear structure helps ensure that every phase, from research to prototyping to testing, is properly considered, reducing the risk of overlooking critical elements or rushing through key decisions.

But what does it mean to establish a framework? At the very least, it means identifying the core stages of the project, clarifying the steps involved in each, and aligning the team around a set of expectations. If we want to raise the threshold, we should aim to provide both guidance and flexibility – enough structure to move forward with purpose, but enough openness to respond to what emerges along the way. In this sense, a framework is not a constraint – it is a support for navigating the complexity and creativity that legal design requires.

Suggestions:
- In the last part of the book we share our Better Ipsum framework for legal design projects (called The Leonardo Framework©). How about using it as a starting point?
- Do you feel brave? Create your own framework to guide each phase!

Challenge 10: Different clients, different organizations – adapting to varied needs

Think about working for a bank, then for a pharmaceutical company, then for an institution. Or a law firm. Legal design projects often involve a wide range of organizations and clients, each with its own culture, needs, and expectations. What proves effective in one setting may fall flat in another. Adapting to these differences requires not only flexibility, but also a careful and informed understanding of the client's context, internal dynamics, and strategic objectives. If you are a professional living in that environment, it is a pro. But you can lose the benefit of the fresh and dynamic perspective that comes from outside. In any case, only staying responsive and attentive, we can navigate institutional differences and deliver solutions that are not only well-designed, but meaningful and effective for the people who will use them.

Suggestions:
- Offer flexible solutions. Provide different options that suit varying levels of design maturity.
- Spend time knowing the client you'll work for.
- When you work for the company, try to start with fresh eyes. Worse than not knowing is thinking that you know.

Challenge 11: The smartest ones in the room

Lawyers are often seen as the authoritative figures – professionals expected to provide clear answers, manage risk, and maintain control. This expertise is unquestionably valuable. However, in the context of legal design, it can inadvertently become an obstacle. Legal design thrives on collaboration, creativity, and user-centered thinking – approaches that require a different posture because they are grounded in openness, iteration, and a willingness to engage with uncertainty.

The process demands not only legal knowledge, but asks for a suspension of certainty, an acceptance that problems may need to be redefined before they can be solved, and a recognition that good ideas can come from anywhere. For lawyers trained to deliver polished conclusions and operate as sole problem-solvers, this shift can be disorienting. There may also be a tendency to equate legal authority with infallibility, making it harder to receive input or critique from outside the legal domain.

The key lies in understanding that letting go of the need to be right, or to be in control, is not a loss of competence – it is a necessary step towards innovation. The process rewards curiosity over certainty, participation over control, and learning over mastery. It does not diminish the value of legal expertise – it simply reframes it as one voice among many, contributing to something more complete, more relevant, and more human.

Suggestions:
- Promote a growth mindset. Encourage humility and openness by framing legal design sessions as spaces for mutual learning, where each participant, regardless of her background, has something valuable to contribute. Emphasize that creativity and innovation flourish when diverse perspectives are welcomed and explored.
- Manage ego with care. Establish clear ground rules at the start of each session, highlighting the importance of active listening, respect for all contributions, and suspension of judgment. Facilitation techniques that equalize participation can help lawyers feel safe stepping out of their traditional authoritative role.
- Normalize iteration and feedback. Reassure legal professionals that iterative processes and constructive feedback are not signs of weakness or error, but rather integral parts of refining ideas and solutions.

Challenge 12: Modification and editability of legal design outputs
Another common challenge in legal design projects lies in the difficulty of editing and modifying the final outputs. While traditional legal documents, no matter how long and dense, can typically be revised with ease by legal professionals using standard word processing tools, legally designed docu-

ments introduce a new level of complexity. These materials often include visual structures, interactive features, and carefully constructed layouts that cannot be altered as simply as updating text in a contract. When documents are created using specialized software or involve integrated design components, even minor changes may require the involvement of a designer or technical specialist. This dependency introduces friction into the process, creating bottlenecks that can limit scalability. Organizations may find themselves facing delays and additional costs when they attempt to update or adapt their legal design assets without internal design capabilities.

Suggestions:
- Work on modular templates that can be easily adapted to different contexts without compromising user experience. Identify core elements that remain constant across projects while allowing for minor adaptations.
- Standardize visual assets. Develop a shared design library with icons, color codes, and typography styles approved for legal documents. This allows for consistency across projects and simplifies future changes.

Insight:
Several of our clients have addressed this challenge by creating internal legal design task forces or appointing in-house lawyers to take on full-time legal design roles. These initiatives not only reduce dependency on external consultants but also help embed legal design into the organization's daily practice. Why not consider doing the same? It could be a strategic way to build internal capacity, maintain continuity, and ensure that legal design becomes a sustained part of how your team works.

Chapter 14:
12 tips for great legal design sessions

Tip 1: Don't let equity partners and general counsels run the show

Legal design, at its best, is a collaborative practice in which every participant has a voice, regardless of title or seniority. In traditional legal meetings, however, hierarchy tends to be visible and reinforced. Equity partners, senior counsels, or department heads often set the tone, and their views shape not only the course of discussion but also the boundaries of what remains unspoken. If the aim is to redesign systems that work for users, the process must reflect that same principle from within. It must be open, inclusive, and willing to accommodate disagreement. Paradoxically, the best sessions are those in which people are not afraid to embarrass themselves.

Legal design thrives when a range of perspectives are genuinely engaged. Some of the most grounded, creative, and implementable ideas emerge from unexpected places – a junior associate, a contract manager, or an intern. These professionals are often closest to the points where legal theory meets daily reality. They see friction where others do not. They encounter inefficiencies that go unnoticed by those removed from execution. Yet their contributions are frequently overlooked or filtered through layers of organizational hierarchy.

Still thinking your legal environment is a different one? Consider how clients are represented in high-stakes negotiation, how contracts are drafted and approved in large organizations, or how legal technologies are selected and adopted. In most of these processes, the final word rests with those who hold formal authority. But the consequences of these decisions are felt most acutely by others. The software that is purchased may not reflect how junior teams and paralegals actually work. The workflow chosen may respond to institutional expectations, but not to the way problems are encountered and solved on the ground. Decisions are taken by those with power, but effectiveness is often judged elsewhere.

Insight:

Power in legal environments is rarely explicit. It does not reside solely in titles or reporting lines. It is expressed through subtle cues – who speaks first, whose contributions are acknowledged, who is interrupted and who is not. It shows itself in behavioral patterns – the unspoken expectation to reply immediately to a message, the inability to decline a meeting, the way some voices are anticipated while others must wait for permission to enter the conversation. The most effective way to challenge this quiet hierarchy is not to speak about inclusion, but to practice it.

Tip 2: Manage interruptions wisely

Interruptions are notorious for undermining focus, and in legal design sessions they can derail the flow of thinking at precisely the wrong moment. They do not merely pause a conversation. They fracture momentum.[1] Managing them effectively begins with setting clear expectations. Ask participants to silence notifications, put phones away, and, where possible, activate a "do not disturb" status. This is particularly important during brainstorming or brainwriting exercises, where continuity and immersion are essential. If the session is remote, encourage participants to keep their cameras on and to refrain from multitasking. Presence, in this context, is not just about being online – it's about being engaged.

For longer sessions, incorporate short breaks to allow participants to address urgent matters or check messages. These pauses reduce the temptation to split attention and help preserve the energy of the group across the session.

Of course, there is no perfect solution. Sometimes a call will come in that cannot be postponed, and someone will have to step away (or leave the session entirely). In this case, regaining concentration after such interruptions won't be easy. However, we should not over-dramatize it when it happens.

Example:

In our experience, interruptions are one of the most underestimated threats to the quality of a legal design session, especially when working online. That's why we always begin online sessions with a clear digital etiquette. We ask participants to close unrelated tabs, silence email and chat notifications, and, where possible, set up a dedicated space where they can focus fully. We have also noticed that sharing the day's agenda and clarifying doubts and expectations give participants a feeling of trust and safety during the session. However, earning participants' attention is becoming increasingly hard. For that reason, we structure sessions to be as dynamic as possible. We alternate formats, use breakout rooms, integrate short polls or interactive boards, and vary the pace. The facilitator plays a key role in maintaining this rhythm and making sure everyone remains part of the conversation.

Tip 3: Be cautious with recording sessions

Recording can be helpful for capturing key points, tracking decisions, or revisiting insights. However, it is a strategy that should be used with caution. In our experience, the presence of a recording device often changes the atmosphere in the room. Participants, especially in cross-functional or sensitive sessions, may feel less inclined to speak openly. The dynamic of a conversation shifts when people know their words might be reviewed later by someone who wasn't in the room. This is particularly true in workshops involving multiple departments, where underlying tensions may emerge.

Example:

Imagine a situation in which the legal team questions how a marketing initiative was handled, or voices doubts about compliance oversight. Would those same thoughts be expressed with a red light blinking on the corner of the screen? Probably not.

Yet, it is often precisely those comments, the informal ones, the "maybe I shouldn't say this" remarks, that prove to be the most revealing and useful for the success of a legal design project. They highlight friction points, misunderstandings, or systemic gaps that would otherwise remain hidden.

If you do decide to record, please be transparent. Inform participants well in advance, explain why the session is being recorded, and if possible, limit the recording to specific segments. This helps to preserve the sense of safety and informality that many legal design sessions require. Finally, make sure any recordings comply with internal protocols and data protection laws, particularly when handling confidential material.

Tip 4: Use AI tools for minutes

Taking accurate minutes is rarely straightforward – especially when ideas are flowing, action points are multiplying, and attention is focused on facilitation rather than transcription. In most cases, the minute-taking happens afterwards. However, given that these sessions are often intense and time-consuming, participants typically need to return to their daily tasks immediately. Expecting them to recall everything, or to follow up in detail, is rarely realistic.

That's why we are increasingly relying on AI-powered transcription tools. These tools can generate real-time notes, capture dialogue with accuracy, and highlight key themes and follow-up actions. Some systems even allow you to create keyword-based tags or extract decision points, making post-session review faster and more structured. This frees up participants to stay present and focused, knowing that the key content is being captured and can be shared later in a clear, digestible format.

That said, it is essential to remember that the use of AI tools, just like recording the sessions, can make some participants uncomfortable. They may not be familiar with the tool, or they may not feel at ease knowing that an external system is transcribing their input. Others may prefer to take notes themselves, either for control or because they're unsure how the data will be stored or shared. In these cases, the principle is the same as with recording – transparency first. Let participants know in advance which tools will be used, why, and how the material will be handled. Clear communication fosters trust. And trust, more than any tool, is what allows a legal design session to work.

Tip 5: Assign homework duties

Assigning pre-session homework can significantly improve the quality of a legal design session. It helps participants arrive with a clearer understanding of the context and a more focused mindset, which often leads to deeper insights and more productive discussions. This preparation might involve reviewing background materials, researching specific issues, or simply reflecting on a given theme or question.

In our experience, the level of engagement with pre-work varies greatly depending on the team and the way the project is framed. Some teams are highly motivated and willing to dedicate time outside of sessions. Others (the majority, to be honest) see the session itself as the only window available for legal design work and may not respond well to requests that extend beyond it.

This is why balance matters. Pre-session preparation should support, not burden. When well-calibrated, it encourages ownership and enriches participation. But when excessive or unclear, it risks alienating participants and creating unnecessary friction. As always, the key is to know your team, set expectations early, and keep the focus on what adds real value.

Pro tip:
If you're providing homework, remember that the key is relevance and conciseness. Assign tasks that directly contribute to the session's objectives and clarify why each task matters. The more the team feel it's useful, the more they'll be inclined to devote some extra time to it.

Tip 6: Adopt forward, not backward thinking

One of the key ingredients for a successful legal design session lies in mindset. Legal professionals are trained to operate within well-established frameworks – analyzing past cases, applying precedent, and prioritizing precision and risk management. Designers, on the other hand, approach problems with a forward-looking attitude, embracing experimentation, empathy, and iteration. To fully benefit from a legal design session, participants – especially from the legal side – need to consciously shift gears. Thinking like a designer means letting go of the need for immediate certainty, being open to ambiguity, and allowing space for ideas to emerge before evaluating them. This mindset does not replace legal thinking – it complements it, making space for creativity to meet rigor.

Our decalogue of forward thinking:
1. Collaborate. Don't isolate.
2. Stay positive. Don't default to doubt.
3. Prototype. Don't chase perfection.
4. Welcome new perspectives. Don't cling to precedent.
5. Create. Don't debate for the sake of it.
6. Experiment. Don't fear getting it wrong.
7. Empathize. Don't presume.
8. Embrace change. Don't resist it.
9. Stay curious. Don't settle for what you know.
10. Act. Don't overthink.

Tip 7: Rely on evangelists

In every legal design project, certain participants naturally emerge as advocates for the process. These are what we call "evangelists". These individuals believe in the value of the project and help energize the group. They play a key role not only in sustaining internal momentum, especially when enthusiasm wanes or resistance surfaces, but also in communicating the value of legal design across the organization. In my experience, the presence of strong evangelists can make the difference between a project that simply delivers outputs and one that leaves a lasting mark on how the team works.

Evangelists are often the ones who first reach out to legal design agencies and consultancies, who advocate for the initiative with internal stakeholders, and who keep the conversation alive with partners, colleagues, or in-house counsel. They are the ones speaking about proactive law and collaboration in adversarial environments. Without them, projects risk losing visibility, alignment, and long-term impact.

To nurture these roles, invite motivated participants to take on facilitation responsibilities, lead specific parts of the process, or share reflections with the wider team. This kind of ownership reinforces their engagement and helps build a culture of collaboration.

Tip 8: Maintain an informal approach

Legal design thinking works best in environments that are informal, flexible, and open to exploration. Supporting this approach requires creating a space in which participants feel comfortable and free from the weight of traditional legal formality. The objective is not to dilute legal rigor, but to create conditions in which ideas can emerge without the pressure of judgment or hierarchy. If played well, legal design sessions can be extremely fun and engaging. Informality improves relationships among teams. That said, be sure to guarantee psychological safety, which in the legal field represents a determining factor for innovation.

Insight:

The smallest details often influence how people interact with a process. Even our clothing can affect the way we think and behave. Would a law firm equity partner tackle an issue the same way dressed in a tailored suit as they would in a hoodie? Would someone in high heels feel equally free to speak as they might in sneakers or barefoot? The same logic applies to physical space. Can a typical meeting room in a law firm truly encourage the same openness and creativity as a more informal, relaxed setting? Probably not. I don't claim to have a definitive answer, but I do know that atmosphere matters. That's why, for our workshops, we encourage an informal dress code and call each other by first name. It's a simple gesture, but one that helps lower defenses, foster creativity, and signal that this space is different from business as usual.

Tip 9: Fewer words, more practice

Talking about legal design is one thing. Doing it is something else entirely. It's a bit like learning the rules of a game, only to realize, once you start playing, that the real challenge lies in the experience, not the theory. That's exactly how many of our clients feel the first time they step into a legal design session or open Miro for collaborative work.

The key is not to hesitate. Encourage participants to experiment, even if the tools feel unfamiliar at first. Start sketching, use mind maps, open a Canva. These tools don't replace legal reasoning – they open new pathways for clarity, structure, and communication. Generally, starting is the hardest part. Once participants realize they don't need to be designers to think visually, or to be proficient in legal design to be creative, something clicks. That's when the magic begins.

Tip 10: Celebrate small wins

Acknowledging progress, especially the small, incremental wins, such as a better contract or good feedback from users, has a powerful effect on motivation. It helps maintain momentum and reinforces a collaborative, constructive atmosphere. Recognition doesn't need to be elaborate – it can be as simple as highlighting a particularly creative idea, giving credit for clear thinking, or sharing a brief progress update with the wider team.

Example:

One of my professors at law school had a rather original habit – he would arrive at each lesson with a generous supply of snacks and sweets. Technically, these treats were meant to be a reward for everyone at the end of the four-hour class. Yet, from time to time, he made exceptions for the most active or effective participants. Unsurprisingly, given the competitive nature that often defines legal environments, we all fought hard to win those candies.

These moments signal that contributions are seen and appreciated. Over time, we can shape a culture where participation, experimentation, and continuous improvement are not only encouraged but genuinely valued. When people feel recognized, they show up more fully.

Tip 11: Manage cognitive load

Legal design sessions demand a high level of mental engagement. They combine analytical thinking, creativity, and collaborative work, often in unfamiliar formats, which places considerable strain on cognitive resources. Participants must navigate complex legal issues while learning new methodologies and adapting to a less structured, more iterative way of working. If this cognitive load becomes excessive, the consequences are predictable – disengagement, diminished problem-solving ability, and difficulty retaining core insights.

One of the most reliable strategies to manage cognitive load is to alternate between divergent and convergent thinking. Divergent moments, such as brainstorming sessions, allow for expansive exploration. Convergent moments, by contrast, help participants narrow the field, identify priorities, and move toward decisions. This rhythm between expansion and focus helps keep energy levels steady, avoids mental fatigue, and supports a more natural creative flow.

Structured breaks are equally important. In sessions that run over several hours, even brief pauses of five or ten minutes can make a substantial difference in restoring attention, boosting cognitive flexibility, and promoting quality thinking.

I would also suggest facilitators remain alert to signs of fatigue, such as waning attention, reduced participation, or repetition. While legal professionals are often trained to power through high-pressure environments, a legal design session calls for a different kind of presence – more fluid, more reflective, and more collaborative.

Tip 12: Defer judgment

Among the habits that make or break a legal design session, suspending judgment is perhaps the most underestimated and the most essential. Legal professionals are trained to evaluate, to scrutinize, to find the flaw in an argument or the ambiguity in a clause. This reflex is a strength in the right context. But in the early stages of a design session, it becomes a risk. When ideas are still raw, fragile, half-formed, the instinct to criticize too early can suffocate creativity before it has the chance to breathe.

In legal design, the creative process unfolds in phases. There is a time to generate and a time to evaluate. These two moments must remain distinct. The reason is simple – judgment alters the room. It shifts the tone from exploration to defense. It makes participants cautious. It pushes people to second-guess themselves, to edit before they express, to play it safe. And safety, while essential for emotional comfort, is not the same as intellectual constraint. Participants need to feel secure enough to share bold or unconventional ideas, but that requires a suspension of the instinct to immediately say, "That won't work", "We've already tried that", or "That's too risky".

Suspending judgment does not mean lowering standards. It does not mean that everything is accepted without scrutiny, or that all ideas are equally viable. It simply means respecting the timing of critique. An idea needs to grow, to be tested and shaped, before it is ready to be judged. Like in brainstorming sessions where quantity precedes quality, deferring judgment allows the collective intelligence of the group to expand rather than contract.

This mindset also helps dismantle hierarchy. When the usual voices of authority hold back from evaluating too early, they make space for others to speak. The intern's intuition, the assistant's observation, the non-legal stakeholder's suggestion – all can become valuable contributions, but only if they are allowed to emerge without being immediately filtered through skepticism.

Pro tip:

Practically speaking, the facilitator should make it clear that early-stage contributions are not about solutions, but about perspectives. It can be useful to remind participants that ideas are invitations, not conclusions. During the divergent phases of the session, all input is valid, even if it's messy, unrealistic, or incomplete. What matters is getting it on the table. The process of refinement will come later.

At its core, suspending judgment is about trust – trust in the process, in your team, and in the idea that something valuable can emerge even from what seems, at first, uncertain or strange. It is about giving creativity space to unfold, before asking it to defend itself. In a legal culture often dominated by control, precision, and risk aversion, it is a radical, but necessary, act.

Letting go of judgment, even temporarily, is not easy. But once embraced, it changes everything. It opens doors, reveals possibilities, and reminds us that innovation does not arrive fully formed. It begins, always, as something fragile, and it needs silence before critique, listening before response, and space before structure. That is the 12th tip, and maybe the hardest one to learn.

References

1 According to a study, it takes 25 minutes after you are interrupted to be focused again. Gloria Mark, Daniela Gudith, and Ulrich Klocke, "The Cost of Interrupted Work: More Speed and Stress", Proceedings of CHI 2008, Florence, Italy, ACM 2008.

Chapter 15:

The 12 most common mistakes in legal design (AKA the best lessons I've learned)

Mistake 1: Thinking you know the user

One of the most common mistakes in legal design is assuming that we already understand what users need, without ever actually engaging with them. This presumption can derail even the most promising projects, resulting in solutions that may be elegant or well-intentioned but ultimately disconnected from the lived experience of those they aim to serve. User research is not a decorative exercise or a box to tick. It is the cornerstone of any meaningful design process, uncovering real friction points, misunderstandings, and behaviors that often contradict internal expectations. It can be minimal, or more structured, but it has to be there.

Legal professionals, particularly those with years of experience, frequently rely on what they believe is intuitive knowledge of their clients. How often have we heard a senior partner say, with absolute certainty, "I know exactly what my client wants"? And yet, when asked how their contracts are actually read, how users navigate their documents, or what is lost in the transfer from legal intention to user interaction, that confidence begins to waver. Legal expertise is not the same as user insight, and confusing the two can be costly.

Insight:

Genuine user engagement remains rare in legal practice. Interviews, usability testing, and document walkthroughs are seldom conducted by lawyers themselves. If any such activity occurs, it is often delegated to marketing or communications teams, disconnected from the design and delivery of legal content. Insights are collected, but they sit unused, failing to inform the structure, tone, or functionality of the actual legal documents.

This gap is more than a missed opportunity. It undermines the effectiveness of the legal service itself. Insights drawn from users often shift the direction of the project entirely. They expose mismatches between what lawyers think they are saying and what users actually hear or understand. They reveal ambiguity where clarity was assumed, friction where usability was expected, and frustration where compliance was presumed.

To address this, legal designers must move from assumption to observation, from projection to inquiry. Without testing, everything is just an assumption. Without listening, everything is just projection. And without users, legal design is not design at all – it's guesswork.

Mistake 2: Considering the contract out of its system

One of the most frequent and damaging missteps in legal design is focusing exclusively on the redesign of contracts or policies while ignoring the wider legal ecosystem in which they operate. It is all too easy to treat legal design as a cosmetic exercise, a way to make documents more attractive or easier to read. But this narrow interpretation weakens its transformative force. Contracts and policies do not exist in isolation – they are part of a much larger and more complex system. Without a broader perspective that considers the full legal journey (from how information is communicated and understood to how decisions are implemented and followed up), any redesign risks remain superficial.

This narrow focus often leads to disproportionate attention to the final output, especially its visual dimension, while neglecting the underlying mechanisms that shape legal interactions. We must not forget that legal design is not about creating stylish templates. It is about questioning how legal services actually function. A contract may be impeccably written and beautifully laid out, but if it sits within a workflow that is outdated, fragmented, or opaque, its real-world effect will be limited. Readability is a necessary condition, for sure, but not the final objective. The real ambition is usability. To reshape the legal experience in a meaningful way, we need to look beyond the words and their layout. We must consider how a document is accessed, how it is navigated, how it is understood, and what it enables or prevents in practice.

Example:

Take, for instance, a mortgage contract that has been redesigned to simplify the language. On the surface, this might appear to be a successful intervention. But if the process for signing the document is cumbersome, if stakeholders cannot easily retrieve critical clauses, or if the obligations it sets out are not integrated with internal systems or operations, then the redesign has failed to deliver its full value. The document is more legible, but not necessarily more functional.

We suggest a broader, more integrated approach. Legal documents do not exist in a vacuum. They interact with people, with procedures, and increasingly with technology. They are read, interpreted, negotiated, and executed across a variety of touchpoints and by a range of users with different needs and levels of expertise. Improving only the document, without improving how that document functions within its environment, is like repainting a door without fixing the hinges. The design will look better, but the experience will not be improved.

Mistake 3: Raising excessive expectations

One of the most frequent missteps in presenting legal design is the tendency to overpromise. The idea that in a few weeks we will rapidly resolve long-standing problems in compliance is attractive, but often unrealistic. Legal design is sometimes framed as a shortcut to transformation, a quick win that will modernize systems overnight and this narrative may be persuasive, especially when pitching to stakeholders, but it risks creating expectations that no design process, however well-executed, can meet. When someone expects a bunch of workshops to radically shift behaviors or assumes that redesigning a contract will automatically generate alignment and understanding on a specific issue, it is likely that stakeholder will be disappointed. Sometimes, the gap between what people hope for and what legal design achieves becomes a source of tension.

To prevent this, I recommend being clear from the outset. Sometimes, it is better not to start a project than ruin the opinion of legal design in a law firm or company. Once partners and general counsels have bad experiences, it's pretty hard to change their minds on what you can offer.

Example:

I remember pitching our legal design services to an insurance company a few years ago. We had a solid proposal and a clear value proposition, but my contact warned me there was little hope. The general counsel had been deeply disappointed by a previous project, where the result was a shorter and better-looking document, but a couple of clauses were null. That experience had left such a bitter aftertaste that it closed the door before we could even open it.

Mistake 4: Expecting legal design to fix everything

This error is subtler but no less damaging. It does not arise from overselling results, but from misunderstanding the scope of the method. Legal design is sometimes approached as if it were a universal remedy – capable of resolving deep organizational dysfunctions on its own. Legal design cannot replace regulatory strategy, fix siloed governance, or compensate for a lack of leadership. It is a toolset, not a miracle cure. Expecting legal design to work in isolation, without structural or cultural support, leads to misplaced expectations and eventual frustration. A well-designed contract cannot overcome a broken procurement process. A clear policy cannot resolve systemic trust issues. This mistake assigns to legal design a burden it was never meant to carry. Unlike Mistake 3, which involves misjudging the speed and scale of outcomes, this involves misjudging the role legal design can realistically play. The most effective teams understand this distinction. They position legal design as part of a broader transformation effort, working alongside policy leads, change managers, and tech experts. They do not claim to solve everything. Instead, they amplify clarity, participation, and usability within a well-defined scope. Recognizing these limits is a sign of maturity. When legal design is integrated rather than isolated, its contribution becomes not only more sustainable but also more powerful in context.

Mistake 5: Losing the initial enthusiasm

Legal design projects often begin with enthusiasm, driven by the promise of innovation, user-centricity, and tangible change. Workshops are energizing, brainstorming sessions feel productive, and the early stages are often accompanied by a genuine sense of momentum. Yet, as the work progresses and complexities arise, that initial energy tends to fade. In many organizations, especially those where legal design is still unfamiliar or viewed as experimental, projects risk stagnating, slipping into conceptual exercises with no lasting outcomes. Avoiding this trajectory requires a deliberate strategy for maintaining engagement and continuity.

A primary reason enthusiasm fades is the consistent underestimation of the time, energy, and attention that meaningful legal design demands. Teams often compare legal design to traditional legal tasks, expecting similar timelines, outputs, and levels of effort. This is inaccurate and misleading.

The two modes of work are fundamentally different. Traditional legal work tends to focus on precedent, risk, and established procedures, whereas legal design involves research, iteration, co-creation, and testing, none of which follow linear patterns or predictable calendars. Comparing the two serves little purpose and often leads to frustration. In this sense, the act of comparison itself could be considered a mistake, one that distorts expectations and undermines the process before it fully begins.

The second reason relates to organizational resistance, practical bottlenecks, or a lack of clarity about how to proceed. In this transition from excitement to execution, one of the most effective ways to maintain the hype is to build in early wins. Celebrating, and possibly communicating, visible, incremental progress helps reinforce the value of the work and keeps morale high. This could include sharing simplified clauses, presenting redesigned templates, or showcasing feedback from users. Regular check-ins, stakeholder updates, and transparent tracking of project milestones may also help create rhythm and remind participants why the project was undertaken in the first place.

Another key tactic (hard to deliver, but highly effective) is embedding legal design practices within the broader organizational framework. When legal design is treated as an isolated experiment, it becomes vulnerable to the tides of internal politics, shifting priorities, or changes in leadership. By contrast, when it is integrated into workflows, decision-making routines, and communication models, its longevity is more secure. This requires cultivating internal champions, nurturing cross-functional collaboration, and offering visibility to the value produced, both in terms of improved outputs and enhanced user experience.

Momentum is not automatic. It must be built, nurtured, and defended. But when it is, legal design evolves from a promising concept into a lasting capability.

Insight:

I remember a conversation with an in-house counsel during a particularly challenging legal design project we were managing. The timeline had stretched far beyond what we had anticipated, and the goal of completing it within the year was becoming increasingly difficult. After some honest discussions, we reached an unusual but effective agreement with her and the company's management – the successful completion of the legal design project would be tied to her performance bonus. Not surprisingly, from that moment on, everything accelerated.

Mistake 6: Treating documents as static artefacts

One of the most entrenched process-related mistakes in legal design is the tendency to treat legal documents as static endpoints rather than as evolving tools. This mindset assumes that once a contract, policy, or set of terms is finalized and signed, it no longer requires scrutiny, unless a regulatory shift or legal dispute forces a revision. This approach reflects a legacy culture where legal certainty was achieved through fixed language and unchanging templates. However, in contemporary legal and business environments, where needs evolve quickly and legal tools interface increasingly with digital systems, this static view is outdated and counterproductive.

Documents are no longer passive repositories of obligations and rights. They are operational instruments, embedded in processes, platforms, and workflows. In many cases, they serve as triggers for automated actions or checkpoints in broader service ecosystems. Treating them as fixed objects neglects the ways in which contracts interact with people, systems, and shifting expectations over time.

Example:

You don't have to go far for an example. Imagine a procurement contract reused for years without adjusting to updated compliance processes, digital signature technologies, or cross-border requirements. This may cause delays, inefficiencies, or even legal risk.

Legal design reframes documents not as final products but as iterative components of a dynamic system. This means establishing regular review cycles, tracking how documents are used in real contexts, and updating them in response to feedback. It also means mapping the full workflow around the document – how users access it, what happens after signature, who depends on which clause, and how legal and operational teams interact with the content over time. When this full picture is ignored, redesign efforts risk remaining superficial – changing the interface without improving the function.

That said, moving toward a more adaptive, process-oriented perspective does not mean compromising legal rigor. It means recognizing that the utility of a document is not fixed at the point of approval. It is earned (and re-earned) through continuous alignment with the systems it is part of. A document that is never revisited is a document that slowly drifts out of relevance. A document that is constantly revised becomes one of the company's greatest assets.

Mistake 7: Assuming our documents are already good enough

Closely related to (but conceptually distinct from) the previous point is the cognitive error of assuming that our legal documents are already optimal simply because they were drafted by experienced professionals, validated by precedent, or used successfully in the past. This mistake is less about process and more about perception. It stems from a deeply human tendency – to equate familiarity with effectiveness, and to trust the authority of authorship over the actual experience of use.

This assumption goes largely unchallenged in many legal contexts. Contracts are circulated internally, edited by senior lawyers, and adopted wholesale from previous matters without thorough re-examination. Sometimes a knowledge manager creates templates out of them, and they become part of a corporate identity. Yet, when tested, whether through user interviews, usability assessments, or even a close reading, it is not uncommon to find contradictions, redundancies, or even basic grammar and syntax errors that have slipped through years of copy-paste reuse. More importantly, these documents often fail to meet the basic standards of clarity and comprehension required by the people who are expected to act on them.

In legal design workshops, we frequently witness this disconnect. General counsels who claim their documents are clear struggle to locate key provisions. Internal users ask for definitions of common terms. Clients misinterpret obligations. These are symptoms of a broader mindset that confuses legal completeness with user readability, and internal consensus with actual utility.

Legal design challenges this false sense of completeness, treating the document as a hypothesis to be tested, not a monument to legal expertise. It invites critique, measures readability, and solicits feedback. We are not aiming to undermine legal work, but to improve its effectiveness. A document is only as good as the outcomes it enables. If users cannot navigate it, understand it, or act on it without friction, then it is not good enough, no matter how robust the legal reasoning behind it may be.

In this light, the idea of "perfection" becomes a trap. It prevents iteration, discourages review, and reinforces a static culture. Legal design promotes a different mindset – one rooted in curiosity, humility, and continuous improvement. It does not ask lawyers to abandon their standards. It asks them to expand them, and to include clarity, usability, and user experience as part of what it means to be excellent.

Mistake 8: Jumping directly to the solutions

One of the most damaging mistakes in legal design (and one of the most common) is the tendency to leap into solutions without first taking the necessary time to understand and define the problem. The urgency to produce visible outcomes often leads teams to bypass the initial discovery phase, assuming that the issue is self-evident or that their professional experience suffices to guide the intervention. This rush to action may yield results that appear promising at first glance, but that frequently address only the symptoms rather than the root causes of legal inefficiencies, miscommunication, or user dissatisfaction. In legal design, success is not measured by speed of execution but by the relevance and durability of the solution in meeting actual user needs.

This mistake is particularly common among legal professionals accustomed to working under pressure and rewarded for providing quick, authoritative answers. The habits of legal reasoning, based on precedent, risk aversion, and technical clarity, often stand in tension with the design mindset, which requires open-ended exploration and tolerance for ambiguity. However, when the problem is not properly framed, teams risk misreading the situation, misunderstanding user expectations, and delivering solutions that are misaligned with the organizational reality. In such cases, even well-intentioned interventions may fail to gain traction, becoming shelf projects or templates that are never adopted in practice.

Adopting a problem-first mindset means accepting that the solution cannot precede the question. Before any redesign begins, we should invest time in understanding the context, needs, and pain points of users and stakeholders. We should reveal not only what is broken but why it is broken, and how different actors experience that dysfunction. Most importantly, we should resist the temptation to assume consensus on the problem. Often, what appears to be a single issue is, in fact, a cluster of diverging expectations, organizational frictions, and overlooked constraints. Clarifying the challenge requires structured dialogue, active listening, and analytical tools capable of distinguishing between causes and effects.

Ultimately, the design phase can only be effective if it builds on a clear and shared understanding of the problem space. When this foundation is missing, teams may produce documents that are visually appealing but functionally irrelevant, or workflows that are technically sound but culturally unfeasible. By contrast, when problem definition is treated as a core competence, and not just a preliminary formality, legal design becomes what it is meant to be – a thoughtful, grounded, and strategic methodology for improving legal communication and operations.

Mistake 9: Lack of interdisciplinary collaboration

Another persistent mistake is the failure to fully embrace interdisciplinary collaboration. Too often, legal professionals approach these projects adopting a lawyer-centric perspective, assuming that legal knowledge alone can generate solutions that are both effective and user-friendly. This assumption overlooks a foundational truth – legal design is not simply about refining legal content, it is about reimagining how legal information is communicated, understood, and experienced. This task requires the integration of skills and sensibilities that extend far beyond the legal domain.

At its core, legal design is a multidisciplinary undertaking. Designers may contribute expertise in visual hierarchy, clarity, and user interface. Psychologists and behavioral scientists may offer insight into how individuals interpret, retain, and act on information. Data analysts may help translate user interactions into patterns that reveal friction points and unmet needs. Technology specialists may enable the implementation of scalable tools that can support dynamic, interactive legal experiences. Of course, some professionals may be multipotentialites, but what matters is that multiple perspectives are better than one.

When legal teams fail to involve professionals from these adjacent disciplines, the results often remain superficial. A contract might look more modern, but if it is not cognitively accessible, contextually relevant, or technologically adaptable, the redesign falls short.

To cultivate such collaboration, legal teams must move beyond siloed thinking. This means creating spaces – both organizational and procedural – where cross-disciplinary work is the norm. How do we do it? Building mutual respect across roles, fostering shared language, and allowing for iterative feedback loops that value diverse forms of knowledge. As you can imagine, this is easier said than done.

Mistake 10: Downplaying resistance to change within legal teams

Another significant barrier to the success of legal design projects lies in the cultural resistance to change that often characterizes legal teams. Legal professionals are typically trained to operate within frameworks that reward precedent, precision, and caution. This emphasis on stability and predictability, while entirely appropriate in many legal contexts, can foster a skepticism toward methodologies that appear less certain, more experimental, or seemingly outside the conventional legal toolkit. As a result, user-centered approaches, visual design elements, and iterative processes such as prototyping and testing are frequently met with hesitation, if not outright dismissal.

This resistance is rarely a matter of bad faith. It stems instead from deeply ingrained habits of thought and professional identity. Many lawyers are conditioned to associate credibility with formality, expertise with textual density, and risk mitigation with control over every word. The shift to consider clarity over complexity, co-creation over authority, and experimentation over certainty, can feel uncomfortable, even threatening.

To overcome this resistance, the best approach is strategic and empathetic. First, try to involve legal teams early, not only as stakeholders but as co-creators. When lawyers are given the opportunity to shape the direction of a legal design initiative, they are more likely to see its relevance to their work and its compatibility with legal rigor. Framing design as a complementary lens for improving communication, usability, and impact helps reduce defensiveness and fosters constructive dialogue.

Another key strategy is building evidence. Showcasing successful legal design projects (especially those in comparable sectors or jurisdictions) can help dispel the perception that design is merely cosmetic or optional. Quantitative metrics, such as improved turnaround times or reduced negotiation cycles, alongside qualitative feedback from users, offer compelling arguments for why the legal design methodology deserves attention.

The third strategy is relying on institutional support. When leadership within law firms, legal departments, or regulatory bodies champions legal design, it creates a culture that encourages experimentation and continuous improvement.

Pro tip:
One of the most effective ways we have found to overcome resistance is to offer targeted training on legal design to legal departments and law firms. While lawyers are generally accustomed to training, it is often confined within the boundaries of their specific area of practice. Rarely do they explore structured learning opportunities outside their usual scope. Legal design, in this context, becomes more than just a novelty. It can serve as a powerful tool to refine their professional approach, improve the clarity and usability of legal documents, and, in the most rewarding scenarios, also contribute to earning CLE credits.

Ultimately, the key to addressing resistance is to recognize that legal design is not an attack on legal competence, but an invitation to broaden its scope. Legal designers do not aim to dilute legal standards, but rather align them more closely with the people and contexts they are meant to serve. I still believe that, with the right framing, participation, and support, even the most skeptical and conservative legal teams can become advocates for change.

Mistake 11: Underestimating regulatory and ethical considerations

While one of the core strengths of legal design lies in its focus on user experience and accessibility, this emphasis must be carefully balanced with the need to respect existing legal frameworks and uphold core principles such as transparency, fairness, and data protection. Legal design projects that overlook regulatory and ethical considerations risk producing outcomes that are visually engaging but legally unsound or ethically questionable. Failure to incorporate these dimensions may result in legal instruments that are misleading, non-compliant, or unenforceable.

Ethical considerations add another layer of responsibility. This is particularly relevant when legal design is applied to digital environments, whether in the form of automated contracting tools, decision-support systems, or platforms handling personal data. This goes beyond GDPR or anti-discrimination laws, engaging with broader ethical questions that shape trust in legal systems. How much control do users retain over their choices? Are the terms presented fairly? Can all users understand the information regardless of background, cognitive ability, or access to technology?

To mitigate these risks, I suggest integrating regulatory and ethical assessment during the design process, and not considering them as an afterthought. This may include working in close contact with compliance officers, consulting with ethics committees when available, and even engaging regulators as stakeholders during the project. These dialogues help identify critical red flags early and guide the project towards solutions that are both legally robust and socially responsible.

Mistake 12: Treating legal design as a one-time effort

One of the most persistent misconceptions about legal design is the belief that it is a one-off exercise rather than a sustained, iterative process. Many organizations approach legal design as a discrete intervention – a single workshop, a redesigned contract, or the adoption of a new tool – expecting it to deliver long-term solutions to deeply rooted usability or communication problems. While such interventions can be valuable starting points, they rarely produce enduring change in isolation. Legal design achieves its full potential only when embedded into an ongoing process of improvement, adaptation, and refinement.

Legal contexts are not static. Regulations evolve, business models shift, technologies change, and user expectations grow more sophisticated. A legal document or procedure that serves its purpose well today may become obsolete within a few years. To remain effective, we have to integrate user-centric strategies into organizational routines that account for this fluidity. This means establishing regular review cycles, treating user feedback as a strategic resource, and ensuring that legal outputs (whether documents, workflows, or digital tools) can evolve in step with their operational and regulatory environments.

In an ideal environment, organizations would develop mechanisms to capture feedback in real time, monitor the performance of redesigned legal tools, and identify emerging pain points. This would allow for manageable and targeted improvements that build over time. Iteration becomes a mindset rather than a phase, and design becomes an embedded competence rather than an external service.

To support this shift, legal departments and firms need to invest in long-term capabilities. This includes upskilling legal professionals in the principles and methods of legal design thinking, establishing multidisciplinary teams with design and technology expertise, and creating collaborative frameworks that bring users, lawyers, and other stakeholders into dialogue. We can also allocate dedicated resources in order to commit to continuous development, testing, and evaluation.

Ultimately, treating legal design as a continuous journey rather than a finite task is what distinguishes impactful innovation from fleeting experimentation. Only this way can we be capable of solving current challenges and adapting gracefully to future ones.

Chapter 16:
Practical applications of AI for legal design projects

Choosing the right engine – a short guide to AI tools

Let's start with the tools, because that is where most curiosity tends to concentrate. Maybe we should begin by being honest – despite the marketing noise and the abundance of AI solutions claiming to be tailor-made for legal work, most legal designers still rely heavily on a few general-purpose tools. The go-to choices tend to be OpenAI's ChatGPT, Google's Gemini, Anthropic's Claude, and Grok by xAI. These are not legal-specific and that is precisely what makes them powerful – they are fast, constantly updated, and highly versatile. In a field like ours, often caught between rigid structures and the pressure to innovate, we need tools that allow experimentation without locking us into narrow formats or predefined answers.

Each of these models has its own identity. ChatGPT has become a sort of universal platform, capable of drafting clauses, simplifying compliance texts, or suggesting user-friendly alternatives to traditional contract language. With the addition of custom GPTs and plugins, it allows legal teams to prototype internal workflows and automate document drafting with minimal technical effort.

Gemini, integrated deeply within the Google environment, proves particularly useful for work related to the Google suite – iterating on contract drafts directly in Docs, mapping timelines in Sheets, or simply analyzing surveys done with Forms.

Another favorite is Claude. So far, it tends to hallucinate less than other tools and explain more. But AI is endless – Perplexity for search, Grok for its infrastructure, the CoPilot environment for Microsoft-based uses. Not to mention the possibility offered by AI additions for Canva, Adobe suite, etc.

Yet none of these tools is neutral, let alone flawless. They generate fluent text, but fluency is not the same as accuracy. They can propose alternatives, but they do not understand the regulatory or ethical boundaries we must navigate. It's hard for them to assess whether a term is unfair under European consumer law, or if a visual contract supports inclusivity or inadvertently reinforces bias. I suggest using them for creative prompts or early-stage proposals. If you like to play, you may also consider them team members, because they help us think more broadly. But the wisdom part is still ours to own. The moment we begin to treat them as decision-makers, we risk delegating not only our work, but our judgment. In legal design, that is never a safe trade.

Building with the machine – prototyping in practice

One of the most promising, yet still underutilized, uses of artificial intelligence in legal design is in the prototyping phase. Traditionally, this stage has been labor-intensive, often requiring a great deal of facilitation, multiple iterative cycles, and the patience to navigate internal approvals. Add to that the frequent absence of meaningful user feedback at early stages, and it becomes clear why many legal innovation projects slow down before they can gain real traction. AI offers a way to reframe this moment – accelerating the conditions under which iteration becomes possible. In this sense, we can see AI as a scaffold supporting the temporary structure, which allows us to test sooner, revise faster, and ask better questions.

We can now simulate user interaction with draft legal products – be it a reimagined contract, a new compliance protocol, or a digital policy dashboard – without needing to wait for user access or full-scale pilots. How about using them to observe potential friction points before a single real user engages?

Example:

In a recent project focused on onboarding policy for a fintech company, we generated synthetic personas based on prior usage patterns. The AI detected where cognitive overload was likely to occur, which branching sequences caused confusion, and which segments might deter engagement altogether. These findings did not replace later user testing, but they allowed us to refine our initial draft to such a degree that the first live session became far more productive.

We can call it "pre-feedback design" – the opportunity to improve materials before they are shown to a real audience. Just as UI/UX designers rely on heatmaps and behavioral predictions, legal designers can now deploy AI tools to walk through a decision tree, predict drop-off points, or identify sentences where clarity fades. These systems may not understand law in a strict doctrinal sense, but they can detect inconsistency, ambiguity, and density in language with surprising precision. They provide a layer of simulated feedback that sharpens our hypotheses and makes every subsequent conversation more meaningful.

There is also a new kind of tempo at play. What once required hours of group facilitation, followed by days of synthesis, can now begin with a single draft and an intelligent agent trained to adjust tone, simplify logic, and surface cultural misalignments. During a cross-border contract review, for example, we used an AI model to assess whether plain language edits were equally effective in different jurisdictions. The result, even in its draft form, was a deeper understanding of how expectations vary across legal cultures – knowledge that is difficult to obtain through traditional prototyping alone.

It is useful to consider AI as a companion within co-design settings. Imagine a workshop where someone challenges a clause's wording, and the facilitator can instantly generate several stylistic and structural alternatives – rendered visually and ready for discussion in real time. This immediacy turns what used to be abstract or deferred conversations into hands-on exploration. It supports inclusion by giving voice to different views, and it strengthens transparency by allowing participants to see the implications of their choices unfold on the screen. Legal design, at its best, is about designing better moments of decision, and AI, used carefully, can help make those moments both faster and deeper.

From drafting to conversating – specific uses of AI

Over the past few years, we've been given the opportunity to test how artificial intelligence can support legal design projects as a means to accelerate and enrich our processes. What I've learned so far is that AI, in our field, should not be approached as a singular solution, but as a set of strategic tools, each capable of unlocking different aspects of the legal design process when used deliberately and with care. Its value lies not in automation for its own sake, but in how it helps us move faster from ambiguity to clarity, from complexity to usability. In all the following scenarios, the value of AI therefore lies in how it extends our reach without displacing our judgment. If we retain control over when and how it is used, it can amplify our capacity to design clearly, to iterate faster, and to think more inclusively.

Among the many ways of working with AI, I find the following the most intriguing:

- *Playing with words*. The most immediate use of AI in legal design is its capacity to work with legal content. Tools like ChatGPT or Claude can assist in highlighting key elements of a clause, rephrasing dense passages, or suggesting structural changes that reflect user needs. This proves especially useful in the early stages of a project, when teams are faced with rigid templates or outdated boilerplate language. In one recent workshop with an in-house legal team, we fed a standard onboarding contract into a GPT model to generate simplified alternatives for a dozen common clauses. The tool offered quick variations in tone, structure, and length, which the team used not as final outputs, but as conversation starters.

- *Text analysis.* One of the less visible yet extremely helpful uses of AI in legal design is its ability to read legal content at scale. When applied to a collection of contracts, terms and conditions, or privacy notices, AI can identify recurring patterns, surface inconsistencies, and detect outdated formulations. These tools allow us to scan entire document sets and flag elements that merit revision, whether from a legal standpoint or from the perspective of user comprehension. For example, during a redesign of a global service agreement, we used AI to run a comparative review across six country versions. The system flagged conflicting phrasings and redundant clauses that would have escaped a manual scan.

- *Preparing to co-design.* Another meaningful application lies in preparing for the co-design phase. AI can help generate user personas, synthesize behavioral data, and model possible customer journeys, especially when past feedback or service records are available. Rather than relying solely on abstract assumptions, legal teams can ground their design work in patterns that reflect real user behavior. This kind of groundwork makes it easier to ensure that the solutions we create are not only compliant, but usable and relevant.

- *Visual support.* AI is also quietly reshaping the visual and structural layer of legal documents. We've been experimenting with systems that provide explanations alongside legal text, modular sections with expandable content, and visual elements that make navigation easier. In one workshop for a tech company, we co-created a dual-view agreement – one version for legal reviewers, rich in legal detail; another version for business partners, focused on narrative clarity and visual storytelling. The interface was built with the support of AI layout tools, which helped us test different structures and adapt the flow depending on audience profiles.

- *Customization*. The capacity of AI to customize and contextualize content deserves special mention. Imagine a tool that adjusts the level of detail depending on the user's function, or a model trained on a company's past contracts, able to suggest variations that reflect not only previous positions but also internal tone of voice and negotiation history. With a bit of work, this is already a realizable scenario. One day, perhaps, we will stop thinking in terms of templates altogether and begin designing documents that are truly responsive to those who read them.
- *Ideation*. The role of AI is not limited to text or layout. It can actively support ideation. In brainstorming or brainwriting sessions, we can use AI to generate alternative framings, provoke discussion, or break creative deadlocks. Despite the concerns regarding human creativity, it often creates friction-rich dialogue that forces us to think more broadly.
- *Cognitive support*. AI can reduce the cognitive burden of repetitive tasks – like tagging clauses, comparing versions, or drafting translations – thus freeing up time and energy for the work that requires judgement, empathy, and imagination. Be ready to review what has been done but also be ready to use it to hasten your process!
- *Providing continuity*. AI can offer continuity beyond the delivery of a legal product. Integrated tools such as chatbots, interactive guides, and smart clause walkthroughs allow end users to engage with legal documents in an ongoing way, rather than passively accepting them. Imagine a contract that responds to your queries, anticipates your concerns, or adapts its explanations based on your previous interactions. In that case, AI would not only help make documents readable – it would help them come alive.

More tools, better questions

We are no longer at the experimental margins of AI in legal design. We are at the stage where its use is becoming routine – embedded in documents, workflows, and even conversations. The novelty is fading, and with it comes deeper responsibility. It is no longer about proving that AI can be useful. That has been established. The challenge now is to decide how we use it, and why. The temptation to impress with speed, automation, or visual flair is strong. But legal design is more than a performance. It is a method for reshaping how legal systems communicate, include, and serve. That requires discernment.

AI can certainly help us draft faster, prototype with less friction, and test assumptions at scale. It can simulate user responses, suggest alternatives, and visualize legal content in ways we could not easily achieve before. But it does not know whether a sentence is fair. It cannot tell us whether a layout invites dialogue or reinforces hierarchy. These are decisions grounded in context, values, and human consequences. When it spots issues in contracts, it may hallucinate. When it provides suggestions of improvement, it may rely on problems that don't exist for that specific scenario.

The role of AI, then, is not to decide for us, but to challenge us, to support our iterations, to extend what is possible without diluting what matters.

The future of legal design will not be defined by the number of tools we use, but by the quality of the choices we make while using them. There is no shortage of AI-driven features. What remains rare – and valuable – is the ability to pause, to edit, to ask better questions before moving forward. In a field that combines law with care, speed without direction is not progress. It is distraction. Our task is not to follow the technology, but to ensure that it follows the kind of thinking we still want to defend.

Chapter 17:
The aftermath – leveraging the learning experience

Gathering feedback and listening for learning

Our clients know this well – the final minutes of each session are always dedicated to feedback. What began almost as a light-hearted ritual – often no more than a circle of voices exchanging impressions – has evolved into a central part of our method. At the end of the day, no session is ever flawless. Even when a session feels well-executed, there are always dimensions that could be improved, perspectives that were underrepresented, moments that left someone behind. This space for reflection is neither cosmetic nor optional. It is a deliberate gesture – a pause that invites listening, a moment of responsibility more than an act of courtesy.

Feedback, when taken seriously, becomes a form of design itself. Each session is a prototype, and every prototype needs to be read through the eyes of those who experienced it. What one participant found energizing, another may have perceived as confusing or too fast-paced. A metaphor that sparked clarity in one group might have felt opaque or culturally distant to someone else. What seemed like a minor detail to the facilitator might have been crucial for someone less familiar with the topic, or for those navigating the session in a second language. Legal design, if it wants to remain inclusive and adaptive, must actively seek out these nuances rather than relying on general impressions.

We typically host a live debrief at the end of each session – a collective moment where participants are invited to share their impressions while everything is still vivid. These conversations are often revelatory – ideas that seemed universally accepted are challenged, quiet voices raise overlooked questions, and tensions that were felt but not named during the session find space to be expressed. The facilitator plays a key role here – not only in holding space, but in actively listening, reformulating, and drawing out patterns. This is about building a fuller picture of what actually happened, from multiple vantage points.

That said, not everyone feels comfortable speaking up in a group setting. Some people process slowly. Others are naturally more reflective and need time to articulate their impressions. And there are those who may feel constrained by hierarchy, language, or dynamics of visibility. For this reason, alternative feedback formats (short written reflections, anonymous surveys, one-on-one follow-ups) ensure that what emerges reflects a true plurality of voices. The format can vary, but the intention must remain consistent – genuine curiosity about how the session was lived, and a commitment to learn from it.

Thoughts:

Once feedback has been collected, it should not sit forgotten in a folder or be skimmed through hastily. It deserves careful reading and/or reflections. We should look at patterns and recurring observations, but also to outliers, as they often reveal blind spots or unspoken dynamics. Feedback is not always easy to hear, especially when it points to moments of confusion, frustration, or disconnect. Yet it is precisely in those cracks that the most relevant questions tend to arise. What do we need to change? What have we overlooked? What assumptions might we be making that no longer serve us? Turning these questions into an action list is a discipline in itself. It is easy to fall into the trap of vague resolutions ("Next time we'll manage time better" or "We should communicate more clearly") but it is more useful to translate insights into tangible changes. Adjust the structure. Rework the instructions. Bring in a different tool. Invite another voice. Small changes, grounded in real feedback, often make the biggest difference.

Maintaining momentum

Whether we are working on a standalone legal design workshop or a longer, more complex journey involving multiple sessions, what happens after the session is as decisive as what occurs within it. Ideas can be powerful, but they are fragile. The moment the room clears, the energy begins to dissipate. Emails, meetings, deadlines – all conspire to make the insights of a legal design session (or project) feel distant, abstract, or less urgent than they seemed just hours before. It is therefore essential to act swiftly and preserve continuity.

Within 24 to 48 hours, I suggest sending a structured follow-up to all participants. This should include decisions made, the open questions, the actions proposed, and the mood in the room. This document, however brief, can serve as a bridge between shared imagination and collective responsibility. When done well, it reminds everyone about the session's logic and helps them see how their contribution fits into the broader story.

The follow-up should also assign responsibilities and set realistic deadlines. Vague to-do lists rarely lead to action. A visual timeline or checklist, even if minimal, allows the group to see where they are going and who is moving with them. In some cases, artificial intelligence can support this work by drafting summaries or extracting key tasks. In others, a participant or co-facilitator might take on the responsibility. Either way, the task deserves attention. Translating insights into action is the hinge on which progress depends.

Thoughts:

In our experience, most participants will not have the time – or the headspace – to dedicate additional effort once the session is over. Many prefer to channel their energy into the legal design session itself, seeing it as a self-contained moment of focus within otherwise saturated schedules. That is entirely acceptable. Not every project requires extensive work between sessions, nor should we assume that follow-up must always involve elaborate tasks. However, what remains essential is a regular cadence of check-ins to keep the project aligned with its goals. These touchpoints – whether weekly, biweekly, or monthly – act as anchors, helping the group stay connected to the trajectory of the work and offering a space to address small misalignments before they become bigger obstacles. Even short conversations can make a difference, as they create a rhythm of accountability, allow for course corrections, and help maintain shared ownership of the outcomes. Legal design is rarely a straight path, and these regular pauses help ensure we are still heading in the right direction.

After the project is done – turning (more) ideas into action

A legal design project does not conclude when the last canvas is filled, or the room is tidied. The sticky notes may be put into the trash and the workshop over, but that is precisely when the true test begins. Now we need to turn those ideas into reality. This transition is where many projects falter – overwhelmed by the sheer volume of inputs, uncertain about where to start, or lacking a clear distribution of roles, the legal design project comes to an end. On the other hand, it is here that strategic thinking meets organizational maturity.

The first step is prioritization. Not everything needs to happen now. Some ideas are urgent; others are valuable but require different conditions to flourish. Categorizing actions into short-, medium-, and long-term priorities provides structure and creates a sense of progression. This approach also helps manage expectations and prevents the frustration – frequent in innovation contexts – of trying to do too much, too fast, without adequate resources.

Pro tip:
One of the best ways to manage a potential impasse is assigning responsibilities. When someone knows that she is directly accountable for an outcome – not abstractly, but concretely – she is more likely to take initiative. Ideally, this distribution of responsibility should take into account not just roles and functions, but also motivation and proximity to the issue. A legal counsel may be best positioned to revise a clause, while someone from product may lead the redesign of a user flow.

Secondly, I suggest setting up lightweight project tracking systems – a shared spreadsheet, a Kanban board, a digital checklist, a shared Google Doc. These tools do not need to be sophisticated. What matters is that they are visible, updated, and collectively owned.

As the work evolves, it becomes important to communicate beyond the original circle. Compliance teams, product owners, customer support, external partners – all may interact with what was designed. A short visual summary of the outcomes can help extend the value of the session. Periodic updates on progress help maintain credibility and create internal champions who can speak to the work's relevance.

Finally, don't forget to develop a moment of structured reflection in relation to the project you closed. This is more about sense-making than feedback. What worked well, and why? What didn't work, and what do we need to change for next time? These conversations should be candid, specific, and future-oriented. Learning from friction points is as valuable as celebrating what went well. Over time, these reflective practices shape a culture that values experimentation without naivety, and rigor without rigidity.

Legal design moves in cycles. In each cycle, the follow-up phase is where intent becomes practice. Treating the soil where ideas are spread with care can make the difference between a session that fades and a project that leaves a mark.

Thoughtful perspective
Sally Guyer

As global CEO of one of the world's fastest growing non-profits, Sally Guyer's mission is to inspire and support the World Commerce & Contracting (WorldCC) team and global community to collectively drive recognition and excellence in commercial and contract management. She is an experienced and accomplished commercial and contracts management professional, holding senior commercial positions at a range of corporate and multi-national organizations. Her focus is on the creation of positive and successful business relationships, constantly striving to ensure that businesses realize their true potential and value. In 2019, Sally was invited to become chair of the board for the Open Contracting Partnership (OCP) and in 2021 she was appointed professor in practice in strategy and innovation at the University of Durham Business School.

Marco: Reflecting on the past couple of decades, how have you observed the role and perception of contracting evolve within organizations?

Sally: That's a fantastic question, and a lot of what you've shared with me while preparing this book has pushed me to reflect deeply on that evolution. At their core, contracts are economic instruments. For many years, however, they've been cloaked in legal formalism. Legal teams are important stakeholders, of course, and legal content is a necessary part of contracts. But fundamentally, contracts are for the business.

We often refer to contracting as the least reformed business process in any organization. It remains fragmented and disjointed, despite being absolutely vital. Contracts are the lifeblood of economies and institutions. That's not my opinion – it was the basis for the Nobel Prize awarded to Hart and Holmström for their work in economic sciences.

Yet contracts remain alienating. Designed by lawyers, for lawyers, and in anticipation of litigation, they are often impenetrable, filled with legalese that intimidates rather than empowers. That's at the core of our mission at World Commerce & Contracting – to elevate contracts so that they are not only accessible, but meaningful to a wider audience. If contracts hold our economies together, then they must be crafted in a way that stakeholders – across sectors, across functions – can actually understand and use.

The real point of friction arises post-signature. That's where value is won or lost. Our research shows that lawyers tend to exit the scene once the contract is signed. Then, business professionals from across departments are expected to perform against that contract, but often, they don't fully understand it. It's not the operational guide it should be. And when things go wrong, legal is brought back in to pick up the pieces. This cycle becomes a self-fulfilling prophecy.

Too much time is spent negotiating clauses that only become relevant in case of failure. Very little attention is paid to designing for success from the outset. Contracting should be a multi-stakeholder effort. It's not just a legal function. It's a core business function, and that's what we've been working on for 26 years and will continue to advocate for.

Marco: I completely agree. In your view, what are the primary drivers behind the transformation of contracting from a periodic administrative task into a strategic business enabler?

Sally: We need to acknowledge the broader economic shifts over the past few decades. Globalization has been a major driver. We've moved from local, product-driven economies to global service-based ones. Today, more than two-thirds of the global economy revolves around the procurement and delivery of services, not products.

This shift has profound implications for contracting. Service-based relationships are more complex and long-term. Yet, our contracts haven't always kept up. Too often, they become massive, risk-averse documents that grow by accretion – new risks mean new clauses, new regulations lead to more boilerplate. We attempt to create certainty in an inherently volatile world through excess, rather than through clarity.

What we need are operational documents that reflect the nature of these evolving relationships. Contracts should function in harmony with relationship management and governance frameworks to deliver the outcomes we aim for. The contract alone isn't sufficient. It must be part of a broader system of alignment and collaboration.

Marco: I find it fascinating how this long-term mindset changes everything. And I love your economic lens – it's exactly the one I use when I talk about legal wellbeing. CEOs and business leaders care about two things – how much money can I make, and how much can I save. When we frame legal work in that context – when compliance becomes an asset, and legal strategy drives direction – then legal professionals earn their seat at the table. Now, I see a major gap between large corporations and SMEs in contracting. What are the unique challenges SMEs face, especially when negotiating with larger entities?

Sally: It's a significant issue. We recently published our "Most Negotiated Terms" report with a strong focus on SMEs. I'm working with a construction sector group in the UK right now, and we see this all the time. Large organizations impose rigid, one-sided contracting frameworks on smaller suppliers. It's often a "take it or leave it" situation. If SMEs want the revenue, they have to sign – regardless of the risk.

We've seen the consequences in high-profile failures. Their collapse pulled down countless SMEs who were contractually trapped. In these settings, the imbalance is clear, and the human toll is devastating. But there's another side. SMEs also need more commercial capability. Many SMEs are ill-equipped to negotiate or even understand the contracts they're signing.

There are positive stories too. Just yesterday, I heard about a UK-based aerospace and defense firm that drastically simplified its SME contracts – from 80 pages to just six. They recognized that simplicity is not just about being kind. It's about efficiency, mutual trust, and operational sanity. The people in those big organizations are overwhelmed too. Over-complication serves no one.

Marco: That example really resonates. I've been tracking post-COVID trends in legal wellbeing because of my UIA role. Initially, big law firms were the main concern – associates and partners earning well but facing immense pressure. But since the pandemic, it's the corporate legal departments that are experiencing the most burnout. Legal teams are shrinking, budgets are tighter, and yet the regulatory load is heavier, especially in Europe. Add to that the rising pressure to integrate AI. Legal professionals now need to implement solutions that didn't exist five years ago. The message from the top is increasingly, "Don't ask for headcount if you haven't tried AI". But we're asking lawyers – often individualistic, skeptical, and non-technical – to pivot fast. It's a perfect storm.

Sally: Absolutely. It's a real concern.

Marco: Let's talk about investment. One of the common objections to legal design is the perceived cost. If you had to name three compelling reasons for investing in better contracting processes, what would they be?

Sally: First, reputation. In a competitive environment, being transparent and easy to work with makes a huge difference. Contracts speak to your values. Are you hiding behind legalese, or are you trying to build trust?

Second, return on investment. Organizations that invest in contract design and simplification consistently report dramatic results. We've seen contract cycle times reduced by 40, 50, even 60 percent. One CEO told us it was the best ROI of any innovation project in five years.

Third, wellbeing and operational resilience. If your processes are unnecessarily complex, you're embedding friction and risk into your organization. Contracting must be recognized as a business process, not a legal one. It needs to be efficient, understandable, and designed for its users – internal and external. That shift improves not just outcomes but morale.

Marco: Now, the big topic. AI is increasingly being integrated into contract management. How do you see AI reshaping the field?

Sally: I'm cautiously optimistic. We're doing extensive research at the moment. There's a lot we still don't know, but curiosity is key. Everyone in this field, no matter their role, needs to be curious about the implications of AI.

What excites me most is the potential to tap into the business intelligence that has always existed in contracts but has remained out of reach. Traditionally, contract data sits in 24 different systems that don't communicate. We haven't been able to see the whole picture, let alone learn from it. Now we can. AI can help us unlock that intelligence.

This isn't about replacing people. It's about helping contracting professionals do what they were always meant to do – serve as the connective tissue of the business, using data to drive performance and value.

Part IV:
The Leonardo Framework©

Introduction to Part IV:
Towards a common ground

Legal design, as it stands today, has no codified methodology, no universally accepted roadmap, no standard path. There are many ideas, tools, articles, and a growing body of practice. But no common frameworks. Some see this absence as a flaw, as a sign of immaturity. I see it differently. I believe that this openness is precisely what allows legal design to remain dynamic, creative, and attuned to people's real needs. Yet even freedom requires form. Even experimentation benefits from clarity. Because when we work with real organizations, real users, real deadlines, we cannot always rely on intuition. We need something to hold onto. A frame that is light but robust, structured yet breathable.

As this realization matured, I began to sketch out the shape of this part of the book – a space devoted not just to case studies or tactics, but to the deeper reasoning behind how we, as Better Ipsum, approach documents, services, and legal experiences. When I first shared this idea with colleagues, I encountered hesitation. "Why open the engine?" they asked. "Why make public what others consider proprietary?" In a field still defining itself, some feared that codifying too much might trap the discipline in premature boundaries. Others wondered why we focus so much on documents and policies, when legal design today touches technology, interfaces, governance, and beyond. My answer was, and remains, simple – because sharing is the point. Legal design cannot thrive in secrecy. It was never meant to.

Legal design is not a solo performance. It is a collective craft. If we believe in clarity, in accessibility, in rethinking law for human beings, then we cannot afford to treat methods like trade secrets. This fourth part of the book is not a marketing move, nor a theoretical detour. It is a direct expression of the values that underpin our work. By making our thinking transparent, by laying out our approach to structuring sessions, shaping documents, and supporting change, we offer a set of coordinates. We do not claim completeness. But we do claim experience – one forged over time, through projects that worked and others that taught us why they didn't.

What follows is our Leonardo Framework©. It is not a doctrine, but a step-by-step guide. An attempt to offer legal professionals, designers, and change-makers a way of navigating the practice of legal design with more confidence and clarity. It is built on three progressive levels, each reflecting a different depth of engagement with legal transformation – from visuals and plain language, to collaboration and co-creation, and finally to structural redesign informed by data, research, and interdisciplinarity. It does not aim to impose a method, but to offer orientation. Like any good map, it is meant to be read, used, annotated, and challenged.

This fourth part is, at least for me, the center of gravity of this book. It represents the moment where theory becomes structure, and practice gains a backbone. If legal design is to grow, it must remain flexible, but also teachable, applicable, and open to refinement. The Leonardo Framework© is one way of doing this. A starting point for conversation, experimentation, and shared evolution.

Chapter 18:
The Leonardo Framework©

Some disclaimers

Before entering the heart of the Leonardo Framework©, a few clarifications are in order. What follows is the result of our work, our method, our way of doing legal design. It has emerged through years of experimentation, feedback, and critical observation. It is not presented as a universal solution, nor as the only viable path. While many approaches to legal design share some common ground, this framework reflects the choices we made, the priorities we set, and the questions we kept returning to. Is it the best method? For us, yes. Because it resonates with the way we think, work, and listen. Could there be others, equally sound, equally coherent? Absolutely.

One of the most delicate paradoxes in legal design lies in its desire to remain open to outcomes. The process should shape the solution, not the other way round. This means that applying a framework across contracts, policies, and legal texts could, in some cases, undermine the very spirit of the approach. Not every problem requires a rewritten clause or a redesigned document. Sometimes, the most meaningful intervention is a new habit, a different interface, a better way of exchanging information. In some cases, the answer might not involve a document at all – it could be a conversation, a video, an interactive tool. A good legal design framework must always leave space for such possibilities.

It is also worth stating that the principal focus of the Leonardo Framework© remains on documents, rules, policies, and texts. Legal design can be applied at many levels, from systems to services to structures, but we choose to work where the written word still carries weight – the clauses people do not read, the policies they ignore, and the rules they find obscure. Our work is grounded in that terrain – where precision meets opacity, and where interpretation must often serve as a bridge between the law and its readers.

At the same time, we are fully aware that legal design does not stand still. It evolves, absorbs, reacts. From a Daoist angle, one might say that naming a method is already a compromise, as any attempt to define risks freezing what should remain fluid. The written word may offer clarity, but it also reduces motion to stillness. And yet, there comes a moment when a structure becomes necessary, not to impose, but to orient. A good framework offers a rhythm. It provides support more than constraint.

This is how we see it. The Leonardo Framework© is our contribution to a broader conversation. It is grounded but not rigid, detailed but not prescriptive. It offers a way forward without claiming to be the only one. In this spirit, we begin.

How about three levels of legal design?

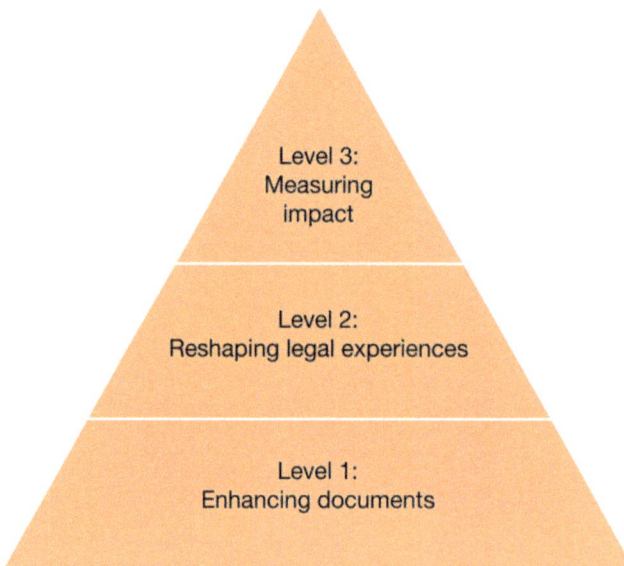

Level 3:
Measuring
impact

Level 2:
Reshaping legal experiences

Level 1:
Enhancing documents

As discussed in the theoretical section, legal design has grown rapidly over the past decade. No longer a niche interest confined to academic circles or isolated innovation teams, it has attracted the attention of institutions, universities, law firms, and in-house departments worldwide. This widespread curiosity has undoubtedly changed the way the legal field interacts with clients, with technology, and with regulatory frameworks. Yet despite this momentum, legal design still suffers from a certain ontological uncertainty. What is it exactly? A method, a process, an approach, a mindset, or a combination of all these? The lack of a shared definition has practical consequences, particularly when one tries to apply legal design in concrete settings. A long footnote could easily be added here, tracing the various interpretations offered by scholars and practitioners alike.

This ambiguity becomes especially relevant when we move to the question of methodology. For some, adding a few icons to a contract or simplifying the layout of a privacy policy is already enough to count as legal design. Others maintain that unless a project follows a legal design thinking logic – with defined stages, iterative cycles, and user involvement – it cannot be considered as such. A more rigorous view pushes the boundary even further, arguing that legal design should only be recognized when it includes structured measurement, turning policies and contracts into responsive, data-informed tools. These diverging perspectives reflect a broader tension – while many associate legal design with documents, contracts, and written outputs, others see it as a means to rethink legal systems, processes, and the role of law itself.

Even where there is agreement on core values – user focus, empathy, inclusivity, transparency, etc. – interpretation varies. What does it really mean to focus on the user? Is it enough to create personas, distribute surveys, and conduct interviews, or does it require legal professionals to truly engage with users' lived experiences? Similarly, inclusivity and empathy can mean different things in different contexts. Do they refer to language choices, participatory methods, or simply the clarity of the final outcome? The absence of shared parameters extends to measurement. Traditional KPIs and return-on-investment models often fall short when trying to capture the effects of legal design. Many of its outcomes – clarity, trust, comprehension, reduced friction – are not easily quantified, yet they are essential. Clients and practitioners alike shift their expectations from project to project, contributing to an evolving, and at times unstable, understanding of what legal design actually requires.

This leads to a final set of questions – are we practicing legal design when we use plain language and a few well-placed visuals in a contract? Or does it only apply when we involve users at every step and redesign the process from scratch? Must there always be co-creation? Must the output be entirely new? These are not rhetorical provocations – they shape budgets, timelines, and expectations. Answers vary widely depending on who is asked.

To make sense of this, we developed a model structured around three levels of legal design, each reflecting a different degree of complexity, awareness, and engagement. This layered structure reflects the practical need for a clearer way of understanding what legal design is and what it involves. Depending on the nature of the problem, the client's needs, and the available resources, legal design can take the form of a quick intervention or a deep transformation. At the end of the day, we do not require the same level of investment for every case, nor do we always produce the same type of result. In short, Level 1 improves our documents, Level 2 reshapes our experiences, and Level 3 measures and validates legal design's effects in practice. These three levels do not represent a hierarchy of value, but rather a spectrum of possible interventions – each appropriate in its own context.

Example:
Let's put our framework in a concrete scenario. A financial institution can start redesigning its mortgage policy at Level 1, focusing on plain language and visual layout. At Level 2, it may decide to transform the onboarding process into an interactive guide. At Level 3, it may want to track the correlation between redesigned content and compliance rates over a year.

This model did not emerge from theory alone. It came out of conversations – with clients who were unsure about what to expect, with colleagues in global think tanks, with researchers, and with professionals who needed a way to talk about effort, cost, and result. Many clients found it difficult to understand where legal design began and ended, what it required, and what it could realistically deliver. The three layers were born to avoid that confusion. They are meant to clarify rather than codify, to offer direction without rigidly prescribing. In the following pages, we present this framework as an orientation tool – one that accepts the fluidity of the field, while providing a concrete structure to support better decisions and deeper understanding.

Insight:
Once we developed the three levels, we realized that they do not pertain solely to methodology but also correspond to different levels of awareness, impact, and commitment. From a business perspective, this tripartition further represents three distinct teams, varying degrees of complexity, different project timelines, and distinct cost structures.

Level 1: The base of the pyramid

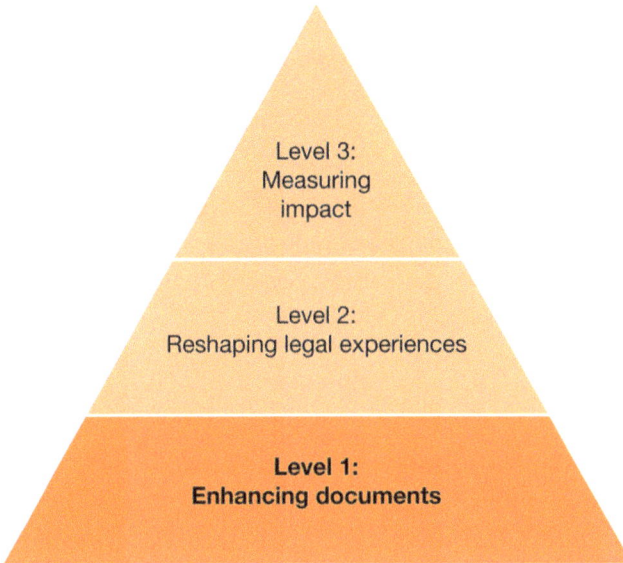

The first level of legal design represents, for most, the typical entry point into the field. It also corresponds to what many newcomers (and, surprisingly, many law firm partners) tend to associate with legal design as a whole. At this stage, the aim is relatively straightforward – to improve our documents and make them more user-focused. The emphasis lies usually on improving the visual and linguistic presentation of legal texts, without substantially altering their structure or underlying content. The central concern is to enhance clarity, accessibility, and usability, always keeping the final user in mind.

This level usually starts with a review of existing materials to identify opportunities for improvement. The interventions might include simplifying language, adjusting layout, introducing icons or infographics, and generally rethinking the way information is presented.

The process often takes the form of a collaboration between a legal professional and a graphic designer. In some cases, a communications specialist with experience in tools like Canva or InDesign may play this role. Occasionally, the legal expert may take on both tasks, although the opposite is less common.

Pro tip:
When the visual side is handled by a designer without legal training, we strongly recommend a final check by a qualified legal professional, as the risk of creating documents that are legally ineffective, or even invalid, is not negligible.

This foundational level of legal design does not demand extensive user research, nor does it rely on complex design thinking frameworks. Instead, it focuses on making legal content clearer and more approachable, by simplifying terminology, removing unnecessary jargon and redundancies, and supporting the text with visual elements. The goal is just to make the document easier to read, easier to navigate, and more engaging. It is a first, essential move toward bridging the distance that often separates legal texts from their audiences.

From a budgetary perspective, this level is also the most accessible. It requires limited time and relatively modest resources. For this reason, we often recommend it to those who are curious about legal design but remain hesitant, whether due to skepticism, limited capacity, or fear of unintended consequences. Starting small allows teams to test the waters without committing to a full-scale transformation. Even modest adjustments, when made carefully, can lead to meaningful results.

That said, this level is not without its limits. By concentrating on the surface of legal communication, it may fail to address deeper structural or systemic shortcomings. It also tends to minimize the role of the user. While documents become more accessible, they are not necessarily shaped around the actual needs, behaviors, or contexts of those who use them. As a result, there is a risk that the redesign remains cosmetic. Still, the benefits are real. A well-executed intervention at this level can enhance a firm's public image, foster internal awareness, and encourage more ambitious applications of legal design down the line. In many cases, it marks the beginning of a cultural shift. Subtle, but decisive.

Insight:
When we shared our three-level framework with colleagues, some of them, especially the most prone to legal design thinking, were skeptical, arguing that this may not be seen as legal design. We would like you to reflect on the focus and the purpose of the discipline.
  •   Is the new document better and more user-centric? Yes

- Has Level 1 helped you think more about the end user? Yes
- Have you made legal content more accessible and comprehensible to a broader audience and spread the seeds of plain language and accessibility on a wider scale? Yes

Then, maybe, legal design may have reached its goal.

Level 2: The magic of legal design thinking

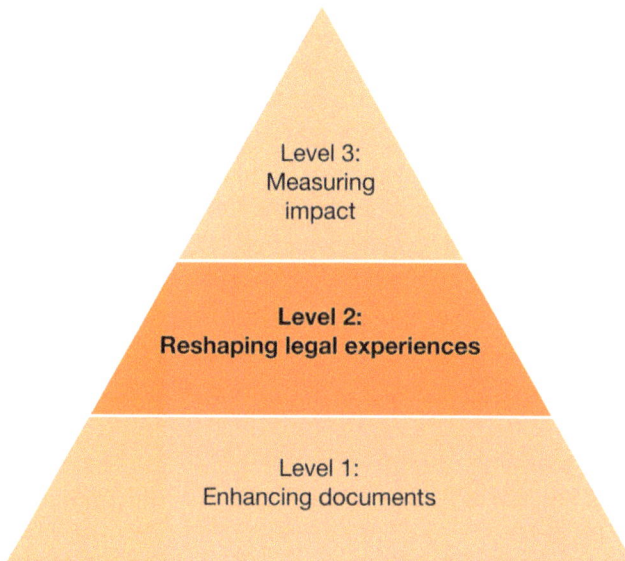

As we move further into legal design, the second level introduces a more structured and deliberate approach, one that fully engages with the logic of legal design thinking. This is where the process shifts from improving the appearance and readability of legal documents to rethinking how legal frameworks themselves interact with users. The emphasis on the end user becomes broader and deeper – no longer limited to clarity and layout, but extending to the ways in which information is organized, accessed, and experienced.

At this stage, legal design thinking becomes a central method, shaping how we gather and interpret data, how we structure legal content, and how we test and refine what we create. We begin by constructing user personas, mapping user journeys, identifying key touchpoints, and pinpointing moments of friction that typically go unnoticed in traditional legal work. These findings are then validated through surveys, interviews, and contextual inquiries. We also pay attention to the tone of voice of the final user, finding the balance between legal precision and human comprehension. Lastly, co-creation becomes a feature of the process – lawyers, clients, designers, and, where necessary, developers work in close collaboration. The goal is not just to make content more appealing or easier to read – it is to ensure that the legal tool, whatever its form, functions effectively for the people it is meant to serve.

While the first level provides an essential base, the second marks a more ambitious transition, redefining how legal information is structured and how legal systems speak to those who use them. It also widens the scope of legal design, from improving documents to improving interaction. This added depth also enables legal teams to understand the wider consequences of their work – not only usability but also organizational coherence, institutional trust, and business alignment.

However, this increased value comes with added demands. Firstly, in terms of commitment – more time, more resources, and more openness to change. The timeline tends to extend, as feedback loops and iterative testing take center stage. Unlike level one, where the process often concludes after a few rounds of revision, here we work in cycles, adapting the design in response to how real users actually engage with it. We create, test, and refine prototypes multiple times.

This shift also brings certain challenges. Many legal professionals are not accustomed to iterative workflows, and the idea of testing legal content before it is finalized can feel counterintuitive. There is also a natural tension between the structure of legal reasoning and the demands of simplicity, clarity, and usability. To work effectively at this level, legal designers must often act as mediators – navigating between the internal logic of law and the external needs of users, between doctrinal constraints and practical expectations. It is not always easy. But it is in this space of tension that legal design becomes something more than visual improvement or stylistic revision. It becomes a tool for change.

Insight:

It is not uncommon that a legal designer starts with Level 1, but then wants to go deeper, whether they decide to intervene on systemic issues, or to work on impact.

Such an evolution requires legal professionals to move away from document-centric thinking and embrace a more holistic approach to legal design. Instead of treating contracts, policies, and regulations as fixed, one-size-fits-all instruments, Level 2 encourages legal teams to explore more flexible, user-responsive frameworks.

Think about the work on an internal policy. We begin improving the document but then we want to transform it into an interactive compliance tool, tailored to different audiences through conditional logic or adaptive content delivery. In that case, involving professionals with expertise in design thinking, UX/UI, and, in cases of digital solutions, legal tech development, becomes necessary.

Level 3: Metricizing the law

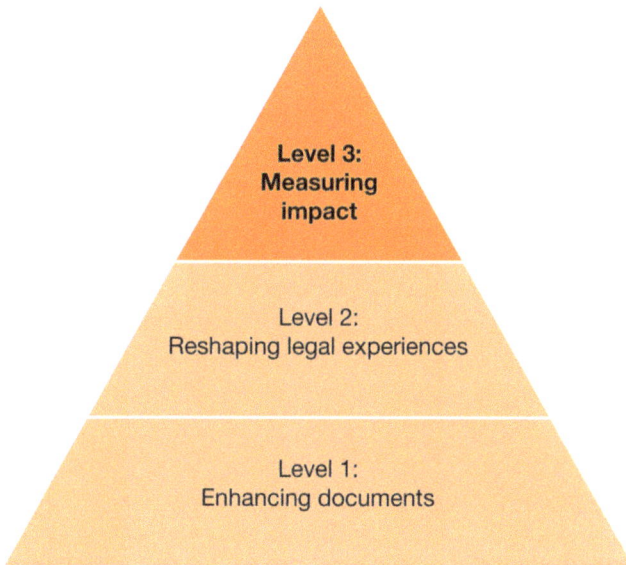

The third and most advanced level of legal design – what we refer to as Level 3 – brings together the full scope of the framework. It builds on the foundations laid in Level 1, where visual and linguistic clarity are improved, and on the structure of Level 2, where user-centered design and iterative processes become central. Yet it moves decisively further. At this stage, legal design does not stop at making documents more comprehensible or engaging. Instead, it aims to demonstrate, through structured assessment, whether these improvements lead to measurable and durable results for users, organizations, and institutions. The focus shifts from creating better documents to understanding how those documents function, perform, and produce value in practice. As this shift deepens, legal documents are no longer seen merely as a series of clauses but increasingly as sources of data – living instruments whose use, interpretation, and effects can be observed, tested, and refined.

This level necessarily calls for an interdisciplinary approach. While lawyers remain central, they are joined by professionals from other domains – in the best cases, economists who understand incentives and modelling, behavioral scientists who examine user decisions, psychologists who study comprehension and perception, and data analysts who can extract patterns and trends from usage. Their collective expertise enables a more layered and nuanced evaluation of how legal artefacts function in the real world. Level 3 is thus characterized by the systematic use of both qualitative and quantitative tools. These might include user testing, eye-tracking studies, behavior mapping, compliance audits, or even economic modelling. By introducing these techniques, the process becomes evidence-based, and legal design leaves the space of intuition to enter into the domain of verification.

At Level 3, every element of the legal document, from its opening clause to its navigational structure, is subject to scrutiny. The central questions become more precise. Are the clauses not only valid but understandable? Do they reduce confusion? Do they change how decisions are made? Can we observe a difference in behavior after the intervention? Can we quantify that difference? These questions speak to the effectiveness of legal communication and the real consequences of legal choices. Redesign is no longer about improvement in the abstract; it is about proof – about tracing the consequences of a legal design process and showing what has changed, for whom, and how.

Level 3 also encourages a shift in how law is conceived. Rather than being reactive – responding only when things go wrong – it promotes a proactive posture. Contracts, when written with clarity and behavioral insight, may prevent disputes before they arise. Compliance policies that use visual cues or behavioral nudges can reduce violations without requiring additional enforcement. Prevention, whether in terms of avoided misinterpretation, error, escalation, or friction, become a trackable element. It is this anticipatory dimension that links legal design to strategic decision-making. When measurable outcomes such as improved compliance, reduced litigation, or faster negotiation times can be demonstrated, the case for legal design becomes concrete, not aspirational.

While the first level improves documents and the second refines experiences, it is in the third that legal design justifies itself fully. Here, it becomes a methodology that can be evaluated, tested, and improved over time. Its contribution is not rhetorical but structural. It offers a path toward legal systems that are not only more humane and accessible, but also more efficient, accountable, and capable of learning from their own results. Level 3 is not the only destination, but it is where the potential of legal design is most fully realized.

Example:

A critical dimension of this analysis involves behavioral insights. Understanding how individuals interact with legal texts allows for iterative refinements. For example, if a newly designed contract reduces negotiation time by 40 percent or increases comprehension among non-lawyers by 60 percent, such data points validate the value of the design intervention. This kind of empirical evidence is particularly crucial when advocating for legal design within organizations or regulatory bodies, as it moves discussions away from aesthetics and toward measurable business, legal, and operational efficiency. Imagine if an impact analysis demonstrates that adopting a legal design framework for a specific contract reduces litigation on a particular issue by 20-30 percent. In that case, such evidence becomes a powerful argument for CFOs, CEOs, and other decision-makers, who are generally forced to cut costs and make savvy economic decisions.

Chapter 19:
Level 1 of the Leonardo Framework©

Preamble – always users first

Level 1 centers primarily on the use of plain language and visual elements. Yet neither of these strategies can truly work unless the user is placed at the core. The starting point for any legal design process should always be the same – who is going to read this document, and in what way? It is not a rhetorical question. The reader's background, level of expertise, and way of engaging with the material all shape how the message is received and understood. These aspects cannot be treated as secondary, nor can they be guessed or assumed. Even if we are not conducting the full set of research methods, such as developing personas or mapping user journeys, some initial inquiry is always necessary. A few targeted interviews or short user tests can make a meaningful difference. They ensure that what we produce is not only beautifully designed in abstract, but relevant and effective for those who will actually use it.

Step 1: Look. Read. Listen

Before anything else – before the tools, the canvases, and the mapping sessions – there is a moment that precedes all others: the encounter with the document as it stands. This moment matters more than it seems. Print the contract in black and white – no color, no brand palette, no design frills. Just the raw text, in its unfiltered state. Then look at the colors. Read the document aloud, slowly and deliberately, as if you were reading it to someone you care about. Then read it again in silence. Change your setting. Switch devices – move from your desktop screen to a smartphone, from a smartphone to a tablet, perhaps even a printed copy held in your hands on a train or a sofa. Watch yourself. How do your eyes navigate the page? Where do they stop? Where do they get lost?

What at first appeared to be a standard legal document begins to reveal itself differently. You notice the density – words pressed into long paragraphs with no visual breathing space. Sentences that stretch beyond what memory comfortably holds. Clauses wrapped in abstraction, drifting from any connection with real life. Maybe it is not immediately obvious what is wrong, but something feels off. The structure resists your attention. The tone pushes you away. You find yourself rereading the same line twice. Or skimming, hoping to locate something that makes sense – a date, a number, a familiar term – only to find the layout offers no clues. This is the experience that too often gets missed when lawyers assess their own work. We know what we meant, after all. But we are not the ones who will have to navigate that meaning from the outside.

Reading a contract in this way – out of context, out of comfort, out of our legal work – reveals not just what is present, but what is missing. Visual cues that could guide the eye. A structure that tells a story. A tone that acknowledges the reader's presence. What emerges is not a list of errors, but a feeling – this is hard to read, and even harder to trust. That feeling matters. If that first impression is one of confusion, fatigue, or intimidation, the rest of the journey becomes compromised before it has begun.

This diagnostic moment is our first act of respect towards the user. A way to see the document not for what it says, but for how it speaks. A contract that cannot be comfortably read will not be comfortably accepted, no matter how precise its clauses. If we skip this step, if we rush straight into solutions without sitting first in the problem, we risk missing the most human part of the design process – the willingness to see things as they are, not as we imagine them to be.

Step 2: Clarifying the language, part one – things to avoid

One of the major steps in legal design is clarifying the legal language, so I have devoted two sections to it[1] – one regarding things to avoid, and another regarding things to do.

The following are some things to avoid.

Archaisms

The use of archaic language in legal documents is one of the clearest obstacles to clarity. These expressions often survive just because they have been repeated for decades, not because they are needed. Why avoid them? Because they create a tone of distance and exclusivity, which may have been perceived as authoritative in the past but today risks alienating readers and undermining trust. Replacing them with current, plain alternatives makes the text easier to understand and reinforces the idea that legal communication can be both serious and accessible.

Archaic term	Modern alternative	Use in context (before)	Use in context (after)
Heretofore	Until now / Previously	The party heretofore known as the Supplier	The party previously known as the Supplier
Afore-mentioned	Mentioned above / Earlier	In accordance with the aforementioned section	In accordance with the section mentioned above
Therein	In it / In that	As outlined in the contract and detailed therein	As outlined in the contract and detailed in it
Forthwith	Immediately / Without delay	The goods shall be delivered forthwith upon receipt	The goods shall be delivered immediately upon receipt
Pursuant to	Under / According to	Pursuant to Clause 4 of this Agreement	Under Clause 4 of this Agreement
Hereunder	Under this	The rights granted hereunder shall remain in force	The rights granted under this agreement shall remain in force

Latin and foreign terms

Latin expressions and foreign terms have long held a place in legal language, often used to convey precision, formality, or authority. Yet in most legal contexts today, these terms function more as barriers than bridges. Their use tends to signal exclusion, creating a communication style accessible mainly to legal insiders. While some Latin terms may still be necessary in specific legal systems or for doctrinal accuracy, many others can be replaced without any loss of meaning. The same applies to foreign words or phrases that could be translated into plain, accessible language. I suggest evaluating each occurrence of Latin or foreign terminology carefully, asking whether its inclusion truly adds value or whether it creates unnecessary complexity.

Latin or foreign term	Modern alternative	Use in context (before)	Use in context (after)
Inter alia	Among other things	The party shall, *inter alia*, provide insurance documents	The party shall, among other things, provide insurance documents
Ab initio	From the beginning	The agreement shall be considered void *ab initio*	The agreement shall be considered void from the beginning
De facto	In practice / In reality	He acted as the *de facto* director	He acted as the director in practice
Bona fide	In good faith	The buyer must act in a *bona fide* manner	The buyer must act in good faith
Mutatis mutandis	With necessary changes	The same procedure applies, *mutatis mutandis*	The same procedure applies, with the necessary adjustments

continued on next page

Latin or foreign term	Modern alternative	Use in context (before)	Use in context (after)
Force majeure	Exceptional circumstances	The clause applies in cases of *force majeure*	The clause applies in cases of exceptional or unforeseeable events
Ex parte	Without the other party	An *ex parte* decision was issued	A decision was issued without hearing the other party

Passive voice

Another effective strategy for improving clarity is to reduce the use of the passive voice. While common in legal writing, passive constructions often obscure responsibility and weaken the immediacy of the message. They make it harder for the reader to identify who is acting and what is being done, which can lead to confusion, misinterpretation, or unnecessary re-reading. I suggest favoring the active voice whenever possible, especially when the identity of the actor is relevant, or the sentence describes a concrete obligation or right. The active voice makes language more direct, transparent, and easier to process. It places the subject at the forefront, where it naturally belongs in any user-centered communication.

Passive construction	Active alternative	Use in context (before)	Use in context (after)
The contract will be signed by both parties	Both parties will sign the contract	The contract will be signed by both parties	Both parties will sign the contract

continued on next page

Passive construction	Active alternative	Use in context (before)	Use in context (after)
The documents must be submitted by the client	The client must submit the documents	The documents must be submitted by the client	The client must submit the documents
Payment shall be made within 30 days	The buyer must pay within 30 days	Payment shall be made within 30 days of delivery	The buyer must pay within 30 days of delivery
The application will be reviewed by our team	Our team will review the application	The application will be reviewed by our team	Our team will review the application

Jargon

Avoiding jargon is another key step in reducing over-formalization and improving the readability of legal documents. Technical terms, insider phrases, and unnecessarily abstract expressions often create barriers rather than building trust. While such language may be second nature to legal professionals, it rarely aligns with how people speak, think, or understand information in everyday life. I suggest replacing jargon with clear, familiar terms wherever possible, without compromising legal accuracy.

Jargon / legal term	Plain language alternative	Use in context (before)	Use in context (after)
Commence proceedings	Start a case / Go to court	The claimant shall commence proceedings within 30 days	The claimant must start the case within 30 days
Terminate the agreement	End the agreement	Either party may terminate the agreement with written notice	Either party may end the agreement with written notice
Remuneration	Payment	The employee shall receive monthly remuneration	The employee shall receive monthly payment
Prior to	Before	The goods must be delivered prior to 1 July	The goods must be delivered before 1 July
In the event that	If	In the event that the supplier fails to deliver	If the supplier fails to deliver
Hereinafter referred to as	From now on called	The Client (hereinafter referred to as 'the Purchaser')	The Client (from now on called 'the Purchaser')

Redundancies

Alongside archaisms, Latinisms, passives, and jargon, another barrier to clarity comes from overused phrases that inflate sentences without adding substance. Legal writing often relies on long-winded formulations that could be expressed more succinctly. These phrases may sound formal or even reassuring, but in reality they dilute meaning and stretch attention. I propose replacing redundant expressions with more direct alternatives, both to save space and show respect for the reader's time and concentration.

Redundant phrase	Clearer alternative	Use in context (before)	Use in context (after)
For the avoidance of doubt	To clarify / To be clear	For the avoidance of doubt, this clause applies to all users	To clarify, this clause applies to all users
Notwithstanding the foregoing	Even so / However	Notwithstanding the foregoing, the payment remains due	However, the payment remains due
In accordance with the provisions of	Under / As provided by	In accordance with the provisions of Article 5	Under Article 5
At this point in time	Now	At this point in time, the supplier is not in breach	Now, the supplier is not in breach
In the event that	If	In the event that the buyer cancels the order	If the buyer cancels the order
Until such time as	Until	The contract remains valid until such time as it is terminated	The contract remains valid until it is terminated

Repetitions

Repetitions in legal writing are often the result of caution. Lawyers tend to restate the same point in slightly different terms, hoping to reinforce meaning or cover every possible nuance. But repetition does not always create clarity. In many cases, it generates confusion, dilutes the message, and increases the cognitive effort required to follow a document. Readers are forced to distinguish between similar phrases, wondering whether the difference is intentional or merely stylistic. This can lead to misinterpretation or, worse, a sense of distrust in the coherence of the document.

Insight:

I recall a very famous Italian lawyer, well known for a peculiar habit that, over time, became almost a personal signature. In every summons he drafted, regardless of the case or the matter at stake, he would stress the same point repeatedly across every page. It was not simply a rhetorical flourish, or an oversight born out of haste. It was a carefully chosen strategy. During an informal conversation with him, driven by a mixture of curiosity and professional admiration, I asked about the reason behind this distinctive style. His answer struck me with its clarity and precision. He said, *"Marco, I want to win. And I believe that if you repeat the same concept over and over again, it will stick in the judge's mind."* (Note: I was in Italy, therefore a civil law country. That said, giving more reasons than necessary to stress a point can make the point weaker, not stronger. Keep in mind the famous phrase reported by Sir Bertrand Russell: *"It is impossible that yesterday evening you saw me drunk, for two very good reasons: the first is that I abhor alcohol. The second is that I had only one glass of wine."*)

Step 3: Clarifying the language, part two – things to do

These are the strategies I suggest implementing.

Prioritize brevity

One of the most effective ways to reduce formality and improve clarity is to prioritize brevity. Legal writing has long favored verbosity, often layering redundant phrases, doublets, and extended explanations in the name of precision. In practice, such excess rarely adds clarity. Instead, it slows the reader down, obscures the key message, and inflates the text unnecessarily. I propose that legal professionals ask themselves a simple question after drafting any clause: Can I say the same thing in fewer words, without losing clarity or precision? If the answer is yes, then revision is not just possible but necessary. Brevity is more about distilling meaning to its clearest form than cutting corners. A brief sentence, if well-constructed, does not simplify the law – it reveals it. And that is the essence of good legal design.

Example:

Before

In the event that the Client, notwithstanding having received prior written notification from the Service Provider regarding the upcoming scheduled maintenance of the platform, which was communicated in accordance with Clause 4.2 of the present Agreement, fails to take the necessary and appropriate steps to ensure data backup or to notify its internal stake-holders of any potential disruption in access, the Service Provider shall not be held liable, to the maximum extent permitted by applicable law, for any direct, indirect, incidental, or consequential losses or damages, including but not limited to loss of data, interruption of business opera-tions, or reputational harm, arising directly or indirectly from the temporary unavailability of the platform during said maintenance period.

After

If the Client does not prepare for scheduled maintenance after being prop-erly notified under Clause 4.2, the Service Provider is not liable for any resulting losses, including data loss or business disruption. This includes both direct and indirect damages. Responsibility is excluded to the fullest extent allowed by law.

Using examples

Examples are one of the most effective tools for making legal writing more accessible. Abstract clauses often remain vague or misunderstood unless anchored in real or hypothetical situations. I suggest integrating examples wherever the reader may struggle to imagine how a rule, obligation, or excep-tion applies in practice.

Example:

Before

The Client shall ensure that all confidential information is stored and transmitted using appropriate security protocols.

After

The Client shall ensure that all confidential information is stored and transmitted using appropriate security protocols. This includes using password-protected files for email attachments and sharing documents only through encrypted platforms.

Including FAQs

Legal documents are often dense, technical, and difficult to navigate. Readers, whether clients, partners, or internal teams, frequently have recurring questions that are not directly addressed in the main text. Including a Frequently Asked Questions (FAQ) section is a practical way to anticipate doubts, clarify complex points, and offer a human voice within a formal structure

FAQs should be positioned either at the end of the document or near key chapters, depending on length and layout.

Example:

Question: Can I terminate the agreement if the supplier misses a delivery deadline?
Answer: Yes, but only if the delay lasts more than 15 days and no alternative delivery date has been agreed in writing.

Question: What happens if I stop using the service before the contract ends?
Answer: You will still be required to pay for the remaining period, unless you have cancelled according to Clause 9.

Being consistent

Consistency is one of the quiet strengths of effective legal communication. It creates clarity, reinforces structure, and builds trust. Yet it is often overlooked in both language and design. A frequent issue in contracts is the tendency to express the same concept in different ways across the document, using varied terminology, shifting tone, or rephrasing obligations without clear need. This can confuse the reader, raise doubts about meaning, and trigger legal uncertainty. I suggest establishing and maintaining a consistent vocabulary from the beginning, especially for key terms like party roles, timelines, rights, and obligations.

> ### Example:
> If "termination" is used in one clause, avoid switching to "cancellation" or "withdrawal" in another unless there is a precise legal distinction. If the client is called "the Purchaser" in one section, they should not become "the Buyer" two pages later.

Step 4: A matter of how

Often, it is not only the content, but also the way it is presented.[2] Structuring documents logically and clearly can reduce the need for formal, dense language. The content is the same, but we receive it in a different way.

The following are some of the best strategies to use.

Using clear titles and headings

A document with clear, well-structured headings allows the reader to follow its logic, locate information easily, and distinguish between topics without unnecessary effort. It supports scanning, digital readability, and fosters a human tone. One of the best ways to implement headings is using them as signposts, guiding the reader through the structure to support faster orientation.

> ### Pro tip:
> - Use verbs or actions when possible ("Terminating the contract" is better than "Termination").
> - Avoid vague labels like "General", "Miscellaneous", or "Other".
> - Reflect the structure visually through size, spacing, or numbering.
> - Keep headings consistent in tone and format throughout the document.

Organizing sections

When sections are clearly grouped by theme and presented in a logical sequence, the document becomes easier to follow, easier to explain, and far more likely to be read in full. I suggest avoiding abstract groupings and instead using titles that reflect the content and relevance of each part. How about organizing the contract in a way that mirrors the reader's experience. What are my rights? What are my obligations? What happens if something goes wrong? How can this be ended?

Pro tip:

Using descriptive section titles like "Your Rights", "Your Responsibilities", or "How to End the Contract" makes the structure feel intuitive and human-centered. This approach supports comprehension without sacrificing rigor and helps shift the tone of the document from defensive to cooperative.

Adding swim lanes and columns

Swim lanes and columns can significantly improve the clarity of legal documents, especially when dealing with complexity or multiple parties. Swim lanes offer a structured way to map roles, responsibilities, and rights across the parties involved in a contract. They divide the page into horizontal or vertical sections (typically one per party), making it immediately clear who is responsible for what, when, and how. This format is particularly effective in bilateral or multilateral agreements, where obligations are interdependent but distinct. In this case we could organize information based on who does what, rather than following a chronological or thematic order. The resulting layout usually provides a sense of visual balance, reinforcing the idea that legal relationships involve reciprocal effort and shared accountability.

Pro tip:

When using swim lanes, how about using a central space to highlight shared duties, such as joint deadlines, review processes, or mutual commitments?

Columns, on the other hand, are a versatile layout tool that enhance comprehension by supporting comparison and bringing structure, rhythm, and clarity to even the most technical content. Don't forget what we mentioned earlier – our brain doesn't read top to bottom, it processes information, looking for patterns, similarities, and contrasts.

Placing smart definitions

Definitions are essential in most legal documents, but they are too often written for the drafter rather than the reader. Over-formal, circular, or buried in complexity, they tend to obstruct rather than support understanding. Place them where they are most useful – either at the beginning of the document if they are few and central, or directly in context if they are limited and local. Whenever possible, add an icon that refers to the concept.

Pro tip:

A smart definition is one that explains the concept as the user needs to understand it, not just as the law would traditionally frame it. This means avoiding circularity ("Confidential Information means any confidential information") and preferring phrasing that anchors the term in reality.

Step 5: Refining our typography

Typography,[3] while often overlooked, is a crucial component of effective legal design. The choice of font, size, spacing, and color can influence how readers engage with the document, impacting both readability and comprehension. While legal design is way more than typography, the latter is certainly a useful tool to make our information more structured and accessible.

Font choice

In legal design, the choice of font is a matter of usability more than style, because it shapes tone, readability, and perceived credibility. Before we get into the concept, take into account that most law firms and legal departments have already made specific choices (such as Times New Roman, Calibri, Garamond), or implemented their own fonts. That said, if you are not bound to house style, I have some tips. Firstly, some fonts are considered better on paper and some fonts better on digital. As an example, Serif fonts such as Times New Roman or Georgia are better to support longer reading and signal formality, while Sans-serif fonts like Arial, Calibri, or Helvetica are often preferred in digital formats, where their clean, modern lines enhance legibility on screens. Choosing according to the platform is always a safe bet.

Second, don't be influenced by habit or precedent. Think about how the document will be read, not the fact that you used Calibri up to now. Third, don't choose too many fonts, and apply them consistently throughout the document, avoiding unnecessary switches that disrupt visual continuity. Two is probably the maximum number I would take into consideration for a document.

Pro tip:

Have you ever considered using a font designed to support neurodiverse readers? There are several options specifically created to assist individuals with ADHD or dyslexia.[4] One of our favorites is Bionic Reading,[5] which modifies the rhythm of text to guide the eye more intuitively and make reading more accessible and focused.

Font size

Font size plays a relevant role in shaping the reading experience. Legal documents often rely on small text, either to save space, squeeze in additional clauses, or replicate a traditional aesthetic. Yet in a design-oriented approach, readability must come first. Text that is too small quickly becomes a barrier. It strains the reader's eyes, discourages engagement, and conveys a subtle but powerful message – this content is not meant to be understood, only followed. I recommend slightly larger sizes for body text, ideally 12 points or more, to support sustained reading without fatigue. Regarding the use of different sizes, many experienced legal and information designers do vary font sizes to guide attention and structure the page. It is a good strategy, but I suggest keeping the variation within two or three levels. Going beyond those risks introducing visual noise rather than clarity.

Pro tip:

When choosing a font, it is also important to consider the company's brand identity, tone of voice, and house style. The font should not feel foreign to the organization's communication culture – it should reflect and reinforce it, while still meeting the standards of readability and usability that legal documents require.

Bullet points

Bullet points can be a valuable tool for breaking down dense information into manageable, readable elements. They support visual clarity, help readers scan content more easily, and reduce the cognitive strain caused by long, unstructured paragraphs. Use bullet points when listing obligations, conditions, exceptions, or step-by-step actions. Limit each point to a single idea and ensure that the list flows logically from one item to the next.

Pro tip:

Not all bullet points serve the same purpose. A numbered list suggests sequence or priority, while letters or roman numerals can imply formality or legal reference. Bullets are best for simple enumeration, but even they carry tone.

Paragraphs

While fully justified text may appear neat at first glance, it often introduces uneven spaces between words, which hampers readability and creates an artificial rhythm that the eye must constantly adjust to. The left-aligned paragraph offers a more natural and readable structure, creating a visual anchor that helps the reader follow the flow of information without distraction or unnecessary effort. Alongside alignment, line spacing deserves equal attention. Generous interline spacing can drastically improve the user's reading experience. It gives the eye room to move, reduces fatigue, and allows the reader to process each line with greater ease. It is a good choice to use at least 1.5 line spacing for body text, and ensuring paragraph spacing is visibly distinct without being exaggerated. A related point concerns margins – wide margins not only make a document feel more open and accessible, but also provide room for notes, comments, or version tracking; elements that are often essential in legal contexts.

Pro tip:

One of the legal designer's tricks is playing with paragraphs. How about using single line spacing for less relevant elements, and 1.5 spacing or more for topics that require more attention?

Coloring and highlighting

While often avoided in traditional legal drafting, color, when used deliberately, can be an exceptional tool to support clarity, structure, and emphasis in legal documents. Think about using colors to highlight key areas, or distinguish between sections, parties, or types of information. I suggest using it sparingly and consistently, making sure it serves a function rather than acting as decoration.

Color must also respect accessibility. We need to maintain high contrast, especially for digital documents or when the text might be printed in black and white. At the same time, we should avoid bright or saturated tones for body text, as they can strain the eyes and reduce legibility. The use of red, in particular, should be handled with care as it often carries emotional weight and may unintentionally signal error or urgency where none is intended. Finally, color should reflect the organization's identity and align with its brand guidelines. Remember that legal documents do not exist in isolation – they are part of a broader communication ecosystem.

Pro tip:

One of the most underestimated elements, regarding color, relates to cultural elements. This may be particularly relevant for multinational companies or law firms with offices worldwide. To provide an example, red, white, and black mean different things in Europe, China, and India.

Contrast

Contrast is a powerful design principle that helps the reader distinguish between different types of information, navigate complex sections, and focus on what matters most. In traditional contracts, the absence of contrast (visually and linguistically) often results in a uniform block of text where all content looks and feels the same. This overwhelms the reader and makes it difficult to identify hierarchy, priorities, or change of tone. Use contrast deliberately to signal importance, structure, or transitions. You can apply it through layout, color (where permitted), or even tone of voice (using plain language summaries alongside technical clauses).

Pro tip:

How about using contrast to play a role in the logic of the document? We can deploy it to distinguish obligations from recommendations, conditions from consequences, or internal rules from external references. When these categories look the same, they risk being interpreted the same, even when they should not be.

Blank spaces

Blank spaces, also known as white spaces, are what allow the rest of the document to breathe. In traditional legal drafting, pages are often filled from margin to margin, leaving little room for the eye to pause or the reader to reflect. In design-centered documents, blank space plays a vital role in guiding attention, separating ideas, and improving overall readability. I suggest using generous margins, clear paragraph spacing, and distinct separations between sections to create a rhythm that supports comprehension. Treat blank space as an active part of the layout, not a leftover but a design choice that shapes the experience of reading. White spaces help reduce visual clutter, help user focus, and prevent cognitive overload. They can signal transitions, isolate key information, or simply provide relief after a dense clause.

Pro tip:

One of our efforts in legal design is "thinking what to cut out". This makes perfect sense. But while we think about this concept in terms of clauses and words, we should also think in terms of information architecture (see below).

Thinking in terms of information architecture

Legal design is not just about rewriting or redesigning individual clauses. It is about rethinking how legal content is structured, accessed, and experienced as a whole. This is where the concept of information architecture becomes essential. A legal document is not a sequence of words – it is a system. It contains layers of meaning, interdependencies, and expectations that must be organized in a way that reflects how real people read, decide, and act. We should approach each document as an environment – something that needs to be navigated, not just read. Map the logic of the document before drafting, identifying what the user needs to know first, what can wait, and what must be clearly signposted throughout.

Information architecture means making choices about hierarchy, sequence, visibility, and emphasis. It means deciding what belongs together, what must stand apart, and how each section connects to the next. It is what turns a contract from a block of clauses into a navigable space. When applied carefully, it reduces the reader's uncertainty, supports understanding, and minimizes the risk of misinterpretation.

Pro tip:
Information architecture reminds us of a truth we often overlook – not every part of a document or contract carries the same weight. Some clauses matter more than others, whether in terms of legal consequences, user attention, or practical impact. If we present legal documents as flat, uniform blocks of text, where each section appears to have identical relevance, we create an illusion of equality that misleads rather than informs.

References

1. The book adopts English as its main language, yet I believe that most of the recommendations can be applied to most Latin languages as well.
2. Regarding layout and visual design, these are the indications provided by M. Hagan in LawbyDesign (www.lawbydesign.com):
   1. Compose top left highest priority/bottom right the least important.
   2. Be careful with redundancies.
   3. Establish visual hierarchy among info.
   4. Maximum of two fonts.
   5. More white space.
   6. Use color sparingly.
   7. Use a grid to ensure content is well aligned.
   8. DON'T USE CAPS ALL THE TEXT (sic).
   9. Never use Comic Sans.

3   For further information, see Matthew Butterick, *Typography for Lawyers*, https://typographyforlawyers.com

4   Examples include Atkinson Hyperlegible, Verdana Regular, and Lexend. For clarification, most of their effectiveness is disputed, therefore take everything *cum grano salis.*

5   For the sake of clarification, bionic reading has been proven not to make a difference: www.sciencedirect.com/science/article/pii/S0001691824001811, https://blog.readwise.io/bionic-reading-results/

Chapter 20:
Level 2 of the Leonardo Framework©

From intervention to intention

The transition from Level 1 to Level 2 marks the moment when legal design moves from surface correction to strategic design. In my view, every legal design initiative should begin with clarity about which level we are operating on – one, two, or three – not as a rigid taxonomy, but as a way to guide intentions and expectations. Everything achieved at Level 1 remains valid. It is always a good idea to bring clarity and accessibility in systems where legal language has long remained opaque. But Level 2 is where the real legal design work begins. It is only from Level 2 onwards that we begin to see the full strategic depth of legal design. If the first level focuses on making a document easier to understand, the second addresses the deeper challenge of making legal communication genuinely useful, meaningful, and aligned with the user's needs and context.

Level 1 practitioners often approach legal design through discrete tools. They simplify the language, introduce icons, restructure content for better readability – all valuable steps. Yet these actions are frequently performed in isolation, without an overarching methodology or a strategic understanding of how each change contributes to the user experience as a whole. The focus remains on the document itself. The user is present, but only as a reference point, not as a central actor in the design process.

By contrast, Level 2 represents a shift in posture. It is the moment where legal design thinking is no longer something one does occasionally, but something that shapes how one works. The steps are no longer performed mechanically but integrated naturally and intentionally. Tools are no longer adopted for their novelty or aesthetic appeal, but because they serve a precise function within a structured process. The user is not an abstract figure, but a real person whose needs, constraints, and behaviors shape every phase of the work.

At Level 2, legal professionals begin to think across disciplines. They understand that innovation rarely originates within the echo chamber of legal expertise alone. They borrow from behavioral science, psychology, service design, and communication studies. They are comfortable with ambiguity, aware that meaningful change rarely comes with certainty. They know how to balance usability with legal robustness, and they make choices grounded in both empathy and precision.

Progression from Level 1 to Level 2, then, is not a matter of quantity – of using more tools or spending more hours – but a qualitative leap. It is the point where legal design becomes a form of reasoning more than an exercise in style.

At this stage, legal design ceases to be a patchwork of interventions and becomes a strategic lens through which to address complex problems.

Step 1: What do we want to achieve? What impact do we want to have?

One of the most valuable starting points in any Level 2 legal design thinking initiative lies in the ability to pause and ask a single question – What are we really trying to do? This moment of reflection should not be treated as a formality nor confined to a sticky-pad on a whiteboard. It requires space, silence, and intention. It means carving out a dedicated time to bring the team together, even if for just 15 minutes, with the sole purpose of defining what success would look like, and why it matters. Not from a project management point of view, nor from a legal one, but from a shared human understanding. What matters most to those involved, both within and outside the organization? What would make us proud, not just as professionals, but as people? Even if we are tempted to answer instinctively, we should take some time to reflect.

On the same level, it becomes important to reflect on the kind of change we aim to spark. Sometimes the ambition is to improve how end-users experience a contract or a policy. Other times, the focus may be on improving internal cooperation, reducing friction across departments, or building stronger bridges between legal and non-legal professionals. Often, the objective is a mix of these elements. But a common trap lies in wanting to fix too many things at once. When ambition is not accompanied by prioritization, confusion follows. That is why one of the first tasks should be to map the impact zones and assign a clear order of priority, asking what truly matters now, and what can wait.

To support this phase, brainstorming remains a classic – a collective, fast-paced exchange of ideas that energizes the group and reveals patterns. Brainwriting, on the other hand, allows each voice to emerge without interruption, offering quieter participants a way into the conversation. Instead of choosing between the two, the real value comes from understanding how to use them wisely, and when. Both require structure, clear timing, and the gentle guidance of someone who can hold the space without dominating it. The goal is not to fill the room with ideas, but to arrive at the ones that matter.

Pro tip:
When guiding a brainstorming or brainwriting session, a few simple but powerful principles can make a tangible difference. First, create a space where quantity is valued over perfection. The goal in the initial phase is not to find the ultimate solution but to generate movement, to unlock ideas that might later evolve into something meaningful. The more ideas surface, the greater the chances of uncovering unexpected connections or paths worth exploring. Participants should feel free to propose rough drafts, half-formed thoughts, or even intentionally provocative suggestions. Sometimes, what seems off-track at first becomes the spark for a completely new perspective.

Equally important is to reassure everyone that this is not the moment for filtering or ranking. That stage will come. By making it explicit that prioritization is a separate step, you help prevent the common tendency to over-edit or silence an idea before it has even been voiced. This is particularly true in groups that include people from different backgrounds or levels, where the fear of being judged can easily inhibit participation. In both brainstorming and brainwriting, the initial aim is not to be right, but to be present. To participate, fully and freely.

Step 2: Empathize
The empathize[1] phase is a shift in posture, a deliberate choice to move away from assumptions and towards attentive observation. It starts with a deceptively simple question – For whom are we doing this? And under what circumstances will they encounter our work? This question cannot be answered through speculation, nor by relying solely on one's legal expertise. It requires proximity. It asks us to sit with the user by stepping into her constraints, her habits, her fears, and the cognitive shortcuts they might use when facing a legal document. Without this perspective, any solution runs the risk of being technically elegant but humanly irrelevant.

One of the most widely used tools to anchor this process is the persona.

More than a marketing cliché, the persona is a way to give shape, voice, and context to those we seek to serve. A well-constructed persona does not reduce complexity but rather helps us focus. Take the example of redesigning a privacy policy for a consumer-facing application. Instead of drafting a generic text aimed at a faceless mass of users, we might imagine Sofia, a 35-year-old parent who values data protection but is pressed for time and unfamiliar with legal terminology. Sofia's persona is a synthesis of patterns drawn from real conversations, behavioral observations, and qualitative data. Her education level, digital habits, professional life, family setting, and emotional triggers become anchors to test every word, sentence, and visual choice.

Pro tip:

Perhaps your marketing team has already defined user personas. Why not start there? They may have gathered insights about client types, expectations, behaviors, and tone preferences that can serve as a foundation for your legal design work. There is no need to reinvent the wheel if valuable profiles already exist. Instead of treating legal and marketing as separate silos, this is an opportunity to align perspectives and build on shared knowledge.

This approach holds true even when designing for broader categories. Whether we're working with a municipality trying to improve transparency with citizens or a law firm looking to make documents clearer for clients, the effort to build fictional but credible personas remains central. In a legal services context, we might imagine Alex, an in-house counsel juggling compliance updates across multiple jurisdictions; Maya, a mid-sized company's HR lead managing employee queries about contracts; or Luca, a start-up founder who needs answers quickly and with minimal legal jargon. Giving these personas names, routines, and pain points allows teams to shift the discussion from generic categories to specific needs. It also reveals potential mismatches between what legal professionals think people need and what they actually struggle with. The questions are endless, but we can start with a few. How is her typical day? What's her motto? What are her priorities in life? What is her confidence with digital tools?

Pro tip:

In many legal design projects, artificial intelligence is treated as a tool, a back-end function, or a silent engine behind the interface. But what if we began to consider it as a persona – an actual participant in the user experience, with its own tone of voice, presence, and role in the interaction? This shift in perspective changes everything. It forces us to move beyond a technical understanding of AI and confront its communicative dimension. Whether it is answering client questions, generating summaries, suggesting clauses, or flagging anomalies, AI is already shaping the user's journey. Ignoring its persona means leaving a key actor undefined, unframed, and unaccounted for.

Once personas are in place, empathy maps can help teams visualize the world from the user's perspective. These maps invite us to ask what our user hears from colleagues or supervisors, what they see on their screens, what they say in meetings, what they truly feel, and what they ultimately do when faced with a legal text. This structured reflection uncovers blind spots in the design process. It often highlights internal contradictions – users who say they understand a document but hesitate to sign it, or those who claim confidence but seek informal confirmation from others. Take into account that empathy maps are not final answers. They are a starting point to refine assumptions that need to be tested through direct interactions, such as interviews, shadowing sessions, surveys, or focus groups.

Example:
Consider a concrete case. If we are designing new contract templates for a procurement department, empathy work might begin with interviews revealing how difficult it is for professionals to interpret cross-references or ambiguous clauses. Users may confess that they copy-paste old contracts because they fear introducing mistakes. Others might reveal that they skim documents, focusing only on bolded terms or highlighted boxes. This kind of insight is often invisible unless sought out deliberately. It then becomes the foundation for design interventions such as clause simplification, visual timelines, tooltips, or interactive formats.

Finally, it is essential to map the user journey. Legal documents are rarely encountered in isolation. They are part of a sequence – an email request, a login process, a contract review, a signature, a storage system. Each stage has emotional, cognitive, and technical implications. Understanding the user's journey means identifying where stress builds, where questions emerge, and where trust breaks down. This holistic mapping allows the design team to locate pain points and redesign not only the document but the experience surrounding it. In this way, empathy becomes a methodology for listening, a tool for decision-making, and a posture that gives the user the final word on what clarity really means.

> **Pro tip:**
> In the empathize phase, interviews and surveys[2] are essential for uncovering how users actually experience legal information, documents, and processes. Rather than starting from assumptions, legal designers listen directly to final users about their frustrations, needs, misunderstandings, and goals. Interviews, especially when open-ended and conversational, offer deep qualitative insight. They allow users to tell stories, express emotions, and articulate pain points that might be invisible in formal processes. A single sentence, *"I signed it, but I didn't really understand it"* can reveal more than pages of analysis. Surveys, by contrast, allow teams to gather input from a broader audience and spot recurring patterns. Used carefully, they can validate emerging hypotheses and highlight themes that deserve deeper exploration in interviews. The strength of this research lies not in isolated answers, but in building a textured picture of the user's world. Legal professionals may be trained to analyze facts and apply doctrine, but in legal design, they must begin by understanding people. Interviews and surveys help bridge that gap.

Step 3: Define

The define phase marks a turning point in any legal design process. It is where uncertainty begins to take form, where scattered observations are distilled into a clear and shared understanding of what truly needs to be addressed. Defining is often treated as a simple transitional step, something to rush through before getting to the tangible part of the work, but this is a mistake. Defining the problem is an exercise in precision, requiring discipline and curiosity. It involves separating surface-level complaints from structural issues, distinguishing what users perceive from what actually hinders their experience. Legal design, in this regard, offers a different lens than traditional legal reasoning. Where the latter tends to leap into predefined boxes (legal issues, regulatory gaps, risk categories, etc.) legal design holds back. It suspends judgement, resists reduction, and asks, What is the real problem here? Not what's legally broken, but what is stopping people from understanding, using, or trusting what we've built? To answer this question properly, one must first examine the inputs that emerged during the empathize phase. Observations, interviews, maps, user journeys, and emotional cues help to trace the boundaries of the challenge and illuminate its complexity. A document might appear too long, but the actual issue may be an internal inconsistency in how clauses are written across departments. A process might seem slow, but what frustrates users might be the lack of guidance during key steps. In other words, what appears broken is often a symptom, not a cause.[3]

This phase is also where tensions and trade-offs begin to surface. Defining the problem means clarifying what matters most, not only to the legal team but to all those involved – users, managers, external partners. It's a moment of convergence, narrowing down the scope to what is feasible, but also a moment of divergence, opening space for alternative frames. In the redesign of a visual contract, the starting assumption might be that users struggle with legalese. But further investigation may reveal that the real barrier lies in inconsistent clause structures, which confuse even the lawyers who drafted them. The problem, then, is organizational, not linguistic. And the legal design team must think about how to intervene.

Example:

Below are some examples of problem identification:

- *Client onboarding process simplification.* A law firm might assume that clients are frustrated by the complexity of its legal documents to start the collaboration. However, by engaging clients, the firm discovers that the real issue is the lack of clear guidance throughout the onboarding process.
- *Contract negotiation bottlenecks.* A corporate legal department faces delays in contract negotiations. Initially, the team assumes that the problem is due to lengthy approval processes. Through workshops with stakeholders, they realize that the main pain points are unclear contract language and rigid templates.
- *Compliance training engagement.* A company wants to improve employee compliance with data protection regulations. It believes the issue lies in the lack of mandatory training sessions. However, after surveying employees, it uncovers that the real problem is that existing training materials are too complex and unrelatable.
- *Privacy policy accessibility.* A tech company believes users are not reading its privacy policy due to a general lack of interest in legal documents. However, user interviews reveal that the real issue is

related to that specific document. If the policy could be shorter, visualized, and clearly understandable, they would read it.

- *Client communication gaps in litigation.* A litigation firm faces frequent client complaints about feeling uninformed during long legal proceedings. The firm assumes clients want more frequent updates. However, through client interviews, it realizes that the real issue is the lack of clarity in updates rather than their frequency.

Ultimately, the define phase is more a foundation than a step in the process, because it sets the tone for the entire project. It allows us to build interventions that are targeted, feasible, and relevant – grounded in real user needs and capable of delivering real change. Whether through a jam, a collaborative workshop, or a quiet moment of reflection, defining the right problem is what makes the difference between design that decorates and design that works.

Insight:

When you deal with the defining step in practice, you also realize that the reality may be way harder than it seems. Some of the issues we struggle the most as the legal design team include:

- *Are we sure the problem we are solving is the real one?* Many legal design projects start with good intentions but end up addressing the wrong challenge.
- *Have we explored the issue deeply enough?* Superficial understanding often leads to incomplete or ineffective solutions. A deep dive into the problem space can reveal underlying complexities that might not be immediately apparent.
- *Have we defined the problem properly?* It is surprising how many times problems are ambiguous and poorly defined.
- *Are we addressing just one problem, or is it part of a broader system?* Problems rarely exist in isolation. They are often interconnected with other issues within a larger ecosystem.
- *What assumptions are we making?* Unchecked assumptions can bias the entire design process. Be ready to challenge these assumptions, validating them through research, prototyping, and stakeholder feedback. This helps ensure that the solution is based on reality rather than perceived constraints.

Step 4: Ideate

The ideate phase is where I encourage teams momentarily forget what they think is possible and open themselves to what could be. It is not about having the right answer immediately, but about creating the conditions for unexpected solutions to emerge. At this stage, I suggest embracing expansiveness and inviting a wide range of ideas without falling into the trap of early judgement. Legal design, by its very nature, demands that we challenge conventions, so this is the time to suspend them. A well-structured brainstorming session, ideally timeboxed and guided by clear prompts, can unlock surprising directions.

I also (often) ask participants to embarrass themselves and include deliberately exaggerated ideas – not because they will be implemented as-is, but because they push the limits of what the team believes to be feasible. In one project aimed at rethinking employment contracts, for instance, suggestions included contracts that could be navigated like a mobile app, clauses explained through short animations, and even voice-assisted guidance through key terms. These ideas may not all survive the next phases, but they serve a crucial role – they free the room from the inertia of the usual.

After this generative moment, we can shift the focus to product envisioning.. Here, the team begins to cluster ideas, identify promising directions, and imagine how they might work in the real world. This is a moment to move from creative enthusiasm to constructive clarity. I encourage the use of scenario analysis to test early ideas against practical variables.

Example:

Say we're working on a compliance dashboard. We should explore how it would perform in different hands. Would a junior employee understand it without further guidance? Could a legal officer find the information they need in seconds? Would it adapt to local regulatory nuances in different countries? By walking through these concrete situations, we begin to understand which solutions have depth and adaptability, and which remain interesting but unworkable.

This phase also brings in the first layer of strategic thinking. I always remind teams that imagination and rigor are companions, not enemies. It's at this point that we begin to ask what each idea would demand in terms of time, tools, collaboration, and organizational change. I'm not advocating for shutting down ideas too early, but for starting to weigh them gently, without losing momentum.

Pro tip:

"How might we?" (HMW) statements are a reliable strategy when we need to reframe problems in a positive, solution-oriented way. For example, if users find a contract too complex, a HMW statement might be, *"How might we make our contract easier to understand without compromising legal precision?"*. These statements guide ideation sessions by focusing on specific aspects of the problem, encouraging open-minded exploration. HMW questions stimulate creativity, prevent overly prescriptive solutions, and keep the team aligned on addressing the user-centered problem.

Step 5: Prototype

Prototyping is where ideas become real. It's the moment where teams move from abstract discussion to tangible form, to stop talking about solutions and start shaping them. We can see it as building to think. Rather than aiming for a perfect result, I suggest beginning with something rough but shareable – a sketch, a journey map, an information flow. In many cases, this first output might be a simple user journey showing how someone interacts with a contract, a policy, or a legal service. It may feel unfinished, and that's the point. The goal is not to impress, but to test.

From there we move to wireframes or low-fidelity layouts. These allow the team to explore the structure of a page, the sequence of actions, the relationship between information and interaction. Even for simpler outputs, like a legal information brochure or a one-page explainer, schematic representations still play a critical role. They let the team check the logic of the message, the balance between text and visuals, the points of confusion that need resolving. How about using AI tools for that?

As feedback starts to emerge, issues will surface – some minor, others fundamental. That's not a sign of failure. It's a sign that the process is working. I insist on keeping iteration at the heart of this phase. Revise, test again, revise once more. Only after several cycles does it make sense to move toward a more polished user interface. At that point, we focus on how visual elements guide attention and behavior. In one project involving an app for reporting workplace incidents, we used color-coded alerts and carefully designed navigation to reduce hesitation and improve user confidence. Every icon, every button, every scroll mattered, not just aesthetically, but emotionally.

Pro tip:
One of the hardest challenges of legal design, especially for lawyers, is using the tone of voice of the reader. The concept of tone of voice goes beyond grammar, structure, and paragraph. It relates to the emotional and cognitive atmosphere that the text creates, the level of formality or familiarity, the sense of authority or accessibility it conveys. It shapes how the reader feels when engaging with the content, and whether they perceive the document as distant or welcoming, rigid or open, cold or attentive. In legal design, tone of voice becomes a strategic tool to build trust, reduce intimidation, and create a relationship of collaboration rather than imposition. Can we use words differently? Can we empathize more with our audience? Can we strengthen the clarity and credibility of the message by making it sound closer, more respectful, and easier to understand?

The mindset in this phase draws from principles like "fail fast" and "keep it simple". These are concepts that remind us to let go of legal perfectionism and embrace fast learning. I often see legal professionals hesitate here, uncomfortable with the idea of showing something that's not yet complete. We have learned in these last few years how important a Minimum Viable Product (MVP) is, in the development of a project. It is the simplest version of your idea, advanced enough that it solves the core problem, but without the refinements that are needed to make the product perfect. It's a way of making a basic version of your product to gather feedback from users. I always make the same point – an MVP is not a weak draft. It's a strategic instrument. It allows us to validate assumptions, surface objections, and confirm direction – without wasting months on a version no one will use. I remember a case in which we released a visual NDA template to a small set of clients. The feedback was immediate, and some of it was critical, but it led us to a stronger, more functional final version, built on real user needs, not imagined preferences.

Rapid prototyping is not about speed for its own sake. It's about learning quickly and adjusting wisely. It creates a loop – design, test, observe, refine. I recommend involving users at every turn, asking them to click, scroll, question, and react. This level of engagement transforms abstract speculation into grounded insight. It ensures that what we're building sounds usable, useful, and trusted. And by the time we reach the final design, much of the risk has already been absorbed and translated into something stronger.

Step 6: Test

The testing phase marks a profound cultural shift for many legal professionals. It calls for something that often feels counterintuitive in traditional legal work – showing an unfinished product and actively inviting criticism. I This is not a weakness but a strength. Testing means stepping outside the internal bubble and listening, really listening, to how users experience what we've built.

There are several ways to conduct testing, and we must select the method looking at the project's complexity and user base. Usability testing is one of the most effective tools. It involves asking real users to interact with the prototype while thinking aloud – sharing what they understand, where they hesitate, and what they expect next. This reveals not only whether something works, but why it does or doesn't. In parallel, structured questionnaires can help gather quantitative and qualitative data around key dimensions such as clarity, usability, trust, and comprehension.

But testing goes beyond usability. It also involves measuring the actual outcomes of the legal design intervention. And it's why we developed an entire level for this – Level 3 of the framework. Increasingly, organizations want evidence that these projects make a difference, not just in perception, but in results. If possible, try incorporating simple metrics early on – improvements in comprehension scores, faster approval times, lower error rates, increased engagement, or even a reduction in clarification emails. These indicators show whether the design delivers on its promise and aligns the project with broader business or policy objectives. The earlier these metrics are defined, the more seamlessly they can be integrated into the process.

Step 7: Refining our work

This is the stage where we examine the regulatory context with utmost precision (sometimes involving external professionals),[4] refine the information architecture, and begin closing in on the details that matter. It's not a final step, but a continuous loop of review and adjustment. Each element, whether legal, structural, or visual, is revisited through the lens of clarity, compliance, and coherence. I often remind teams that this process doesn't truly end. Legal design thrives on iteration, and even as we polish the final product, we remain open to revision. The goal is not perfection, but a version that works – for users, for lawyers, and for the system in which it lives.

Refining, therefore, is the ongoing rhythm of legal design more than a step at the end of Level 2. Every choice made along the way comes back into focus here – the tone of a sentence, the placement of a clause, the sequence of steps in a service. It is also the moment where we face the regulatory framework in its full complexity, making sure that usability never compromises legal soundness. While the legal element has always been in the background and taken into account, now it takes the lead. How will counterparties react to this icon? And how about judges? Are we covered by insurance if something happens?

This is where the design must find its coherence – where content, form, and function come together with purpose. And even here, the work remains provisional. What we are building is a living tool more than a final product. Something that evolves with its users, its purpose, and its context.

References

1   While the 5 step (sometimes 7 step) Design Thinking Process from Stanford School of Design is a standard in many design thinking fields, it is not the only one. One of our favorites is also the double diamond model (discover, define, develop, deliver).

2   Some clients ask us which tools work best for interviews and surveys. One of our favorites is Google Forms, but some teams prefer Microsoft Forms because of its integration with the Microsoft Suite. We also highly recommend Typeform, which is simple, effective, and easy to use.

3   To dig deeper, we often turn to investigative tools that help expose the layers beneath a complaint. One such tool is the Five Whys method, attributed to Sakichi Toyoda. It offers a way to resist the temptation of superficial fixes. Imagine a scenario in which junior lawyers complain about a frustrating document management system. At first glance, the instinct might be to replace the software. But asking "Why?" repeatedly might reveal something else – a lack of consistent filing rules, fragmented onboarding processes, or a culture that discourages questions. With each "Why?", the conversation shifts from frustration to diagnosis. From tool to practice. From patch to purpose.

4   If you're conducting a legal design project in a big law firm, try involving the specialist of the department. Especially in the regulatory scenario, support from lawyers specialized in areas such as insurance, pharma, TMT, etc. can improve dramatically the quality of the document. Moreover, those lawyers will be more in tune with legal design, its premises, its effort, and maybe they'll aim to be involved in the next project!

Chapter 21:
Level 3 of the Leonardo Framework©

From Level 2 to Level 3

The final level of the Leonardo Framework© is where legal design reveals its full potential – not just as a method, but as a culture of accountability. This evaluative dimension is often overlooked, yet it is what transforms legal design from an inspired practice into a reliable model for change. I suggest approaching it not as a bureaucratic requirement, but as a genuine opportunity to ask ourselves, "Does it work?" "For whom?" "Are we better professionals because of it?"

At this level, the focus is no longer on the elegance of a visual layout or the tone of a clause. What matters is whether the intervention has produced a measurable shift in how people understand, use, and trust legal tools. It's easy to state that legal design improves clarity, usability, and engagement. But unless those claims are grounded in evidence, they remain hopeful assumptions rather than verifiable outcomes.

Most professionals consider impact analysis as a checkbox, but I prefer looking at it as an integrated, layered process that invites us to look beyond surface improvements. For this reason, I suggest using a structured approach that goes deeper than subjective impressions or anecdotal praise. Whether we are redesigning a compliance workflow, rewriting a privacy policy, or co-creating a visual contract, we must be able to assess whether the changes lead to greater understanding, better decisions, and stronger adherence. This means also asking hard questions. Did it reduce errors? Did it lower the number of clarification requests? Did it improve time-to-signature, or satisfaction levels, or accessibility for those with limited legal literacy?

Insight:

In the process, we can embrace both qualitative and quantitative tools. Interviews, A/B testing, readability tests – all can contribute to a fuller picture. But the most important shift is in the mindset. Instead of focusing on whether a document looks better, we should ask whether it works better. Whether it enables rather than confuses. Whether it creates trust, rather than merely reducing risk. These are not easy things to measure, but they matter. And they can be measured with the right approach.

Not every intervention will map neatly onto standard KPIs or deliver a predictable return on investment, but this shouldn't stop us from trying to understand what success means, and how to capture it. At Level 3, legal design becomes a conversation between cultures – the culture of law and the culture of evaluation. And we redefine what "success" looks like in a legal setting. Not just compliance, but comprehension. Not just delivery, but usefulness. Not just reduction of risk, but increase in agency. In this sense, I believe Level 3 is where legal design becomes fully mature. It is no longer simply about doing things differently, but about proving that different is better.

This shift reflects a broader evolution in the legal field. As contracts become interactive tools, as legal processes produce and consume increasing amounts of data, and as users demand more meaningful interactions with the law, we propose a new kind of legal professional – one who is not only trained to interpret norms, but to read metrics. To understand feedback as seriously as precedent. To see usability, not as an accessory, but as a foundational element of legality. In short, we may be entering a time in which every lawyer becomes, at least in part, a data lawyer. And legal design can be the bridge between the two.

Why we need to measure impact

Failure to measure impact is more than a technical oversight. It's a missed opportunity for credibility, learning, and influence. Without clear metrics or structured evaluation, even the most promising interventions risk being seen as decorative. They become invisible and tend to be dismissed – irrelevant, unscalable, or untrustworthy.[1]

That is precisely why the third level is more than an afterthought. Without a culture of measurement, legal design cannot justify its costs, evolve meaningfully, or demonstrate strategic value. At this level, a compelling story is transformed into a compelling case. Because if we can't show where the needle moved, why should anyone invest in scaling what we've done?

Measurement becomes the lever for internal advocacy, helping communicate success, foster buy-in, and build bridges with departments driven by performance data. I've already shown how the absence of metrics blocks growth within teams. If we don't track what worked, we can't replicate it. If we don't listen to outcomes, we can't improve. Without feedback loops, even the most creative teams operate in the dark.

Pro tip:

While impact analysis can be extremely complicated, I suggest starting small. You don't need a PhD in evaluation. You just need the will to ask, "What would we like to accomplish, and how would we know if we reached our goal?" Later, you can ask, "How can we achieve that goal again?" Then, you need to start working on it – by far the hardest part.

This gap is structural more than cultural. Legal education has traditionally neglected empirical thinking. Most lawyers are not trained to define baselines, build testing frameworks, or analyze performance data. Many hesitate to even begin, unsure of where to start or fearful of exposing flaws. However, legal design requires this shift, calling for a new professional posture – one that combines the intuition of a drafter with the discipline of a designer and the mindset of a researcher.

That's why I propose making measurement an organic part of the process. Something to build in from the start more than the cherry on the top at the end. We must define what we hope to change, and how we will observe that change. If the aim is better comprehension, then we must test understanding. If the goal is faster approvals, then let's track process times. If the focus is accessibility, then let's check reach and inclusiveness across user groups. These metrics don't need to be perfect. They just need to be present. Because what we track, we tend to improve.

Working towards an impact analysis

Often, it is not just what we do in legal design that matters, but how we do it. The moment you start thinking in terms of outcomes – real, observable, verifiable outcomes – something shifts. Aesthetics become more than decoration, usability becomes more than convenience, and our work acquires a new layer of depth, grounded in purpose and driven by value over time. It's no longer just about making something look or feel better. It's about making it work – for the people who use it, the teams who manage it, and the systems that depend on it.

To make this possible, I recommend defining a clear set of success criteria from the very beginning of each project. These should be more contextual than generic. This way, we can be aligned with the scope, goals, and constraints of each specific intervention.

Of course, not all projects are alike. When the output is not a contract or policy but a platform interface, a notification system, or a data dashboard, traditional legal evaluation tools may fall short. This is why we should apply a Level 3 lens *cum grano salis* – with discernment, flexibility, and a willingness to tailor. There is no universal KPI because legal design at this level is no longer a one-dimensional intervention, but a multi-perspective strategy. The good thing is that there is always something we can measure, and often more than one thing.

The document perspective

This perspective focuses on the internal architecture of the legal text – how it is built, how it reads, and how it guides the user. Here, we must pay attention to both structural and stylistic features, as these directly influence clarity, usability, and accessibility. You can look at indicators such as word count, sentence length, and paragraph structure. You can review the number of clauses and articles. You can also use readability metrics like Flesch-Kincaid or Gunning Fog to provide a baseline and offer quantifiable insight into the ease or difficulty of the language. A simple analysis carried out with a couple of tools may put you ahead most of your competitors.

The user perspective

This perspective shifts the focus from the document itself to the people who interact with it – clients, partners, suppliers, citizens, or any external stakeholder. Look at this dimension as a way to evaluate not only what users read, but how they feel while doing so. It includes readability, of course, but also emotional tone, accessibility, and overall satisfaction.

You can start taking notes about timing. How much time does the user need to read everything? Then you can get into other elements. Does she perceive us as trustable? Innovative? Reliable?

If you want more details, eye-tracking studies help identify areas of confusion or disengagement, showing where users pause, skip, or stumble.

> **Pro tip:**
> When it comes to tone, perceived relevance, and overall user satisfaction, interviews and surveys offer a solid starting point. I recommend balancing different formats and approaches when you start using this tool. Combine

open-ended and closed questions, use rating scales from one to ten, and always include space for honest reflections and suggestions for improvement. This mix not only encourages more thoughtful responses but also helps you capture both measurable impressions and more personal reactions that might otherwise be missed.

The business perspective

This perspective centers on how contracts perform once they leave the drafting table and enter the real world. Here, documents should be considered as living tools that either accelerate or obstruct business processes. What we measure here is their operational effectiveness – how much time they consume, how often they trigger questions, and how smoothly they lead to agreement. Key indicators may include time to review and signature, the proportion of contracts executed without modification, and the number of clarification requests raised during the negotiation phase. These may sound like internal metrics, but their consequences are strategic, touching cost, speed, and client satisfaction all at once. When a contract moves faster, it's usually because it's clearer. If fewer clauses need to be explained or renegotiated, it's often because the structure is more intuitive, the language more neutral, and the layout more supportive of comprehension. I've seen how a well-designed NDA,[2] with modular clauses, visual guides, and simplified definitions, has cut the negotiation time from weeks to a matter of days. That kind of efficiency doesn't just please legal teams – it frees up resources, shortens deal cycles, and improves the overall tempo of collaboration.

Beyond human interactions, contractual efficiency also involves technical readiness. I propose assessing whether a document is structured in a way that supports automation, for instance, through clause tagging, metadata, and standardization. Compatibility with contract lifecycle management (CLM) systems adds another layer of value – it reduces manual handling, cuts administrative errors, and enables faster tracking and updates across large portfolios.

The team dynamics perspective

Legal design doesn't just change documents. It changes conversations. One of the most overlooked, yet powerful, effects of a well-executed legal design intervention is how it reshapes internal dynamics. Look at how teams interact with legal content before and after a redesign, because the difference is often striking. Fewer requests of approval, fewer internal redlines, and less reliance on external counsel are all signs that a legal document is doing its job – aligning expectations and enabling decisions.

This perspective also focuses on how legal and business teams (marketing, sales, procurement, etc.) collaborate. When legal documents are unclear or overly complex, legal departments often become bottlenecks, forced to interpret, rephrase, or explain content that should have been accessible from the start. Think about the time legal professionals spend explaining basic legal concepts. If that time drops significantly after a design intervention, it means that the design has enabled autonomy, increased internal trust, and freed legal professionals to focus on higher-value work.

I've seen this happen in procurement teams who, after adopting redesigned templates, could finalize vendor agreements with minimal legal support. Or in HR teams empowered to use plain-language offer letters without needing a lawyer's constant review. These cultural shifts reflect a move from legal control to legal enablement. They foster a more integrated, less adversarial relationship between legal and the rest of the organization.

Reflections about scalability

Scalability remains one of the most persistent, and paradoxical, challenges in legal design. On the one hand, legal design is built on empathy, context, and deep user understanding. It thrives on specificity. On the other, long-term success in many legal settings depends on consistency, repeatability, and the ability to scale.

Unfortunately, the very strength of legal design – its capacity to tailor solutions to specific users, needs, and regulatory contexts – can also be its main obstacle when it comes to scalability. Many projects involve long workshops, iterative testing, and fine-tuned adjustments to meet the expectations of a clearly defined audience. This attention to nuance ensures quality, but it also makes it hard to generalize. Unlike traditional contracts, which can often be tweaked with minor edits, legal design outputs are typically embedded in a particular experience. Transferring them wholesale to another jurisdiction, department, or client often requires extensive rework. In that sense, scalability in legal design can feel like chasing a mirage, especially when the focus is intensely user-centered.

Yet scalability is a necessity, particularly when legal content lives within digital ecosystems or is required to support operations at scale. A scalable contract is one that can be adapted quickly across offices, reused with minimal legal review, or plugged into document automation systems without sacrificing clarity or legal rigor.

Pro tip:

Can we look at scalability as a design requirement in its own right? Even in this case, it would be about making intentional choices early in the process – using modular structures, designing with metadata in mind, and building for systems, not just individuals. On that level, scalability may be evaluated through several lenses, such as reduced negotiation cycles, fewer clarification needs, lower ambiguity (and by extension, lower dispute potential), and increased efficiency in contract lifecycle management. We may also look at integration with platforms and tools, whether it's a contract automation software, a smart contract interface, or an internal knowledge base.

In practice, scalable legal design shows up through measurable results. You might see a 70 percent reduction in negotiation time across regional offices thanks to a well-structured NDA. Or a policy framework that retains both tone and legal precision when localized across multiple jurisdictions. Indicators of scalability include the ease with which a template adapts to different use cases, its compatibility with document assembly software, and its resilience across changing regulations. Whether we are speaking about functioning across jurisdictions, integration into automated systems, or supporting high-volume, high-speed operations, legal design may be an enabler of departmental efficiency.

That said, scalability still feels like an elusive goal for many legal design projects. It happens frequently that requests for scalability are not well thought out, or the resources to reach this objective are not proportionate to the task. For these reasons, it is rare to find projects that have achieved success in this field. Even so, I believe it's essential to keep it in view. The value of a design is also what it enables in the future. Legal design that scales, even imperfectly, transforms not just one document, but the entire legal function.

Pro tip:

Legal design does not always lead to a new process or service. Sometimes, its most tangible outcome is a redesigned template or an internal play-book. Have you ever considered applying legal design principles to the playbook of your organization? It could be a powerful way to turn abstract policies into clear, user-friendly tools that actually get used. That playbook may be used by a multinational company for all the legal departments worldwide, and scalability may be closer than you think.

Delving into A/B testing

One of my favorite, quick, and highly implementable tools for evaluating the effectiveness of legal design work is A/B testing. It's simple in concept, powerful in practice, and capable of producing insights that go well beyond opinion or intuition. We typically use it in two ways – either by comparing our redesigned work with the previous version, or by comparing our output with that of competitors or standard industry templates. Both approaches offer clarity, structure, and, most importantly, evidence.

Comparison

In this setup, we take two versions of a legal document or interface – one that reflects our legal design intervention (Version B), and another that represents a standard, more traditional version, often from a competitor or from widely used sector templates (Version A). We then test them with distinct user groups under controlled conditions. This comparison gives us a clear picture of how our approach performs not just in isolation, but in context, against what users are already encountering in the market.

The parameters we observe are varied, but always grounded in practical impact. How quickly do users find key information? How long does it take them to read the document? How confidently do they make decisions? Are fewer clarifications needed? Do users report a higher level of satisfaction or trust? Do they consider our company innovative? Once again, these are not abstract concerns. If our redesigned NDA or privacy notice leads to better comprehension, shorter interaction times, and more positive feedback compared to the industry standard, we have not only improved a document. We've created a competitive advantage.

This method is particularly valuable when working with clients who are unsure whether legal design will "really make a difference". A/B testing gives them evidence. It shifts the conversation from "We believe this is better" to "Here is what the data shows". It also helps us refine our own approach, based on real-world feedback, not just internal assumptions.

Before/after

The second method – Before/After testing – is even more practical, especially within organizations where competitor benchmarks are not available or relevant. Here, we take the original version of a legal document or service (the "before") and compare its performance to the redesigned version (the "after"), using consistent metrics.

Once the legal design work is completed, we test the new version using similar methods – surveys, completion time analysis, comprehension questions, user interviews, etc. The goal is to detect measurable improvements – less time spent explaining terms, fewer misunderstandings, higher task completion rates, greater confidence from users.

Pro tip:

Paradoxically, I usually suggest this approach when a baseline of legal design already exists – an onboarding policy, a sales contract, or a set of FAQs already in use. Here, the law firm or the company believes that they already did a great job. Then, you show them that even the easiest and most comprehensible documents have lots of margins to be improved! Another strategy would be using it when the legally designed document is already in circulation and the goal is to demonstrate how we directly improved the user experience.

While this approach may lack the rigor of a sophisticated impact analysis, it often delivers faster results and requires fewer resources – an advantage in organizations with tight timelines or lean teams. In any case, the objective remains the same – to move beyond intuition, aesthetics, or internal consensus, and to ground our work in measurable, verifiable outcomes. This method, when used thoughtfully, shows that legal design is more than a matter of making things look better. It's about making them work better. That is a claim we should always be prepared to prove.

The measure of maturity

Level 3 is where legal design grows up. It's no longer about polishing the surface, simplifying the language, or making documents visually pleasing. It is where we ask tougher questions. Does this actually change anything? Does it reduce friction? Does it help people understand, decide, trust? At this stage, we become accountable, and we move from a matter of style to a matter of effect.

I believe this is where legal design reveals its real power. Not when it creates something beautiful or new, but when it proves that what it creates delivers. Metrics replace assumptions and the user's experience is not just imagined, but measured. This is the shift from intuition to rigor, from creativity to credibility, from design to decision-making. It is the shift between how something looks and how well it performs in real-world legal and organizational contexts.

Once you start working this way, it's difficult to go back. The moment you begin treating usability, comprehension, efficiency, and trust as things you can track – not just feel – you begin to redesign not just legal documents, but legal thinking itself.

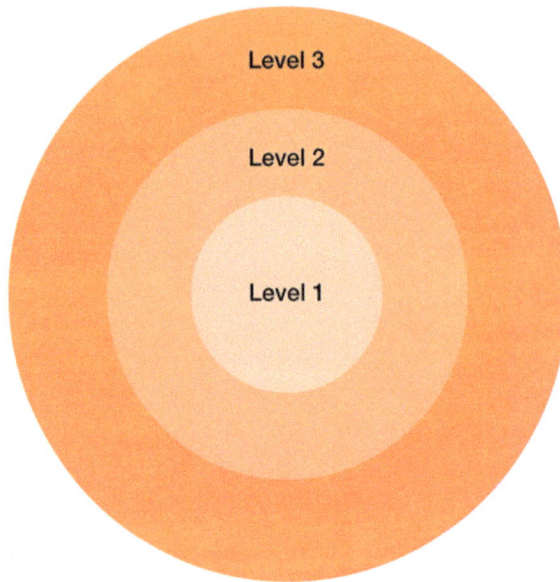

Three levels and Dante's Paradise

One of my favorite literary works has always been *The Divine Comedy*. Among its many unforgettable passages, one resonates with particular force – the moment Dante arrives in Paradise and beholds a vision of God. His attempt to describe this unique encounter with the Divine is both lyrical and elusive, culminating in the image of three radiant circles, perfectly inter-twined. Each stand for one person of the Christian Trinity – the Father, the Son, and the Holy Spirit – distinct, yet entirely contained within one another, a unity beyond the reach of language.

I know that invoking such a sacred image in the context of legal design, and especially in relation to the three levels of the Leonardo Framework©, may seem bold, even uncomfortable to some. Yet I find it an evocative way to express the structure I have in mind. The Mayan pyramid might offer a more familiar representation of a stepwise ascent, where levels are built one upon the other. But what I envisage draws more closely from Dante's vision – not a linear climb, but an inward journey. I picture three concentric circles, each enveloping the next, from the broader scope of Level 1 to the focused center of Level 3. These are not separate steps to be conquered and left behind, but interconnected dimensions. They exist in dialogue, where meaning does not simply accumulate, but grows deeper. Each level draws strength from the others, and together they form a system where direction is not upward but inward, not hierarchical but relational.

And as I am writing the closing paragraph of this book, there's no better way than returning to Dante, the poet who placed the Roman emperor Justinian in Paradise only for his (huge) effort to cleanse the law of confusion and excess. Not for his own quest for glory, but through divine inspiration.

Perhaps anyone who strives for clarity and coherence in the law carries a similar desire – to move closer to justice, not just through doctrine or reasoning, but through a form of harmony that words alone cannot fully contain.

...Cesare fui e son Iustiniano,
che, per voler del primo amor ch'i' sento,
d'entro le leggi trassi il troppo e 'l vano..."
Paradise, VI, 10-12[3]

References

1   For further info about impact in legal design, check out Katri Nousiainen, *Measuring the Impact and Value of Legal Design in Commercial Contracting within the Law and Economics Framework*, Hanken School of Economics (2023).

2   Regarding NDAs, a necessary mention is for Electra Japonas' 1 NDA initiative, www.onenda.org/about

3   *Caesar I was, and am Justinian,*
    Who, by the will of primal Love I feel,
    Took from the laws the useless and redundant.
    https://digitaldante.columbia.edu/dante/divine-comedy/paradiso/paradiso-6/

Thoughtful perspective
Matthew Butterick

Matthew is a writer, designer, programmer, and lawyer. He has written the books Typography for Lawyers, Practical Typography, *and* Beautiful Racket. *Matthew designed the fonts in the MB Type library, including Equity, Concourse, and Triplicate. As a programmer, he created Pollen, a programming language for web publishing; a document-layout system called Quad; and Archetype, a font-editing app. As a lawyer, he's currently serving as co-counsel in class-action lawsuits against multiple generative AI products. Matthew has a visual-studies degree from Harvard University and a law degree from UCLA. He lives in Los Angeles.*

Marco. Hi Matthew. If you had to name the single most common mistake lawyers make the moment they open a Word document, what would it be?

Matthew: In my book, *Typography for Lawyers*, I start by discussing the issue of using two spaces between sentences. People often misinterpret that as my top priority, but that's not the case. I open with it because, at least in American typographic practice, it's a clear and unambiguous rule. And it's a good way to introduce the idea that, in typography, some things are a matter of rule, while others are about judgment.

If I really had a magic wand to change just one thing about legal typography, it would be the overuse of capital letters. We could also talk about underlining, bold, or italics, but capitalization is particularly overdone. Of course, people can have differing views on how much is too much. Personally, I usually suggest that a single line in all caps can work. But lawyers love to capitalize entire sentences or even paragraphs. It's simply too much.

The issue with this is what I call self-defeating typography. When someone uses all caps, they're usually trying to say, "This is important, pay attention". But in practice, large blocks of capital letters are harder to read, not easier. The eye doesn't track them as well. So instead of drawing the reader in, you risk

273

pushing them away. It becomes something people want to skip over. It's a strange habit, and not a helpful one. That's definitely the one thing I'd change.

Marco: I completely agree. One of the visual design principles I use in my workshops is "never capitalize everything". In American writing, capitalization is often overused. Whereas in European legal or editorial practice, we tend to only capitalize the first word of a title. That said, today many contracts and legal documents are being transformed into different formats – interfaces, videos, comics, chat-based interactions, UX interfaces. What role does typography play in these hybrid legal experiences?

Matthew: Well, my view is that typography is the visual element of the written word. So, whenever a word appears, whether on paper, in a PDF, in a user interface, or on a website, someone has to think about typography. The good news for lawyers is that, over the past 15 years, screens and print have started to converge. By that, I mean the gap between what works in print and what works on screen has narrowed because of the huge improvements in screen resolution.

Today, whether it's a mobile phone, desktop, or laptop, these devices all offer high enough resolution that the same typographic decisions made for print can often be applied digitally. Will lawyers actually make good decisions in those contexts? That remains to be seen. But I hope they will pause and think. This is an opportunity to break away from Times New Roman and create something more reader-friendly.

Marco: Let's discuss AI. Everyone is talking about it, and rightly so. It feels like the biggest transformation since the Industrial Revolution. With AI now capable of automatically generating informative legal text, what remains irreplaceable in human typographic sensitivity? Is there something about human typography that machines can't replicate?

Matthew: That's a real challenge to answer. As a lifelong programmer and someone who enjoys technology, I love the idea of AI, but not the reality. As you may know, I'm involved in a series of lawsuits in the United States challenging the legal foundations of current generative AI systems. Even assuming we get to a legally sound version of AI, the issue I see is that these systems are, at their core, statistical modelling machines. They are designed to predict the median, the most statistically likely output. So the result is often boring.

And that matters, even in law. People assume lawyers don't need out-of-the-box thinking, but I disagree. The essence of good lawyering is to look at facts with fresh eyes and an open mind. Sometimes, the best argument is the unexpected one.

I worry about AI imposing conformity. Tools that promise ease often come with defaults. And people love defaults. Think of early CSS frameworks on the web. Rather than inspiring creativity, most people just used the standard templates.

This is not new. Look at LaTeX. People are still using the same layout templates from decades ago. AI is just the latest version of a very old tendency – accepting the default instead of pushing boundaries. And that's my concern. It presents itself as something original, but instead it may limit how we think.

Marco: Typography and law seem worlds apart. They engage different parts of the brain. Yet you've brought them together. What can lawyers learn from typographers, and vice versa?

Matthew: It's a good question. To me, the thread connecting both fields is the written word. Whether you're making a legal argument or designing type, you're shaping how ideas are conveyed to someone else.

When you write on behalf of a client, you're applying logic, structure, critical thinking. Then, as a lawyer, you publish – you're also making typographic and design choices. So I've always been drawn to that full arc – from idea to presentation.

What can lawyers learn from typographers? *Typography for Lawyers* is based on that question. Typography matters. It works. It makes a difference. I often tell lawyers, you wouldn't show up to Court in a wrinkled, coffee-stained suit. So if I don't have to convince you of the value of laundry, why should I have to convince you of good typography?

As for typographers learning from lawyers – that's more subtle. My experience practicing law has helped me think more practically about how fonts are used. For example, I ship my fonts not just in a modern OpenType version but also in simplified formats – one with just text, another with proper small caps.

That sounds outdated, right? But it's the only way to get true small caps in Microsoft Word, which is still the standard tool for lawyers. The "small caps" button in Word does nothing useful. So if you want to help lawyers use better typography, you have to work within the constraints they face.

Marco: That connects perfectly to legal design too. Everyone loves InDesign, Canva, Figma. But at the end of the day, most lawyers still use Word. Not only for convenience but also because they need editable documents. Even if a design is perfect in Canva, the minute you need to change a sentence or bullet point, things fall apart. So Word remains central – for now.

Here's a related question. If you could banish one font from legal documents forever, which one would it be?

Matthew: That's tricky. I don't really think in terms of banning fonts. But I do have a strong view on banning Court rules that require specific fonts.

Some Courts demand filings in Times New Roman, Arial, or Courier. I find that problematic for two reasons. First, lawyers should have the freedom to choose typography that best serves their argument. We don't tell lawyers what clothes to wear to Court. There's an unwritten expectation, yes, but not a dress code. Typography should follow the same logic.

Second, fonts are software products. They're commercial tools owned by companies. So, if a court says, "You must file in Arial," that's essentially mandating the use of a product licensed by a certain corporation. I don't think access to justice should depend on owning specific software.

Marco: Let's talk about neurodiversity. Some chapters in the book address it directly. There's been a growing movement toward fonts tailored for dyslexia or ADHD. What do you think about this? Is it feasible? What are the limitations?

Matthew: I think the motivation behind it is good, but we need to be rigorous about the evidence. Some fonts claim to support specific neurodivergent readers, but many of those claims don't hold up under testing.

I've seen some of these fonts tested with users who have genuine visual or cognitive processing differences, and the improvements often don't materialize. So we have to ask, what are we gaining?

Interestingly, I've had many conversations with readers and customers over the years – people with all sorts of visual needs – and what I've seen is that assistive technology at the system level has improved a lot. That's great progress.

But designing for everyone with one font? I'm skeptical. Once you embed a font in a document, it's the same for every reader. Yet the needs of dyslexic or ADHD readers vary widely. A one-size-fits-all approach doesn't really work.

That's why I prefer solutions that allow for individualization. Screen readers, OS-level settings, high-contrast modes – those give real autonomy to users. And I've adapted some of my own work to better support those systems.

Marco: I had a similar experience. At first, I considered using a special dyslexia-friendly font for this book. But after testing, it became clear that each reader had unique needs. Some fonts made things worse. Eventually, I dropped the idea. That said, I personally benefit from tools like Bionic Reading. The bolded-letter technique really helps me stay focused.

Matthew: That's excellent. If it works for you, that's a good sign. But let's also take a step back. PDFs are particularly problematic here. They're essentially simulations of paper, and they inherit all of paper's limitations.

I'd argue that PDFs are one of the worst formats when it comes to accessibility. Unlike web pages, which let users customize fonts, sizes, or contrast, PDFs are static. Adobe has been slow to improve their accessibility features, and even now, many are inadequate.

I hope future generations of legal professionals – those who grew up with Markdown and better systems – will eventually phase out PDF and Word. When they're running law firms, I imagine they'll look around and ask, "Why are we still using these tools?" Because let's be honest – they don't serve us or our readers as well as they should.

Marco: One last question. You've created not just one font, but many. What have you learned from the process?

Matthew: Type design is a very particular kind of work. It's not like graphic or page layout design. People who move from layout to type design often find it frustrating or tedious.

Fonts are not just visual artefacts – they're software. They have to work at a deep technical level with operating systems and applications. That alone makes type design unusually intricate. You're working in thousandths of an inch. And you have to mentally translate how a letter will appear in its final, small scale, not in the large preview.

It also involves a lot of programming. Many type designers today use Python to automate parts of the process. I've gone further – I wrote my own font editor from scratch in Swift. That way, I can work exactly how I want to. And that's rare in the design world.

No graphic designer would say, "I built my own layout software". But for type designers, building your own tools feels natural. That, for me, has been a real pleasure.

Conclusion:
Legal Design and the Ikigai – a pathway to holistic fulfilment

Originating from Japanese culture, Ikigai provides a profound and compelling framework for both personal and professional fulfilment. The term, which translates to "a reason for being", encapsulates a philosophy deeply rooted in the balance of purpose, passion, and contribution.

Ikigai is composed of four fundamental elements – what one loves, what one is good at, what the world needs, and what one can be paid for. When these four components intersect, they create a powerful alignment between personal aspirations and professional endeavors. Within the realm of legal design, this intersection invites professionals to reimagine their work in a way that is not only economically sustainable but also deeply meaningful, socially impactful, and intellectually stimulating.

Traditionally, the legal profession has been perceived as a rigid and highly structured field, often prioritizing technical expertise and procedural efficiency over creativity and human-centered approaches. However, the introduction of legal design has begun to challenge these conventions. Can we move beyond the conventional expectations of lawyers and legal experts to become true designers of legal experiences? Can we overcome the notion of law as a static framework and instead view it as a dynamic, evolving system that adapts to human needs? More importantly, can we find a way to practice law that not only meets professional obligations but also brings a profound sense of personal fulfilment?

These questions are not merely theoretical – they strike at the very heart of how we approach legal work in the modern world. The legal field has long been associated with high levels of stress, long working hours, and a focus on compliance and risk management rather than innovation and creativity. Many legal professionals, despite achieving traditional markers of success, often struggle with job dissatisfaction, burnout, or a sense that their work lacks broader significance. Integrating legal design into the legal profession presents an opportunity to reshape these experiences, making legal practice not only more effective but also more fulfilling. It suggests that legal professionals can achieve professional excellence without sacrificing personal wellbeing, and that their work can be both intellectually rigorous and emotionally rewarding.

Looking ahead, legal design has immense potential to transform the way law is practiced, perceived, and experienced. By embracing a model that incorporates personal fulfillment into professional engagement, we can move beyond legal design as a set of isolated tools or techniques and instead embrace it as a holistic, evolving philosophy. This philosophy does not simply seek to simplify legal processes or enhance compliance mechanisms. Rather, it aspires to make legal systems more humane, transparent, and adaptable. The future of legal design lies in its ability to cultivate a legal culture that values creativity, inclusivity, and sustainability. In its most transformative form, legal design allows legal professionals to approach their work with renewed purpose. It encourages a shift from a purely analytical and reactive mindset to a proactive, user-centered approach that prioritizes accessibility, engagement, and innovation. Through legal design, we may bridge the gap between personal values and daily work, fostering a practice that is not just about serving clients but also about making a meaningful difference in people's lives. This shift in perspective enables lawyers, policymakers, and legal innovators to see their roles as not merely transactional but deeply relational – rooted in empathy, collaboration, and long-term impact.

As I reflect on the (long) journey of writing this book, I am even more convinced of the transformative power of integrating personal passion with professional endeavors. It is at this intersection that true fulfilment is found – not just in the tangible outcomes of legal work but in the process itself, in the way professionals engage with their clients, their colleagues, and the broader legal ecosystem. When legal professionals align their expertise with their intrinsic motivations, they do not just improve their own work experiences – they contribute to the evolution of the entire legal field.

The challenge ahead is to ensure that this shift becomes more than just an intellectual exercise. It requires a collective effort from legal professionals, designers, educators, and institutions to foster a legal culture that embraces innovation without losing sight of its core values. By carrying forward the ethos of legal design, we can create a legal profession that is not only more effective but also more sustainable – one that prioritizes wellbeing alongside efficiency, impact alongside precision, and meaning alongside success. This, ultimately, is the promise of legal design – to offer legal professionals a pathway toward a more enriching, impactful, and fulfilling career.

One where their work is not just a job but a true reason for being.

About Globe Law and Business

Globe Law and Business was established in 2005. From the very beginning, we set out to create legal books that are sufficiently high level to be of real use to the experienced professional, yet still accessible and easy to navigate. Most of our authors are drawn from Magic Circle and other top commercial firms, both in the United Kingdom and internationally.

Our titles are carefully produced, with the utmost attention paid to editorial, design and production processes. We hope this results in high-quality publications that are easy to read and a pleasure to own.

In 2021, we were very pleased to announce the start of a new chapter for Globe Law and Business following the acquisition of law books under the imprint Ark Publishing. Our law firm management list is now significantly expanded with many well-known and loved Ark Publishing titles.

We are also pleased to announce the launch of our online content platform, Globe Law Online, which allows for easy access across firms. Details of all titles included can be found at www.globelawonline.com. Email glo@globelawandbusiness.com for further details and to arrange a free trial for you or your firm.

We'd very much like to hear from you with your thoughts and ideas for improving what we offer. Please do feel free to email me on sian@globelawandbusiness.com. Happy reading and thank you for your time.

Sian O'Neill
Managing director
Globe Law and Business
www.globelawandbusiness.com

9 781837 231195